103010

Being an Effective Expert Witness

- the technologist in the courtroom

Derek A. Smith

PhD, MSc (London), CChem, FRSC, CEng, FIM, FInstD

Thames Publishing
London

1993

"To Simon Cooke, philosopher, elder statesman and friend, who, a quarter of a century ago, taught me that the word Expert is compounded from 'x', an unknown quantity, and 'spurt', a drip under pressure"

© **D. A. Smith 1993**

Published 1993 by
Thames Publishing
14 Barlby Road, London W10 6AR

British Library Cataloguing in Publication Data

Smith, D. A. (Derek Anthony)

Being an Effective Expert Witness

ISBN 0-905-21094-8

Printed in Great Britain by the Lonsdale Press Ltd, Queen's Park, London

Contents

AUTHOR'S PREFACE

This book relies on the author's experience gained in giving expert evidence in various jurisdictions as well as helping to prepare cases for trial, acting in alternative dispute resolution (ADR) and helping to select suitable Expert Witnesses for specific cases. It is therefore a hands-on account which differs from some previous books on this subject which explain what ought to be done and ought to happen. The text is written in non-legal language and without assumption of any legal knowledge. It is therefore suitable to introduce the new or inexperienced Expert Witness to the legal environment and to give a flavour of the duties which he or she will be expected to perform. While different subject matter, personalities and the nature of disputes will preclude uniformity of preparation, it is hoped that introduction of some basic concepts will foreshorten the instruction necessary by the legal practitioner to get the novice Expert up to speed. This understanding should help to improve the cost-effectiveness of Experts who are hired to assist in the resolution of technology disputes whether through Court proceedings or by prior settlement. Such improvement may be achieved by shortening both preliminary instruction and ultimate proceedings through a closer focus on technical matters of direct relevance to the precise issues between the parties and/or before the Court.

The text is also intended to help corporate clients new to litigation (e.g. directors of manufacturing companies, insurers, and their senior managers) to better understand how a technically qualified and experienced scientist or engineer approaches the task of giving expert evidence. This will assist productive dialogue with solicitors about matters such as the appointment of Experts, the venue of litigation experiments ... whether 'in-house' or at an independent laboratory ... and other matters involving significant costs. Experienced solicitors, counsel, patent agents and others in the legal profession who are already familiar with the role of the Expert may also find the book useful in instructing their new recruits as part of their familiarisation and training in litigation practices. The contents are likewise intended to assist both Attorneys and potential witnesses in foreign jurisdictions, particularly in the USA. Some relevant information is also included relating to US legal practices to help the British Expert Witness when deposed and in the US courtroom. Because so much of the origin of corporate litigation is the USA, any UK witness will also find it advantageous to have some awareness of US procedural differences.

The authors' relevant experience has been mostly in the resolution of Intellectual Property (IP) disputes, often in Patent Courts concerned with chemistry, polymer technology & engineering ... but it has also included work on product liability, forensic problems (particularly in connection with fire losses), misuse of secret information and criminal injuries. For twelve years, as managing director of QMC Industrial Research Ltd (QMC-IRL), a contract research company with academic links, he specialised in the design and performance of litigation experiments. Throughout the text, examples have been included based on personal experience or the experiences of close colleagues or associates. Where specific incidents or quotations are included which could easily be related by a skilled reader to individual Actions, these are particularised. In other cases, such as most of those cited to exemplify mistaken strategy or tactics, experience and conclusions based on fact have been generalised and sometimes incorporate a synthesis of incidents from a number of disparate disputes. Any of the more scurrilous stories are therefore not relatable to individuals.

As to style, although the prime object has been to impart information and guidance, an aim has also been to "intermingle jest with earnest"[1]. But there is also included a more serious chapter which is an attempt to reconcile differences of outlook between scientists and those instructing them.

There is no need to apologise for the occasional use of gentle satire[2] or for the liberal use of quotations[3] which are included to remind readers that man's method of settling disputes has its roots set deep in his culture. Western civilisation owes an early debt to rather few important books, amongst them the Holy Bible and tracts such as 'Ship of Fools' and 'In Praise of Folly' published some five hundred years ago during the Renaissance, a redressing of the imbalance between the dominating influence of superstitious churchmen and that of pragmatic and intellectual scholars, mostly self-styled 'humanists'. However, though the basic faults and vanities of man were underlined and sadly remain virtually identical today, until science writings began to emerge, little constructive prose was written to explain Nature and thereby attempt to improve the human condition. Of course Poetry and the Theatre succeeded where the preachers and pedants had failed and these have been equally influential in the advancement of our culture.

---

[1] Francis Bacon (d.1626)   Essay 'Of Discourse'

[2] "Satire, being levelled at all, is never resented for an offence by any"
J. Swift (d. 1745)   A Tale of A Tub

[3] "A book that furnishes no quotations is, *me judice*, no book ... it is a plaything"
T. L. Peacock (d. 1866)   Crotchet Castle

Science, as we now recognise it, began to be taken up again in the sixteenth century from where the Greeks had left it and it has flourished in essentially its present form for well over three hundred years. Regrettably, some impetus was lost early in the nineteenth century with the development of so-called 'political science'. This, perhaps due to its deceptively easy creed and simple (if sometimes erroneous) teaching by self-opinionated Victorian economists, partially usurped the position of scientific philosophy, represented by such modest and self-critical 'main-stream' figures as Hume and Whewell, in the public mind. This legacy of mispresentation still causes untold confusion amongst otherwise educated people even today.

As a result scientists are still widely supposed to 'discover facts' using something called 'the scientific method', vaguely involving 'hypothesis' and 'experimentation'. We are supposed to prove 'the truth' of such 'facts', which we then promulgate in oracular announcements called 'publications'. That we may often be proved 'wrong' by subsequent investigations then surely demonstrates the fallibility of both 'science' and 'scientists', who should henceforth 'never be trusted'. This is an extraordinary mixed bag of misconceptions and untruths but, to our misfortune, many educated non-scientists still seem to accept unquestioningly this representation of the straw man. They might ponder the view of Sir Peter Medawar F.R.S., one of the most brilliant minds of his generation and not an immoderate critic, who writes[4] with feeling:-

"The equation of science with *facts* and of the humane arts with *ideas* is one of the shabby genteelisms that bolster up the humanist's self-esteem'

In Chapter 3, the author therefore digresses from his main theme in order to try to set this record straight. Therein, he attempts to explain how scientists actually deal in concepts and probabilities varying from the highly speculative to the near-certain.

It is the unwarranted expectation of some old-school lawyers that they have hired a scientific Expert to 'prove the Facts' of their case. This is often at the root of occasional misunderstandings between Expert Witnesses and those instructing them. At worst, the scientist feels pressurised, misapplied and utterly misunderstood whereas the lawyers believe themselves cheated of the specific legal proof which they feel they need to convince a Court.

---

[4] Sir P. B. Medawar   The Art of the Soluble   'Two conceptions of Science' Methuen & Co. 1967 reproduced by permission of Methuen & Co.

Technologists do have an important contribution to make as Experts and this contribution can be better applied if there is greater public awareness of what science is and how its practitioners think. Hopefully, one additional function of this book will therefore be to ventilate this difference of approach and in future enable each side of the hiring equation to see the other's point-of-view more clearly.

• The author wishes to thank his many friends in the legal profession and industry who assisted him both by encouragement and in the correction and clarification of the text, particularly:-

Dr D M Gaythwaite of Bird & Bird who read the first draft and made invaluable suggestions concerning content and particularly the order of presentation of the subject matter; his colleagues Graham Smith and Trevor Cook who were also kind enough to make useful general comments; Simon Cooke and Edward Nodder of Bristows, Cooke & Carpmael who disentangled the garbling of numerous grammatical and legal niceties; Dr James Green formerly of the CBI and 3i and now a Director of Venture Scientifics Ltd who commented in detail on the licensing matters in Chapter 2; Dr Gaythwaite (again) who corrected some residual errors and infelicities in the second draft. Any remaining rubbish is now the sole responsibility of the author.

• He also acknowledges several kind permissions to quote previously published copyright material given by the authors and their publishers which are mentioned in footnotes to the text. In accordance with the grant of a non-exclusive licence to reproduce copyright material issued by Penguin Books Ltd, the author acknowledges in their prescribed form the use of the following such material by James Thurber:-

Short quotations from "The Scotty Who Knew Too Much" from FABLES FOR OUR TIME (Hamish Hamilton, 1939) copyright © James Thurber 1951; from "The Cane in the Corridor" from THE THURBER CARNIVAL (Hamish Hamilton, 1945) © James Thurber, 1945; from "The Lady from the Land" from CREDOS AND CURIOS (Hamish Hamilton, 1962) © James Thurber, 1962 ... Reproduced by permission of Hamish Hamilton Ltd.

Derek Smith   October 1993
26 Devonshire Place
London W1N 1PD

1   Introduction

Expert Witnesses are needed to assist both the civil and criminal courts. That is to say they are expected to advise the Judge or Judges ('the Court') by giving evidence and opinions on technical matters on the basis of their particular technical expertise. Their work in the civil courts is in helping to decide disputes between Parties involving some element of technology i.e. science and/or engineering; architecture and town planning; medicine; and many other technical fields. They do this in three main ways by:-

• interpreting technical documents and data;

• explaining the state of technical knowledge in specific places at specific times;

• giving opinions on the likely technical consequences of actions taken by the parties.

Experts should be truly independent of the parties in dispute. They must treat the gathering and presentation of evidence objectively in order to assist the Courts in reaching impartial decisions on matters which often involve genuine differences of opinion and even of 'fact', sometimes overlaid with commercial chicanery. An Expert should have :-

• appropriate knowledge and training;

• a capacity for original thought leading to his own conclusions (which he can defend);

• the self-discipline needed to deliver work of high quality on time; and

• the self-knowledge, tact, restraint and communicative skills which will enable him to work in a multidisciplinary team constructively and without friction.

The Expert is expected to identify the root technical causes of a dispute and free them gently from their overburden of prejudice. He then has to advise his Counsel how to present to the Court the best completely honest case he can for the party which retains him based on the technical facts which are

1

available or can be adduced by experiment. Another similar Expert will do the same for the opposing party. It is tacitly understood that, while fairly representing the technology involved, the Expert will normally try to present the positive aspects of his client's technical case in the best possible light while answering honestly and directly under cross-examination when taxed with the negative features.

On the basis of diligently researched 'Facts' (meaning 'observations') and their thoughtful interpretations by these opposing Experts in the form of Evidence or Opinions, the Court is thereby presented with a spectrum of evidence which will assist the preparation of a fair and balanced judgement. This is in accord with the adversarial system which we in the UK, and in the USA, believe to be just and efficacious in resolving disputes.

Much of this book is limited to discussion of the role of the independent Expert who is a scientist, technologist or engineer in Intellectual Property (IP), mostly Patent, litigation ... in the English Courts and those of the USA The word 'Expert', with a capital 'E', denotes an independent professional and distinguishes him from many other witnesses (usually 'witnesses of 'fact') who may also be required to give evidence as experts in their subject. This introductory chapter first sets this limited topic in a less circumscribed scene in which many kinds of Experts are used to assist the resolution of a variety of disputes; this gives some idea of what they do.

Legal procedures require disputes to be settled at Trials of Actions heard by Courts who pronounce Judgement in favour of one or other of the disputants. A Court consists of a Judge or group of Judges who hear Evidence and Argument and base their decisions on a series of rules called The Law. In the USA, and in some other jurisdictions, technical cases of the kind dealt with in this book are sometimes heard by lay Juries presided over by an elected Judge, usually a lawyer. By way of contrast certain matters, particularly Patent disputes, are heard in the English courts by a scientifically-knowledgable lawyer-judge sitting alone.

The Law consists of Common Law, Statute Law enacted by national or supra-national governments, augmented by Case Law in which interpretation of the Statutes has been established by previous Courts considering comparable but different situations. Although the Statutes are amended only rarely, Case Law evolves progressively as each Judge, the

Appeal Court or the English 'supreme court', called the 'House of Lords' [1], adds its application and interpretation in the context of the new subject matter of various cases. Formerly the judiciary defended the fiction that they were not 'making new law' but simply confirming in their judgements what the Statutes had always meant! Nowadays the complexity of legal decision-making is better acknowledged, the Statutes being regarded more as albeit-strict guidelines, a framework into which each Trial Judge inserts specific interpretive detail.

At a Trial the Court receives written and oral Evidence which may be Evidence of Fact or Evidence of Opinion. The latter is most acceptable when given by suitably qualified and experienced Expert Witnesses who are required to be independent of the litigating parties so that they can offer impartial technical opinions to advise the Court. It is such 'Expert Witness' which is the subject of this book. At subsequent hearings, in the Court of Appeal and/or in the House of Lords, without hearing further evidence the Lower-Court decision may be overturned. That this happens not infrequently is a cause of protracted hope or fear and a considerable expense for litigants.

This first chapter is a tour d'horizon of matters discussed in greater detail later in the book together with an indication of the very broad field over which Experts are employed.

Kinds of dispute

Many civil disputes are of a commercial nature and most involve attempts to gain, or avoid the loss of, large sums of money [2]. Actions are often started to obtain rightful compensation for theft of knowledge, customers, staff and so on. Others commence because of unfair competition which has led to the establishment of price-fixing and other practices which are not seen to be in the public interest. Most such actions are between corporations who use litigation as one of the tools by which they establish or retain their market position or embarass their competitors. Most have a legitimate and specific grievance based on theft, fraud, infringement of rights or unfair competition. Commencement of litigation by a Company may sometimes require a decision at Board level. It may even have to be disclosed to shareholders, for

[1]   Actually a sub-committee of the UK parliamentary Upper House

[2]   "I wish my deadly foe no worse
Than want of friends; and empty purse"
Nicholas Breton (d.1626?)   The Court and Country

instance at General Meeting, and can have a deleterious effect on investor confidence. Such a decision is not usually taken lightly.

In addition there is a growing tendency also for individuals to try to use civil court procedures to rectify a real or imaginary disadvantage they believe they may have suffered at the hands of a company. For instance, following a lead from the USA, consumers and other members of the public are becoming far more aware of their 'rights' and of the recompense they may expect as a result of legal Action. At the same time some less scrupulous politicians have found that they can achieve temporary popularity by espousing the cause of often unnecessary and usually burdensome consumer and public safety legislation, abetted by the media who make money from sensational suggestions or disclosures. As a result many who would formerly have suffered in silence are now getting a fairer deal from Society. However a new breed of claimant has arisen, often supported by public funds, who expects compensation both for genuine accidents and for self-inflicted hardships. Their first call is usually on their insurer who forthwith increases the premium for cover to such a level that needy customers cannot afford it and have to forego protection.

One may question whether such trends represent a net advance in the progress of civilisation. Most of us would like to see a simpler, cheaper, earlier and more certain outcome of disputes involving 'real people'. On the other hand disputes between corporations are likely to continue even when these too might seem to be avoidable or capable of being readily resolved. They nevertheless deliberately continue unresolved and give rise to litigation for wholly commercial reasons rather than in any attempt to redress an injustice. It is often cheaper to pay lawyers to keep a dispute warm than to pay the recompense required by a settlement and, what is more, the cost of doing this is usually tax-deductible. This would seem to be an abuse of the legal system, albeit a well-established one. And these 'commercial reasons' are not always immediately obvious to the newcomer to commercial litigation. The resultant paradox can puzzle and concern the novice[3].

In an early case that involved him as a Witness in the USA, the author felt that he could see immediately the large area of common ground and minor

---

[3] " We must not make a scarecrow of the Law
Setting it up to fear the birds of prey,
And let it keep one shape till custom make it
Their perch and not their terror"
William Shakespeare (d. 1616)   <u>Measure for Measure i</u>

4

area of technical dispute between the parties and asked his instructing Attorney if he might write a short report which should be of use as a basis for settlement:-

"I wouldn't do that" said the Attorney "These parties are good friends and have carved up the market between them. They have relied for years on keeping a trickle of litigation going to show that they are genuine competitors, which keeps the anti-trust authorities off their backs".

In short[4] :-

"Both parties join'd to do their best
To damn the public interest"

However one views the desirability of the trend, technical litigation for commercial reasons is on the increase (see Chapter 14). This means that there is an ever-increasing need for Experts who are capable of giving reliable, coherent and articulate evidence within the confines of the disciplines in which they are competent. Valuable commercial produce can emerge from a superficially unprepossessing farmyard of corporate litigation. Provided that it knows what it is doing, a corporation will not and should not flinch from the dirt involved in protecting its interests.

One's less-enthusiastic academic colleagues, who are nevertheless among the beneficiaries of industrial enterprise, might usefully learn to look more deeply into the many reasons for litigation and develop some appreciation of them. They will find that great good can come from the defence of a weak licensee or the chasing away of a marauding intellectual property thief. In the light of this knowledge, they may feel more prepared to offer their Expert services to assist the resolution of disputes by legal process. Neither would they wish that the 'right of might' should prevail in the market place. The professional Expert Witness therefore needs to have 'commercial awareness' among those qualities summarised earlier and discussed in detail in Chapter 3.

It is important that those who are instructing Experts should consult with them fully on both the technical and commercial factors likely to influence the case but should on no account press their Expert to change his evidence in any way to 'support' a particular technical line which may for the time

---
[4]   Samuel Butler (d. 1680)   Hudibras Part III

5

being appear attractive to their client. This is a delicate matter, further discussed in detail elsewhere in this book, but suffice it to say here that this happens rarely if at all in respectable circles. If as an Expert one has the unusual misfortune to meet it, it is the Expert's duty to resist such pressure, if necessary to the point of relinquishing the assignment. But when more general suggestions concerning necessary evidence are made by his instructing solicitor whose job it is to the conduct the case, the Expert should not be quick to fear the worst. He should not jump to the conclusion that he is being pressurised until that is abundantly clear in which case his display of limited enthusiasm will normally be sufficient to lead to a rapid rethink of tactics by those instructing.

Brief History

There are now a number of forums in which an Expert may be called upon to advise. Since the passage of the 1949 Patents Act, there have been specialised patent courts in the UK which provide a generally more satisfactory service than the mish-mash of trial procedures conducted in other non-specialist courts which is still the practice in many other countries today.

•   In the UK, the Patents Act 1949 has been superseded by the Patents Act 1977, abetted by the Copyright, Designs and Patents Act 1988. Even today a few "old Act" Patents continue to be litigated.

•   The European Patent has made its appearance and the main venue in which attempts are made to invalidate patents ("Oppositions") is now the European Patent Office (EPO) in Munich.

•   The UK Patents County Court (PCC) has opened its doors, and is intended to offer a quicker, simpler and (nominally cheaper), if not as rigorous, route to resolution of infringement disputes. This brings the Expert into play at an early stage of preparation because of the need to present a coherent technical picture for the 'Preliminary consideration and review' by the Court which is a special feature of PCC proceedings.

Like changes have taken place in other fields of litigation, particularly in the increase of activity concerning product liability, professional negligence and the resolution of insurance disputes. Corporate litigation has steadily become more international so that the strategy of a dispute is constrained by events which have already taken place overseas or which are pending in other jurisdictions. One such litigation, *General Tire v Firestone*, commenced in the 1950s and ran world-wide for well over twenty years during which infringement of the basic patents for oil-extended rubber continued. Despite eventual rulings in favour of the Patentee, niggardly awards of costs and damages provided an inadequate reward to the Plaintiff who had invested many millions of dollars in what was intended to be an effective defence of corporate commercial interests. As a result of this poor decision it became an established commercial strategy to pay lawyers rather than royalties. Today such strategy is well understood and tacitly accepted. Corporate justice has to do with making money and this is why any competent Expert now needs to be well versed in the commercial facts of life.

Another factor which has for many years been of vital importance in the USA, and is now of increasing importance in Europe, is that of 'anti-trust'. This means that the aggressive assertion and defence of monopolies which can be shown to be in restraint of trade may viewed unfavourably by the Courts so that, in practical terms, licences may eventually have to be offered to dangerous competitors. This is an area of change. In recent years there are signs that upholding the rights of their patentees is seen by the US authorities as both necessary to stimulate innovation and keep foreign competitors out of the market, and as a useful technical barrier to trade. In the European Commission, it appears that DG XII may like patents because they stimulate product development whereas DG IV seems overly concerned with competition aspects and preventing the abuse of granted monopolies.

While formerly, virtually all instruction of Experts in the IP field was by Solicitors acting for clients, the field is now more open and, particularly, Patent Agents often instruct and conduct litigation directly for their clients, pleading in the EPO and even in the PCC. This development is being watched with interest. Whereas all contact between Expert and Counsel used to be 'through the solicitor', nowadays more direct lines of informal communication often proliferate, usually through the new breed of technically-qualified Junior Counsel. While some instructing solicitors prefer to stick to the old conventions, many of the younger ones are quite content to see the job done as efficiently as possible by means of more direct communication.

In many branches of court and claim work, UK cases are heard by competent lawyers with no special knowledge of or deep interest in science and technology. Despite their patience and diligence in trying to get to the bottom of a technical dispute, one sometimes fears a situation of polite non-comprehension which is so familiar from one's own dinner parties[5]. This problem is exacerbated in the U.K criminal courts where much of the technical evidence is presented only by the Prosecution. This is discussed further in Chapter 14.

In general the life of the Patent Expert is now easier than before because so many Patent practitioners: Solicitors, Counsel, Patent Agents and indeed some Patent Judges are technically qualified, while all are scientifically literate. This solves many of the former communication problems. However this is by no means the case in the other fields and there remains, even today, a special responsibility of the Expert to couch his technical opinions in language which, though rigorous, is readily comprehended by non-scientists. All Experts do not possess such skills. Those who do not have them must needs seek to acquire them. And indeed it is more than a question of just 'using the right words'. Professor Dawkins deals with such a 'teaching' need lucidly in the following passage[6]:-

"Explaining is a difficult art. You can explain something so that your reader understands the words, and you can explain something so that the reader feels it in the marrow of his bones. To do the latter, it sometimes isn't enough to lay the evidence before the reader in a dispassionate way. You have to become an advocate and use the tricks of the advocate's trade"

But, at the same time, the Expert should try to harness his skills in pleading to the lively and interesting explanation of a genuinely held technical opinion and not allow them to stray towards arguing of his client's case. Such work is the job of the barristers or attorneys.

To make things easier for today's Expert, the technological back-up, particularly communication aids such as facsimile and videotape, have transformed both preparation and presentation. Perhaps the greatest change has come in the rapid accessibility of technical information, so that

---

[5] "'Wonderful thing, technology' said Minturn 'wonderful thing, wonderful thing ... I want a drink''
James Thurber (d. 1961) The Cane in the Corridor Hamish Hamilton

[6] Richard Dawkins The Blind Watchmaker Longman 1986 reprinted by permission of the Peters, Fraser & Dunlop Group Ltd

scrabbling about on dusty library shelves and the laborious abstracting of weighty bound volumes has all but vanished. It is steadily being supplemented and, in the USA is already being replaced, by the interrogation (via the PC) of CD-ROM and on-line database, presently with keyword indexes but, in the not too distant future it would seem with some form of free-text search facility.

It is no longer practicable for the Expert to spend his time and client's money 'searching the literature' for relevant citations. It makes more sense to employ specialist information searchers to find the information that the Expert needs, for[7] :-

"Knowledge is of two kinds: We know a subject ourselves, or we know where to find information upon it"

Expert evidence at Trial

The form in which assistance is given to the Court is primarily as Evidence, both written and oral (often supplemented with photographs and videotapes or films). Unless a special application can be sustained for a hearing *in camera*, which is rarely favoured by the Court, evidence is given in public. It is subject to cross-examination, usually by the other party's barrister.

At Trial of an Action, the Court considers the Evidence and how it has been sustained by witnesses under attack, and also Counsel's arguments based on the evidence before coming to a decision in favour of one or other of the Parties. In a typical Action, independent Experts usually appear alongside in-house corporate experts who, when giving their opinions, are often assumed to have the righteousness of their employer's case more firmly in mind, making them less than truly independent. The technical evidence is completed by the 'witnesses of fact' who are not required to give technical opinions. In Patent Actions there is often need to locate (or synthesise) an 'unimaginative, skilled man' who is capable of reading the Patent and, if it is properly drafted, carrying out its instructions in the light of his 'ordinary skill and knowledge' of the particular industry which is involved. However he is required to be incapable of 'invention'. Such a man has little basis in fact and some weaknesses of the concept of the 'Skilled Man', much beloved of the Courts, is further examined in a subsequent chapter.

---
[7] Dr Samuel Johnson Boswell's 'Life' ii

For the time being, we can perhaps gently caricature him as[8]:-

"Unlearned, he knew no schoolman's subtle art,
No language, but the language of the heart,
By nature honest, by experience wise,
Healthy by temperance, and by exercise"

The basis of the Court's Decision is carefully reasoned in a (usually 'reserved', that is delayed) Judgement which sets out the opposing arguments and the weight which should be attached to each. This Judgement may often be the subject of a subsequent Appeal to a higher court where the lower-court decision may be reversed.

Witness attitudes and beliefs

As we have seen, different independent Experts are employed by each of the parties in a dispute. They will normally try to portray the positive aspects of their client's case while answering honestly when taxed with the negative features. This approach is unremarkable and is inherent in the adversarial system on which English trial procedure is based. It derives from the well-tried and historic procedure of 'the Debate' in which decisions on contentious issues are prefaced by presentation and discussion of fairly-based alternative cases. But this tradition is not always understood and appreciated by committed scientists called to give evidence. For instance while denigrating the procedures of the university debating society and thereby appearing to claim some moral superiority, a leading scientific thinker and communicator writes[9]:-

"In one respect I plead to distance myself from professional advocates. A lawyer or a politician is paid to exercise his passion and his persuasion on behalf of a client or a cause in which he may not privately believe. I have never done this and I never shall. I may not always be right, but I care passionately about what is true and I never say anything that I do not believe to be right"

However this stricture is not applicable to the work of the Expert Witness because, as has already been said, it is not the job of any Expert Witness to

---

[8] Alexander Pope (d. 1744) Epistles and Satires of Horace imitated

[9] R. Dawkins The Blind Watchmaker loc. cit.

plead the client's case to the Court but rather to supply his barrister ('learned counsel') with the necessary technical background so to do. Some nominally-independent Experts do seem to find it difficult to make this distinction with sufficient determination and clarity either washing their hands of the whole judicial procedure as some great cheat or, alternatively, becoming unhealthily identified with their own perceived 'justice' of their client's cause.

They should take a leaf out of the lawyer's book[10]:-

"A lawyer has no business with the justice or injustice of the cause which he undertakes, unless his client asks his opinion, and then he is bound to give it honestly. The justice or injustice of the cause is to be decided by the Judge"

In any adversarial system somebody has to 'come second' and it would be utterly unjust to deny that party the benefit of as skilled technical advice as is made available to the winner. Likewise it is equally vital that the criminal defendant should benefit from the same quality of dispassionate technical evidence as does the Crown prosecutor.

The 'passionate' approach would not seem to admit that there is an important job to do in preparing, and in putting forward in Evidence, the best possible honest and truthful technical case for a party which, privately and irrelevantly, the Expert Witness may regard from the outset as the potential loser. It is a matter of professional responsibility that[11]:-

"No worthy doctor ever fled
Because his patient was half dead"

As for saying things which one "does not believe to be right", Dawkins's final sentence is an acknowledged creed for most Experts. Were it not so, they would soon be found out and discredited by the efficient Trial procedure of cross-examination!

---

[10]   Dr Samuel Johnson (d.1784)   Boswell's   Tour to the Hebrides   (1773)

[11]   Sebastian Brant (d.1521)   Das Narrenschiff ch 38,   translated by William Gillis as The Ship of Fools for the Folio Society, London 1971

11

The Court Expert

Occasionally in the UK[12], but much more frequently in overseas jurisdictions, an Expert or Experts may be appointed by the Court in order to advise the judiciary directly and so facilitate discussion of technical matters during the course of an Action. He may be asked to produce a Report which, with the permission of the Court, can be subject to cross-examination by either Party and he can in certain circumstances carry out experiments. The Expert's fees and expenses are included in the Costs of the Action. Alternatively a 'scientific adviser' may be appointed to sit with the Court during the hearing or to report on "any question of fact or opinion not involving a question of law or construction". By way of example, Dr Sydney Brenner advised the Court of Appeal in the *Genentech* case and is currently (July 1993) advising Aldous J. in the lower court hearing of the *Chiron* HCV case. Such 'Court Experts' are often delegated by the Court to carry out inspections and to perform crucial experimentation aimed to resolve differences between the client-sponsored Experts.

The author's limited experience of such appointments overseas, in France and in Sweden, suggests that the system works quite well provided that the Experts involved are not too opinionated or dictatorial. Experts being 'independent' as they are (Chapter 3), there is always the risk of conflict of opinion. Where Experts appear for the parties and are subject to cross-examination such conflict can be resolved by the Judge but where several are employed directly to advise the Court this would appear to introduce an added complication to the Judge's already formidable task. And the use of only one Court Expert could risk unfair technical partiality.

Other functions of the Expert

The above description is of what might be called the 'primary function' of the independent Expert as it relates to the legal process of dispute resolution. But it is important to note that only a small percentage of such disputes actually reach Trial. Many are settled by private negotiation between the parties, others go to various forms of Arbitration or 'Expert Determination'. More still are resolved after completion of some of the preliminary stages of litigation such as service of the Summons for Direction (see Chapters 5/6).

---

[12] The specific rules and duties are listed in Order 40 of the Patents Act 1949 to 1961 and 1977 and, for the scientific adviser, in Order 104 rule 15

Experts are therefore employed in many other ways later listed (in Table 4.1). In particular they may advise corporations (or individuals) informally on their technical strength in an incipent claim or dispute. This often includes planning and execution of experiments to test the strength of the client's own position. More & more frequently they now act as referees in settling disputes round a table by alternative dispute resolution 'without the need for lawyers'.

Experts acting as industrial consultants usually advise on a *proactive* basis, suggesting to corporate clients how to pre-empt disputes. They can usefully complement the work of more traditional practitioners who are more used to specialising in the cost-effective resolution of existing contention when approached on a *reactive* basis by already-troubled clients. Now that many legal firms are deciding to reconstitute their partnerships on a broader activity plan[13], often offering aspects of management consultancy, particularly 'risk management', there is abundant opportunity for the retention of Experts by these firms to handle technical aspects of their clients' problems.

Corporate attitudes to disputes

Lack of technical advice at an early decision point can have dire consequences on the health of any business and the UK has been particularly slow in recognising this. Recent discussions with a Lloyds Agent make one wonder whether the recent debacles in the market which have lead to the ruin of scores of Names need not have happened had the ill-starred Underwriters kept properly abreast of the technical state-of-the-art in the technologies they were insuring. Neither is there much sign that the lesson has been properly learned even today when the scale of potential losses through pollution, explosion, subsidence, storm damage and other causes has reached unprecedented levels. Technical risk management is still an unfamiliar subject in these circles. In stressing the need for better technical information, one may hope that someone somewhere is going to realise that this is an area where serious money can be made by the simple application of existing scientific and engineering knowledge.

Corporations consist of people and it is senior individuals who decide how a

---

[13]   See, for example, R. Susskind   "Why lawyers should consider consultancy"
Financial Times   13 October 1992

13

dispute should be handled, particularly how it is to be resolved. Like a first world-war general, many a vice-president, convinced of his firm's invincibility and the rightness of its every cause, has poured millions into fruitless confrontation, usually against the advice of both his in-house and external legal advisers but with the grudging support of his brow-beaten Board of Directors. In such disputes and consequent litigation, the independent Expert may find himself ploughing a difficult furrow; he has to fight hard against a natural but professionally fatal cynicism. Nevertheless, he must continue to advise the Board responsibly[14], even if it's legal case is technically flawed. In such circumstances the Expert's period of appointment is usually mercifully short.

In preparing their evidence, Experts often have to come to grips with difficult relative concepts such as what is 'safe' and what is 'harmful' in a given situation. Often it involves the onerous responsibility of apportioning blame for serious injury or loss of life. The opinions of qualified technical experts can be invaluable in assisting the court in such cases. Led from the USA, the onus of liability for injury and death is shifting more and more on to the product manufacturer even when one's common sense may suggest that product or process has been employed in a careless, thoughtless or even negligent way.

The whole concept of 'personal safety' has changed radically during the author's own lifetime. Having as a youngster made (and detonated) gunpowder and nitrogen tri-iodide, when at school in the 40s he remembers identifying cyanides by sniffing 'bitter almonds' (hydrocyanic or prussic acid) at the mouth of a test-tube. As a college student he duly learned to put out the occasional solvent fires by smothering them with his lab coat without too much breakage of glassware and to manipulate the potent carcinogen benzene in an open dish from which he inhaled copiously, day after day. In his first job, handling mildly radioactive solutions protected by a pair of surgeons gloves (and the results of an occasional urine analysis) was quite routine. Knowledge about materials and processes has advanced over the intervening years and what was normal routine *then* is often regarded as highly irresponsible *now*.

To reverse the sentiment of an old judgement[15]:-

---

[14] "I am not bound to please thee with my answer"
     William Shakespeare (d.1616) The Merchant of Venice iv

[15] Lord Macmillan, in *Read v Lyons* English High Court 1947

" ... in a progressive world, things which at one time were reckoned reasonably safe come to be regarded as highly dangerous".

Now just about everything is 'toxic' ... even carrot juice!

Of the greatest concern, both to corporations and to their insurers, is the growing tendency of Courts to award substantial damages for long-term effects on health attributed to exposure, often decades earlier, to noxious materials such as asbestos which were not then sufficiently recognised as hazards. It is particularly taxing to an Expert to have to give evidence on oath that a chance, or even fairly regular, exposure nearly half-a-century ago is substantially responsible for a rapid decline in old age, particularly if the decline is of such a nature (e.g. cancer) as to be relatively common amongst groups of people who have not suffered exposure to the supposed hazard. Much as one applauds the protection of the individual from possible exploitation by rich uncaring capitalists (and governments), it is the capitalists who actually provide much of our employment and economic growth and directly or indirectly (through taxation) fund much of the scientific research which leads to betterment of the human condition. They too must be protected by the Courts, in this case from frivolous or unfairly based claims.

It is therefore very important for Experts employed in liability work to avoid any hint of emotional or political bias, and to form their opinions purely on the basis of the technical facts before them and with a genuine understanding of the state of knowledge at the relevant time. If such knowledge was poor, it is up to them to say so and to indicate clearly any necessary assumptions in bridging the gaps in their evidence. At the end of the day, it is Counsel who is paid to argue the case and the Judge (or, particularly in the USA, the jury) who must decide on its rights and wrongs. All that Experts can really be expected to do is to give an honest opinion based on the information available. And they should be ready to concede the possibility of different interpretations where these can be argued with equal strength. In this connection, it is important not to overstate the strength of one's observations[16]:-

" ... we can never prove that fairies do not exist. All we can say is that no sightings of fairies have ever been confirmed, and that such alleged photographs of them as have been produced are palpable fakes"

---

[16]   Richard Dawkins   The Blind Watchmaker (loc. cit.) ch.11

15

This may seem a pedantic way of putting it but it is not ... it is merely an accurate one. 'Precision of what is claimed' is vital in giving evidence.

Questions of liability

The recent Court of Appeal decision in favour of *Cambridge Water* against *Eastern Counties Leatherworks* (subject to Appeal to the House of Lords) seems to go even further than has been previously suggested (see Chapter 14). It apparently establishes that an act involving solvent contamination of the water table which even if reprehensible was not illegal at the time that it was committed may become illegal, and a cause for damages, through intervening changes in legislation coupled with the tightening of European standards. If this judgement is finally upheld we may expect a flood of litigation which could be highly damaging to many older industries on which the UK economy still depends for its survival. In the absence of a legal 'Noah's Ark', there seems every chance that a number of our remaining few manufacturers could find themselves drowning in Cambridge water.

In dealing with such matters in court, Experts should not choose to express opinions in accord with the views of those who are instructing them until they have thought long and hard. They should consider particularly whether or not any individual, however experienced, can really claim the infinite breadth of knowledge and wisdom which would have to be integrated into 'the whole truth', as opposed to 'an informed opinion', when the subject matter concerns spillages or other contamination dating back a century or more.

The crucial question of exactly what sort of evidence a conscientious scientist can be expected to give is addressed in Chapter 3.

2 Intellectual Property: how it is protected, licensed for use and traded

'IP' is a comprehensive term applied to a rather mixed bag of industrial assets consisting of novel ideas, inventions, designs, copyrights, trademarks, confidential information and certain widely-recognised identities, which have commercial value in that their use is restricted by law to the owners of the assets together with their authorised licensees. More important, others can be stopped by legal process from using such IP and forced to pay substantial sums for having infringed the owner's legal rights. Copyright does not even need to be registered and owners of certain other assets are entitled to some lesser degree of protection. IP is described fully in a number of widely-available publications[1] so that what is given in this Book is the briefest of summaries.

The main sub-divisions of IP are Patents, Trademarks, Copyright and Registered Design. Of these the commonest disputes involving Expert witnesses concern Patents and Copyright. The author's recent personal experience is chiefly in the 'IP' field.

The price paid for seeking legal protection of novel technology, usually by patenting, is that other parties (individuals, corporations, governments) can become aware of exactly what technology it is that your business depends on. Too strong an IP position for any single enterprise can often attract attention from governments concerned at abuse of the possible monopoly thus established in a particular technology which may be or may appear to be 'against the public interest'. In the USA, anti-trust suits are a way of life and there are signs that the European Community may follow suit.

So important and valuable are IP assets that they can be regarded as the main-spring of many a major company's competitiveness. Where would 'Polaroid' be without its camera and film processing patents? Or where Battelle without xerography? Unfortunately, it follows that, in the commercial jungle, it may often seem to be worth a modicum of risk to try to participate either forcefully or surreptitiously in the benefits of a competitor's IP or, if that fails because the victim shows some fight, to try

---

[1] See for example the excellent pamphlets "Inventions, Patents & Patent Agents", "Trade Marks, Registered Trade Marks & Patent Agents", Industrial Designs Copyright & Patent Agents" all published by the Chartered Institute of Patent Agents, London WC1V 7PZ; and various publications from specialist IP law firms such as "From Idea to Market-Place: An introduction to UK Technology Law", Bird & Bird, London EC4A 1JP.

17

to 'break the spring' by putting a competitor out of business. It is in such commercial strategic discussions that the seed of much litigation is sown. The risk of infringement is often coolly balanced against the likely price of taking a licence to employ the particular IP. Because of this risk, which could lead to costly litigation, licences can usually be negotiated with an iron hand in a velvet glove. The potential licensor must have firm targets but also show considerable flexibility in reaching a deal. On the other hand, there is no point in owning IP unless you are prepared to defend your monopoly!

In fact the cost of licences in various types of industry have been established by tradition and must be big enough to leave the licensor, who has borne the costs of innovation, a profit but small enough to allow the new entrant to the market to make some sort of a living in it. Various formulae are used to allow a toe-in-the-water approach, with escalating payments as the newcomer becomes established as a serious rival. There are often advantages to the licensee to rely on the brawn of big brother who will usually take on predator infringers who are too large a match for the minnows.

Likewise there are often advantages to the licensor, such as avoiding anti-trust law by deliberately introducing an albeit toothless competitor to the market place or sometimes deriving income from licensing technology outside the area of the owner's core business. One thing is certain, that licensing and potential litigation, while nominally independent, are in practice indissolubly mixed. In no field is it truer that[2]:-

"Every one lives by selling something"

Licensing and Litigation as commercial "cost centres"

Based on the output of a competent R & D facility, such licensing can soon become 'the tail that wags the dog'. For instance Texas Instruments made losses on manufacturing operations in both 1990 and 1991 but received income[3] from licences over this period of a reputed $428m.While the licensing of patented technology may be highly profitable to large corporations, the position is often less happy for the small high-technology research company seeking a licensee among the corporate majors. This

---

[2]   Robert Louis Stevenson (d.1894) Across the Plains xi 'Beggars'

[3]   See M Nakamoto "Financial Times" 16 July 1992

requires prudence and agility. It is probably rather like feeding elephants: one false move and you're trampled to death. Licensing negotiations should not be entered into lightly. If one of the parties withdraws precipitously or prematurely leaving the other believing itself thereby disadvantaged, the seeds of disharmony are sown which will often sprout a rich crop of litigation. This is particularly likely when the potential licensee has requested full and detailed disclosure/demonstration of the technology to be licensed and subsequently, or even concurrently, has been found to set up a production facility based on such disclosure.

Contrary to popular belief 'going to law', when properly managed, can make money. Several corporations now manage their 'Litigation' departments as cost centres, assessing not only the sums won from settlement of patent infringements such as Honeywell's recent $127m from Minolta but also counting 'money saved' in stemming the losses which would have been caused by failure to take decisive legal action to bridle infringers. Such winnings constitute a 'war chest' to fund future litigation.

This makes good sense, ensuring that IP matters figure on all the agendas of Board Meetings and properly valuing the huge annual investments made by the corporations in their R & D programmes which have usually generated these valuable assets. The British accountancy practice of 'writing off' research expenditure (for tax reasons) in the year in which it occurs usually leads to an actual devaluation of these important assets in the minds of the owners. Were industrial 'R & D' to be capitalised, still within a generous tax shelter, managements might show a greater interest in seeking proper returns through licensing out. But at present only the very brightest stars of UK industry seem to carry out proper technology audits and employ technically-qualified financial advisers who can help them capitalise on the knowledge locked up in their laboratories. Unfortunately where research is capitalised for start-ups, as is sometimes done for instance in Australia, trading of stock in the USA can become more difficult because of the less-rosy picture of the company's financial state in its balance sheet.

Patents: a brief introduction

In the UK, 'patents' (sometimes referred to as 'specifications') are monopolies of (usually) up to 20 years duration granted by the Crown for disclosing details of an invention, a new product or process of practical industrial and commercial use. The national governments of other countries offer like protection and there are 'federated' patents such as the European Patent. The monopoly was formerly that defined strictly by the actual words used in the claims of the 'letters patent', that is to say strictly a matter of 'construction' of the patent in a legal sense. However Courts now take a broader view, often admitting a 'purposive construction' (much like, though rather less broad than, the US 'Doctrine of Equivalence') particularly in defining the scope of a claim (as discussed in Chapter 5). In deciding the breadth of such a construction they will usually seek the advice of Experts, asking them what a skilled addressee of the patent would think that the teaching of the claim actually meant in the relevant industry at a specific date.

Patents are first filed as 'Applications'. The date of first Application is known as the Priority Date and is internationally accepted by convention as the date on which the invention was registered and therefore (in most countries) deemed to have been made. Up to one year later, a fuller document based on the Application but containing Examples and Claims is filed. Under certain defined circumstances the full Patent can contain 'added matter' but, in order to retain the 'priority date' for international filings, this material must be 'fairly based' upon the disclosures in the original Application. One common cause of disputes, resolved with the help of Expert testimony, used to be 'lack of fair basis' of the full Specification but under the 1977 Act this or 'ambiguity' no longer exist as a grounds for attacking a patent.

To assist the Experts and the lawyers to reach a conclusion, some Patent Offices (such as the US) make available the so-called 'File Wrapper' which contains, or is supposed to contain, all details of the Inventor's submissions, together with any other correspondence with the Patent Office Examiner who has responsibility for examining the Application and determining whether there is a patentable invention correctly described and claimed. However very little such documentation is available to public inspection in the UK which is perhaps to be regretted.

Amendments during prosecution

Novice Experts may be surprised to see the major changes which a patent can undergo during its prosecution when subject to mauling by the

20

Examiner. The most usual amendments are introduced to circumvent 'prior art' adduced by the Examiner as rendering the Application (as submitted) either 'obvious' (in the light of the common general knowledge of skilled men, as of the Priority Date) or 'anticipated' by a specific disclosure of exactly the same invention in one of the Examiner's prior published citations. One of the arts of the Patent Agent is to amend the Patent progressively during prosecution to meet the Examiner's criticisms, usually limiting the scope of its claims in such a way that the commercial value is retained but the essence of the Invention is clearly distinguished from anything previously published. The ingenuity here demonstrated can sometimes reach the limits of credibility. But even after attempts to amend, Opposition Proceedings can still result in Revocation of a badly drafted Patent.

Qualifications for grant of a Patent

Patent applications may be rejected because of:-

•   Prior Publication ('It has been described before'), or

•   Obviousness ('It could have been conceived and brought into practice by an non-inventive, but informed, technician')

•   Prior Use ('It has been made/offered/sold before')

•   Insufficiency ('Not enough instruction to understand or recreate the technology described')

At least in Europe, examination by the Patent Office Examiners is usually restricted to 'novelty' (Has it been done before?) which is done by comparison with a limited range of Patent Specifications and readily available publications. However US examiners can concern themselves with obviousness and occasionally with insufficiency. Even if the Patent is granted by the appropriate Patent Office, any of these deficiencies can constitute grounds for revocation in subsequent Court actions. Formerly Patents could also be bad for:-

•   Inutility ('Does not work')

but curiously under the present (1977) Act this ground for invalidity has been withdrawn.

Under the 'old' Act the Inventor also had to disclose the 'best method' ('best mode' US) of performing his invention. A Patent could be found bad by the Courts if this was not done. However this requirement is also missing from the more recent legislation with the result that modern draftsmen sometimes tend to obscure the actual way of doing that which is claimed while still attempting to cover performance aspects sufficiently to justify a claim to an 'enabling disclosure'. While this may certainly gain commercial advantage by confusing potential infringers and attracting genuine licensees (who will of course receive for their license fee a 'know-how package' showing clearly how the invention is actually carried out), it does make for difficult reading of the patent literature. The EC has woken up to the competition aspects of this and is questioning whether the principle of 'the award of a monopoly (by the Crown, or perhaps, soon, the President of a new United Europe?) in exchange for publication of the Invention for the benefit of a grateful populace' is perhaps being abused.

It is often necessary, or at least advisable, to try to find out if an invention has already been patented before proceeding too far with its expensive development. This involves doing, or having done, a 'patent search', usually in specific subject areas and of a limited range of patents (say, for example US, European and, in some subject areas, Japanese). However, this is neither facile nor particularly reliable. Coupled with obscure titling, a delphic abstract, and a rather too general computer classification in the UK Patent Office, it has become only too easy to miss significant patents even in a topic one knows well. Such a search is often best entrusted to a Chartered Patent Agent with specific experience in the subject matter of the invention. Computer searches may be of assistance for art published since the 1970s but few files yet exist for earlier material which may be relevant.

It is naturally undesirable to include deliberate falsehoods in applications and, if later found out, these could formerly invalidate the Patent for False Suggestion. However the 1977 Act does not recognise a specific attack on this ground and so such falsehood has now to be introduced and attacked as a sub-species of 'insufficiency'. In the USA, if the deception is sustained in correspondence with the Patent Examiner who is thereby persuaded to grant a Patent which might otherwise have been denied, this constitutes the serious offence of 'Fraud on the Patent Office' which makes the Patent unenforceable and exacts certain penalties. One common 'deception' is the omission of citations to prior art which the inventor considers irrelevant but the examiner might find pertinent to obviousness or anticipation. When filing in the US it is presently better to err on the safe side by over-citing and disposing of the citations in the preamble to the Application. However in the UK, unless the facts are irrefutable, it is less common for one of the parties to charge the other with skullduggery at a personal level. As one counsel put it:-

"It is generally a bad idea to attack character. Judges can faint at the sight of blood".

But in the USA they may be less shocked by it. Moreover in the (common) jury trials of technical cases, it is the jury which has the right to decide the level of royalties and damages to be paid by the loser. As in libel actions, if they have come to believe that they are righting some deep injustice, juries can be overgenerous in disposing of other people's money.

Some limitations of patenting

In 'hot' topic areas, it often happens that a number of persons or groups, working independently, come up with more-or-less the same invention at the same time. In the UK, and in most other civilised countries which have signed the Patents Cooperation Treaty (PCT), the Patent is granted to the first *applicant*. In the USA it is granted to the first *inventor*, as may be established from evidence such as (witnessed) laboratory notebooks. The American system, also used in the Phillipines and until recently in Canada, was intended to give the private inventor an equal chance against the big corporations.

• In practice the US rule causes untold difficulties mostly centering on the establishment of 'proof of invention' and who first 'reduced it to practice'. A foreigner can only 'swear back' to the date he lodged his application but a US citizen can swear back to his earliest records. This is a form of protectionism. It can entail much waving of smeared and encrusted pages of laboratory notebooks replete with indecipherable figures and jargon (requiring further interpretation by Experts). These were apparently witnessed by Dr Scrabble, the inventor's alleged then supervisor, who reputedly left his employers soon after signing the crucial page(s), without a forwarding address ... possibly to research the taxonomy of the pink-winged shrike in Outer Mongolia ... This aspect of US law is to be reviewed by Congress in 1994 with some likelihood of its being brought into line with the rest of civilisation.

Disclosure before application

In the UK, Europe and Japan, there is a strict rule that, except under confidentiality circumstances or where the disclosure was 'non-enabling', no breath of it, whether written or oral, demonstration or other representation, must escape the inventor prior to filing, otherwise his application is invalid. This is particularly harsh when applied to academic inventors whose jobs depend on a steady flow of publications and the sensible Americans here temper justice with mercy, allowing limited publication within a finite period (the "One Year" rule). Moreover the incautious US inventor may himself be caught out when he publishes as permitted in his own country but subsequently tries to file in foreign countries, including the UK, which may then invalidate his filings on the basis of his prior publication. It is a rule which some British academics find particularly difficult to understand:-

• Professor A. Nonym, of a leading London college, even offered QMC Industrial Research Ltd a novel device for patenting and exploitation which, it eventually transpired, had been reported at three international conferences, together with demonstration of a working model, and then exported in an attempted licensing deal to a Swedish manufacturer. The firm had replied, as do so many, expressing polite interest but mentioning that they already had a 'very similar' device undergoing trials in their laboratories. The Inventor was deeply offended when QMC-IRL declined his offer.

But now at last there seems to be a very real possibility of greater harmonisation, if not of an agreed 'world patent' emerging, which might combine the best features of the US and European systems i.e. 'first to file' and 'permissible limited disclosure prior to filing'.

Oppositions

Oppositions to grant of patents may be filed after publication (or, more usually, grant) of a Patent on the basis of any or all of the aforementioned grounds for invalidity and they will normally be heard at mini-trials held within the Patent Offices involved (including the EPO but no longer in the UK Patent Office). In the UK, it is usual for the firm's Patent Agents to prepare the case which they may plead themselves or instruct junior counsel. Commonly, independent Experts are employed to assist in the preparation and, where required, to swear Statutory Declarations containing technical evidence to put before the Examining Officer. Occasionally they are also called to give oral evidence at the hearings.

Alternatives to patenting

Aside from its relatively high cost, the main corporate deterrent to patenting is the requirement to allow publication by the Patent Office within 18 months of Application. Publication of even a 'strong' Patent Application in a key area by a reputable company is usually followed by flurries of me-too and look-alike activities in competitor's laboratories.

• In the early 1950s, when employed by a large UK chemical corporation, the author learned that it was common research policy to make application for about twenty or so patents for each invention. Of course one application contained the valuable technology and the other nineteen were decoys, 'paper patents', untried and specifically intended to waste the time of our competitors' research teams. The fun started when our team accidentally found that one of the decoys actually worked better than the process in the 'real' patent.

Protection by secrecy

There is a strong temptation to avoid the need for publication and to pass up, either temporarily or for evermore, the opportunity for the legal protection offered by the Patent. The information is designated 'secret' within the Company. As such it is precarious, being protected only by the discretion of the employees and their restraint under their contracts of employment.

• A leading tyre manufacturer is well-known to have pursued a secrecy policy with success for many years but it is said that this has been due in large part to a very stable work force with miniscule turn-over of senior technicians. This in turn was aided by a very liberal staff policy including high salaries and related benefits and perhaps the inability to find suitable alternative technological employment in the Clermont-Ferrand of yesteryear where the Auvergnats main industries often seem to involve doing natural things with smelly animals to make rather good cheese. Had their factory been in Birmingham or Akron, where staff poaching used to be rife, the story might possibly have been different.

Breach of confidence and Trade secrets

Every now and then an employee leaves such a company and may then be alleged to have spilt the beans to his new employer or used the previous employer's novel ideas in creating his own competitive business. Such actions are unwelcome to the previous employer who will naturally want to take all possible steps to protect his commercial position. Whereas most contracts-of-employment restrict the ex-employee from operating in the main field for a fixed period (of say one year) and subsequently prohibit any use or disclosure of secrets learned at his former workplace, the Courts have historically taken the view that an ex-employee is entitled to use his common general knowledge in his new post, this being part of the "tools of his trade".

In order to succeed in establishing mis-use of a Trade Secret in civil proceedings, a distinction has therefore to be established between, on the one hand, the legitimate tool of the trade and, on the other, the intellectual jemmy used by an unscrupulous (and perhaps revengeful) ex-employee to burgle the technology storehouse of his former employer. Such a distinction is difficult to make by the Court in the absence of technical evidence and Independent Experts are employed to establish in particular the industry knowledge of the relevant technology as at the date of the ex-employee's severance.

Defensive publication

An effective corporate strategy is to encourage early publication of each and every invention omitting only the key details which enable these inventions to be actually put into practice. Such defensive publication can act as a deterrent to all but the most informed and sophisticated corporate competitors from filing their own patents in a field in case the Patent Examiner may subsequently regard these as 'obvious'. Furthermore much research will have to be done by the challenger to find the missing link, with no certainty either that it will be found or that, if and when it is, there may not be some other patent 'in the pipe-line' which will restrict or prevent its use.

A complementary strategy of corporate patent departments often involves the submission of numerous Applications covering the key features of the technology which are filed and then abandoned just before compulsory publication becomes due. This results in the invention remaining secret (a policy called, in industry, 'file & drop'). A few days before withdrawal of the old one, a 'new' Application is normally filed which looks remarkably like its predecessor (plus any later discoveries) so that all that is lost at each substitution is the 'priority date' for any future patent, which moves forward by a few months. This continues until the corporate grapevine transmits a message that a competitor's research lab has commenced active cultivation of the patch. At that moment, the then-extant Application is rapidly converted to full patent, the disadvantage of 'publication' notwithstanding. Delay in patenting can confer several benefits:-

•	establishment of a commercial time-lead without need for disclosure of the novel technology

•	prolongation of the monopoly to match a slow market development

•	deferment of patent support fees

... but at the serious risk of leaving the technology vulnerable to a competitor's interim filing of a similar patent which he decides to pursue.

Because even a large corporation cannot usually afford to patent every one of its in-house inventions, which infants are to be 'left exposed' is a delicate corporate decision. However in the USA the monopoly runs from the date of issue, not the date of filing, so they can play a further game in delaying final grant by the Patent Office for as long as possible.

Of course it is not beyond the wit of research labs to lay false trails in the form of utterly bogus patents or other publications designed to panic competitive technologists into disclosing their hands by filing their own patent applications. This is done with the intention of surveying the competition without incurring the heavy costs of mounting a full investigative programme. To do this effectively requires a more than usually commercially-aware Research Director and a particularly loyal corporate research staff.

Many Research Directors nurture their self-images as scientists and are reluctant to tarnish them by descending to this level of 'corporate gamesmanship'. Perhaps this is for the best since to proceed beyond the 'Application' stage incurs the risk of falsehood (as discussed earlier).

Infringement as a policy

When faced with a block in the market in the form of proprietary technology, an all too-common strategy is simply to infringe. A larger and more reputable company will usually do this only on the basis of legal advice, usually that the infringed Patent is almost certainly 'invalid'. The smaller company may take a chance, rather than any advice, believing that its market share is likely to be too small to incite the patent-owner to costly and uncertain retribution.

From such ill-judged acts stem numerous Patent Infringement Actions. The US courts recognise 'wilful infringement' of valid patents in which the infringer is reckless as to whether or not he infringes and he may be punished in terms of triple damages and payment of all the innocent party's attorneys fees. In fact, without the most strict controls and such exceedingly stiff financial penalties, the marketplace would soon be ruled by the age-old principle[4]:-

"   The good old rule
Sufficeth them, the simple plan,
That they should take, who have the power,
And they should keep who can"

---
[4]   William Wordsworth (d. 1850) Memorials of a Tour in Scotland (1803)

28

3   Lawyers, Scientists, and Expert Witnesses

Court procedures, with their wigs, their robes and their ceremonials, can sometimes seem to outsiders like hybrids between the mechanics of an established religion and of a state theatre. This is neither reprehensible nor altogether surprising. All these institutions are, or should be, concerned with the advancement of truth and the negation of evil. Insofar as this is practicable, their processes and presentations aim to remain independent of the ephemeral and occasionally baleful influence of politics and politicians. Law, theatre and church all try to pass down their teaching by way of 'decisions', performances or edicts to their supposedly credulous customers without directly inviting dissent or debate. But dissent and debate nevertheless occur both within and outside the institutions. In contrast, scientists try to throw open their tentative conclusions to peer review at the earliest possible stage and, even after a lifetime's work, should be ready to welcome debate on alternative explanations of their findings. Hitherto these cultural parallels and contrasts have not been much explored and so this Chapter is devoted to trying to make such a comparison by liberal use of quotations from the scientific, liturgical and dramatic gurus.

As mentioned in the Preface, lawyers do not always see eye-to-eye with the Experts whom they hire and, though we Experts can be intransigent, misunderstandings may sometimes also arise because of the failure of the lawyer to comprehend the true nature of Science and of scientists. It is equally true that the scientists who are hired do not always ponder sufficiently the nature of the legal processes in which they are required to play a part. For the sake both of practitioners and their clients, it is obviously desirable that such cultural problems should be debated and then, if possible, resolved.

Intellect , Emotion and Presentation

Though the Law may try to persuade its customers that it operates at a dispassionate and wholly intellectual level, decisions are more often reached partly on emotional and, very occasionally, even irrational grounds. Many of us would have some sympathy for the view that[1] :-

"Opinion is ultimately determined by the feelings and not by the intellect"

---
[1]   Herbert Spencer (d. 1903)   Social Statics ch 30

Decisions may depend not simply on the factual material of a case but also on the quality of the *mise-en-scène* devised by the solicitors and the oratorical skills of the barristers as the 'actors' they have hired to present it. But this is not going so far as to suggest crudely that, in each and every legal Action, 'principals can outsmart principles'. Nevertheless consultation of the league table for successes by individual barristers (and firms of solicitors) shows, in the view of many of their would-be clients, a level of 'wins' not simply related to the quality and integrity of their briefs but also equally reliant on the selection and emphasis placed on particular aspects of the evidence made available to them. There is little doubt that a good barrister is a past-master of the art of diminishing the significance of the inconvenient fact. The art of 'pleading' is perhaps a matter of[2]:-

"All things are lawful for me, but all things are not expedient".

At any rate, the legal profession like any other recognises star quality and expects clients to pay the appropriate premium for a barrister with an international reputation for winning cases. Judges must all have experienced, as will have witnesses[3]:-

"How the heart listened while he pleading spoke!
While on the enlightened mind, with winning art,
His gentle reason so persuasive stole
That the charmed hearer thought it was his own"

For a barrister or attorney to win consistently, on a random series of briefs and in defiance of the law of averages, might suggest a gift for selection and presentation of the most favourable evidence above the norm. This is an aspect of the litigation scene which sometimes causes alarm and despondency[4] among the lay public less familiar with the inherent fairness of the adversarial process.

Scientists can be equally sceptical of 'the legal system' but, in reality, we can be even more endangered by a too-firm belief in our own 'objectivity'

---

[2]   Holy Bible   I Corinthians x

[3]   James Thomson (d.1748)   To the memory of the Lord Talbot

[4]   "What makes all doctrines plain and clear?
About two hundred pounds a year.
And that which was prov'd true before,
Prove false again? Two hundred more."
Samuel Butler (d.1680)   Hudibras pt iii

than are the lawyers, perhaps because some of us trust in this objectivity far too sincerely, even using it as a substitute for any more profound belief.

Many scientists need to know themselves better[5] for, unfortunately, some of us do not rate as highly as we think on the scale of self-knowledge. In studying some new phenomenon, the weaker scientist may form but a single theory and then seek avidly for the experimental facts to support it. If this search yields meagre results, it is particularly important not to be dismissive of contrary evidence or to denigrate those who are brave enough to advance arguments based upon novel material.

Thanks to the defective philosophy of certain influential Victorian writers, there is still a widespread public misapprehension about the so-called 'scientific method'. As a result, the abilities and achievements of scientists can too often be regarded either with awe or with derision and our pronouncements are too easily received by different groups of society either as divine ordinance or as superstitious mumbo-jumbo. Society's views of scientists as gurus can therefore become undesirably polarised, either very positively or very negatively.

In an era of poor education, much of what we write is politely ignored by non-scientists as 'too difficult' because they are not trained to interpret it. This communication problem is, in part at least, the fault (or the misfortune) of scientists who so often have not learned to handle words as well as they handle concepts or materials. The root of this may well be in the too-early specialisation of school-children, whether destined for scientific careers who are no longer required to become fully literate in order to qualify for university entrance, or for arts careers which gives them a premature escape from the beneficial rigours of science and maths.

So there is a precursor problem to be solved before it is possible to consider the qualities of the scientist which make him a good Witness. This problem is no less than discussing in a few paragraphs firstly 'what science is' and secondly 'how a professional scientist attempts to practise and communicate it'.

---

5   "Ful wys is he that can him-selven knowe"
Geoffrey Chaucer (d. 1400) Canterbury Tales: The Monke's Tale

Science and the work of Scientists

Several eminent writers have begun to tackle this problem of communication of science, one of the first and most successful being Medawar in his thoughtful essays[6]: 'Two conceptions of Science' and 'Hypothesis and Imagination'. So important are his conclusions that an attempt is now made to to summarise them.

What Science and scientists are ... and what we do

• Scientists are in the business of having ideas, mostly about natural phenomena. We compare these ideas with available data and are concerned with the testing or trying out of our ideas, which usually involves measurement. By using an *idea* (or 'hypothesis' or 'theory' or ..) as a starting point, we narrow and focus the amount of experimentation or testing which has to be done to show a probable fit with observable 'facts' and so enable extrapolation from the particular to the more general.

But we risk ending up with a poor correlation with real-world behaviour, showing that our theory was erroneous; and this negative result means starting again with a new theory[7]:-

"The great Tragedy of Science ... the slaying of a beautiful hypothesis by an ugly fact"

• Scientists are critical and analytical. We require hard evidence upon which to advance an opinion, this evidence usually being an amalgam of the related work of others which for good reason we feel able to rely on, plus consistent data of our own obtained by a variety of independent experimental observations, preferably using differently-based techniques.

• Before crystallising an opinion, certainly before publishing it, we scientists need to ask ourselves and others whether there may be other equally plausible, or more plausible, explanations for our observations, data or 'results' upon which our opinion is going to be based.

---

[6]   Sir Peter B. Medawar   The Art of the Soluble   Methuen & Co. 1967 (loc. cit.)

[7]   Thomas Henry Huxley (d. 1895)   Collected Essays xii The Coming of Age of the Origin of Species

As the scientist's work develops, tentative conclusions reached in respect of a wider and wider range of facts give place to[8]:-

" .. more general statements of steadily increasing explanatory power and compass".

The attitudes and beliefs of research scientists are well summarised by the poet T. S. Eliot, not quotable here because of copyright restrictions. To crudely paraphrase some magnificent verse[9] and apply it to the matter in hand, i.e. the definition of 'research method':-

The beginning and the end may be one and the same thing. One starts from the 'hypothesis', the 'beginning', and explores in greater and greater depth until one is as certain as is humanly possible that one fully understands the path taken through experiment to reach again the hypothesis ... now as an experimental conclusion, the 'end' ... so confirming its 'correctness'. Only then can the Scientist say for the first time that he 'knows' about the system he is studying.

What Science and scientists are not ... and what we do not

• Scientists do not deal in certainties, only in likelihoods. In mathematical terms, we deal in 'probabilities'. Unlike most lawyers, we are not in the *absolute* business of proving that something is 'true' and another thing is 'false'. Applied to our technological studies, we believe that this sort of 'lawyers' language' would take us into the realm of metaphysics because such categorical statements are not relatable to opinions derived from observation.

• Competent scientists are not 'narrow specialists'. We have steadily become less and less specialised in that we are capable of drawing on and adapting for our purposes a very wide range of investigative techniques, computing methods and engineering technology.

• Despite the confident assertions of the non-scientific Victorian apologists, science is not principally about 'deduction of hypotheses from facts' or even about 'induction'. The latter heresy, which has caused so much of the confusion, has been defined as:-

---

8   Sir P. B. Medawar (loc. cit.)

9   T S Eliot (d. 1965)   Four Quartets: "Little Gidding" Faber & Faber 1968

"a logically mechanised process of thought which, starting from simple declarations of fact arising out of the evidence of the senses, can lead with certainty to the truth of general laws".

Many scientists believe that the so-called 'scientific method', based on an inductive approach, is a myth. They do not even subscribe to the concepts of 'certainty' or 'truth', only to that of 'probability at a given level'. If anyone else wishes to equate a 95%, or 99%, or 99.9% probability with 'certainty', then they are welcome to do so; that is up to them. But even '99.99% certain' still suggests to the scientist the possibility, however remote, that there exists a 0.01% probability of being 'wrong' and that this could possibly be substantiated by further investigation, either now or with better techniques to be developed in the future.

The Scientist as 'Expert'

What is the relevance of the scientists psychology and working methods to his abilities as an Expert? Quoting again from Medawar[10], who goes to the heart of the problem facing the instructing solicitor seeking his Expert Witness:-

"Are scientists a homogeneous body of people in respect of temperament, motivation, and style of thought? (Obviously not: but we talk of *the* scientist nevertheless.) Is there such a thing as a 'scientific mind'? I think not. Or *the* scientific method? Again, I think not. What exactly are the terms of a scientist's contract with the truth? This is an important question, for according to the interpretation of the scientific process which I myself think the most plausible, a scientist, so far from being a man who never knowingly departs from the truth, is always *telling stories* in a sense not very far removed from that of the nursery euphemism ... stories which might be about real life but which have to be tested very scrupulously to find out if indeed they are so."

And, albeit in a footnote, Medawar even raises the possibility that less successful research scientists may have to use 'fancy' to fill in the gaps in their stories and 'some people tend to overdo it'. Of course in Expert Witness work there may be nothing inherently wrong in deploying 'fancy', provided that the speculation involved is clearly identified and the need for it, in bridging to perfect an argument, is made clear.

---
[10] Sir P. B. Medawar (loc. cit.)

34

But the way in which such fancy or speculation is introduced should never be confused with advocacy for one's client's case.

Because practising scientists are perpetually involved in debate as to the most probable explanation of their work, whether it be theoretical or experimental, they can risk appearing to outsiders as an argumentative, even a cretinous lot[11]. This does them less than justice. Scientists are simply used to working in a world where every move, every idea is freely open to question and, within (or very rarely beyond) the conventional bounds of common politeness, their every belief and every thought can be, and usually is, challenged by their peers and the fellow-members of their team[12]:-

"He that wrestles with us strengthens our nerves, and sharpens our skills. Our antagonist is our helper."

Indeed, most academic scientists are unhappy in working any other way ... but as Medawar goes on to say:-

"Though imaginative thought and criticism are equally necessary to a scientist, they are often very unequally developed in any one man. Professional judgement frowns upon extremes. The scientist who devotes his time to showing up the inadequacies of the work of others is suspected of lacking ideas of his own, and everyone loses patience with the man who bubbles over with ideas which he loses interest in and fails to follow up"

In no field is this more true than that of Expert Witness, where a proper sense of balance between positive presentation of a case and the ability to see flaws in the opposing argument is a highly valued attribute.

The amalgam of Law and Science which underlies the work of the Expert Witness is therefore an imperfect binary system, presently marred by culture conflicts, by ambition and by self-delusion, and so typical of the 'real world'. It is with this system that the novice Expert must grapple honestly from time to time during his period of instruction before giving Evidence. In so doing he should remind himself from time to time of the advice of

---

[11]   See the happy moron,
        He doesn't give a damn,
        I wish I were a moron ...
        My God! Perhaps I am."
        Anon.   Eugenics Review   July 1929

[12]   Edmund Burke (d. 1797)   Reflections on the Revolution in France

Francis Bacon[13] :-

"Read not to contradict and confute, nor to believe and take for granted, nor to find talk and discourse, but to weigh and consider".

Self-Management

The Expert Witness must possess both the self-knowledge and decisiveness of a good senior manager. The ground rules for this were laid down by Machiavelli[14], with the warm approval of Bacon[15] :-

"We are much beholden to Machiavel and others, that write what men do, and not what they ought to do"

Following Jay[16] on 'managers', the independent Expert should ideally be 'part Yogi and part Commissar': that is to say a combination of the intellectual, contemplative, thinker with analytical skills and an original slant on all technical aspects of the subject matter, with the energetic, well-organised and self-motivated 'army officer' who can accept, nay welcome, the arcane organisational structure by which the Law business operates. He must needs learn to deploy his technical knowledge to best advantage within this structure without continuously questioning the way in which lawyers go about their business or, worse, trying to force upon them his own concept of how technical preparation of a case should proceed.

To combine such dissimilar traits is rare; to combine them in balanced proportions almost unique. At one extreme, it is possible to fulfil the role of Expert Witness as a Yogi with no more than a smidgen of Commissar in one's psyche ... just enough to withstand the brow-beating of powerful personalities during preparation and examination without withdrawing into some protective inner shell wherein it seems possible to breath the less-tainted air of fundamental truth.

---

[13] Essay 'Of Studies'

[14] Niccolo di Bernardo dei Machiavelli (d. 1527) The Prince transl. George Bull, for Penguin Books Ltd, based on the edition of Mazzoni and Casella, Florence,1929.

[15] Advancement of Learning II, xxi

[16] The basis on this and many other management matters is that excellent, amusing but serious treatise by Antony Jay Management and Machiavelli Hodder & Stoughton, London 1967.

At the other extreme, the Commissar with but a hint of Yogi is pretty useless in the job. Often lacking sufficient capacity for the necessary intellectualization of the material, he will be tempted to efficiently recycle the original ideas of others fed to him in preparation without having evaluated them in any independent way and, when he finds himself giving evidence, such absence of independent thought is likely to become painfully apparent. Since the value of Expert Witness to the Court is primarily for the quality of his independent opinion, in the absence of any such opinion his presence in the witness-box may become superfluous. One need only recall the evidence of a very early Expert in the construction industry, who was so careful in his answer that it could have helped the Court not one iota[17] :-

"The Lord stood upon a wall made by a plumbline,
with a plumbline in his hand,
And the Lord said unto me, Amos, what seest thou?
And I said: A plumbline"

Amos had effectively given his evidence not as an Expert but as a witness of fact. Sadly even on this basis, though no doubt truthful, the evidence was clearly of little value.

The need for Yogi characteristics notwithstanding, the Commissar's capacity for organised and productive hard graft is a most valuable attribute. Whereas the Yogi may develop interesting theories and explanations based on a fairly superficial coverage of a few basic papers in the case, the Commissar will rapidly read, absorb and, if required, act on every paper thrown at him. He will order, classify and retrieve these for all the world like a Périgord swine grubbing for truffles. His is the tenacity needed to get the most out of Discovery (see Chapter 6).

Working with The Team

Because of the way litigation is organised, the Expert must necessarily be a team player. We have seen that the adversarial system requires his team to represent the client's technical case correctly and fairly but in such a way that its strengths are clearly expressed to the Court while any weaknesses are underpinned to the best of the Expert's technical ability. Since each team does this, the Court receives from each of the Parties to a dispute a clear

---
[17]   Holy Bible Amos vi

indication of the best technical case which can be made for that party.

Much depends on the team leader, usually the instructing solicitor, who must instinctively evaluate, react to and harness the Yogi-like and Commissar-like attributes in the various members which constitute the team, allocating preparation work and promulgating information in such a way that everything gets done in the most effective way according to a pre-set timetable. The timetable is that leading to Trial and is agreed by the Parties with the Court, usually at the procedural stage known as Summons for Directions. The solicitor therefore bears much of the burden for success or failure in presentation of the case; in fact, he needs quite remarkable resistance to stress in staying the course up to Trial.

The solicitor's crucial work as *de facto* leader is often made more lively by the existence of a titular Leader, Leading Counsel, who will expect to direct operations whenever he has the time and inclination to attend any meetings. Although this relationship is often a delicate one, it works no less well than in the Board Room of many an industrial company, wherein the executive Managing Director is responsible for the efficient running of the enterprise on a day-to-day basis but must try to maintain, at least in public, the illusion that the distinguished and colourful non-executive Chairman is the company's main-spring and inspiration, the *fons et origo* of all successes, even though he may sometimes be found absent elsewhere (on urgent company matters) at times of stress and failure. In practice the relationship during litigation is sustained both by the friendship prevalent in a small community such as the Patent Bar, and by a mutual dependency: the barrister on the solicitor for his further instructions and the solicitor on counsel for his services in the High Court wherein solicitors themselves are not (yet) permitted to plead.

Rapport with Counsel

As Trial approaches, the advocate role of Leader does become more and more important and, at the Trial, like any good producer who has launched his Hamlet on to the boards, the instructing solicitor, while continuing to feed the hungry mind which is flying from his nest, must really prompt and pray. At this moment, the Expert Witness has a complex role which requires not only the marshalling of technical facts and opinions developed over perhaps years of preparation but also the rapid distilling of these to drops of that priceless elixir which can stimulate Counsel in the right way and at the right time. Any unanticipated hesitation or prevarication by the Expert can lose the Leader's confidence either in the correctness of the science or technology on which he is expected to rely or in the Expert's ability to deliver it as his Evidence to the Court. Fine judgement is needed at this stage as to whether to dig in and insist on explaining, in one's own way and at one's own speed, a complex but vitally important technical principle which may alter the whole of Counsel's putative argument, or whether to temporarily drop the point in the hope of reinjecting it in simplified form. This may conveniently be done at some later stage of preparation, when it can help to have in mind[18]:-

"Men must be taught as if you taught them not,
And things unknown proposed as things forgot"

And so both personal judgement and advanced communication skills are important Expert attributes. At conferences, as so often, Bacon's recipe[19] for handling difficult matters can come to the rescue:-

"In things that are tender and unpleasing, it is good to break the ice by some whose words are of less weight, and to reserve the more weighty voice to come in as by chance"

Alternatively, communication, *in absentia,* of a short written note (perhaps with a longer explanatory appendix) may do the trick.

However they learn to work together, towards the end of preparation there should be but one joint objective: complete confidence and understanding between the Lawyers and the Expert. This understanding should encompass the nature of the arguments, the principle supporting evidence for them, the ability of Counsel to argue each point coherently and link them together into a chain of argument, and the ability of the Expert to support this argument with facts and opinions which will stand up to determined critical scrutiny.

Some Counsel and some Experts develop this rapport to a marked degree; others do not, and the presentation of their client's case suffers accordingly. What is certain is that the chance of developing such a working relationship

---

[18]   Alexander Pope (d. 1744) Essay on 'Criticism'

[19]   Francis Bacon (d. 1626) Essay 'Of Cunning'

is much enhanced by social contact during the preparation of a case, which gives opportunities to both Leader and Expert to meet as ordinary people.

The Expert under fire

Novice Experts often complain that their words or opinions are "twisted" by Counsel whether in preparation, at conferences, or under examination in the court, more particularly under cross-examination by opposing Counsel. It is therefore important that the Expert should try to enter the barrister's mind, to understand his objectives and see how he tries to achieve them. It is the mental equivalent of 'keeping an eye on the ball'. But it is difficult to introduce this concept to the novice Expert without first giving some idea of what goes on during examination of a witness. In order to illustrate how things may develop in an actual examination, there is now interpolated, by way of a caricature, a short fictitious Example (Appendix A) to give the reader in advance a flavour of what the inexperienced Expert might have to face up to when actually giving evidence (as discussed fully in Chapter 11).

This black-and-white Example, called 'A disastrous cross-examination', is included simply to illustrate how easily the Expert can forget the framework in which he is replying and be led into new and dangerous territory wherein he has not properly formulated his opinions.

The Essence of Independence

Critics of our trial system, indeed some who are a part of it, sometimes suggest that true 'independence' would only be demonstrated by an Expert who recognised and treated the technical weaknesses of a case in exactly the same way as the strengths. But those who have instructed independent Experts will know that this is exactly what does happen, any weaknesses in the case being exposed to the best of the Expert's ability in pre-trial conferences, so that they can be considered and, if possible, dealt with. If the Expert cannot be satisfied that the weaknesses he apprehends are minimal or tolerable, he may not be called to give evidence and will often withdraw from the Action. Other equally 'independent' Experts may see the case differently, these disagreeing with the first Expert's opinion as to sources of weakness and therefore being more suitable to represent this particular client's case in court.

Presuming that an equally independent Expert is appearing for each side, some critics go on to say that they would then expect both Experts to give 'identical evidence' to the Court. That this does not happen they attribute to the inadequacies of the system, closely allied to the corruptibility of Experts ... more particularly by those instructing them. Such criticisms are, in the author's view, unjustified and without proper regard to the realities either of Science or of the Law. The issues which surface as contentious at Trial are not necessarily, or even generally, of a simple, factual kind. In practice it is rare to find marked divergence of opinion of Experts concerning 'the facts' insofar as these are observations of processing or experimentation. Disputes which give rise to litigation often concern commercially valuable but technically ill-defined products and processes.

Experts are, or should be, hired not as oracles to give *ex cathedra* pronouncements as to absolute 'rights' and 'wrongs' but rather to give their honest assessments of technical probabilities. This is what scientists do naturally in the course of their ordinary professional work and it is all they would expect to be able to offer in court. It is therefore unsurprising that different Experts are quite likely to make different assessments; indeed, were they to agree in all details this would surely be *prima facie* evidence for lack of independence, probably through collusion. It is in the *interpretation* of the facts and the conclusions that are drawn from them that Expert opinion will naturally vary. This is a consequence of employing intelligent people to give considered opinions on difficult subject-matter.

In practice, independence is more a matter of being prepared to stand up as Devil's Advocate against a 'party line', to be prepared to tell a client or his adviser to his face that one believes his technical case is flawed, to be able to ask for modifications in an approach and expect such a request to be taken seriously. The guiding principle[20] is:-

"Be so true to thyself as thou be not false to others"

What if, after "full and frank discussion", reconciliation of the Expert's considered view with that of his clients or their advisors proves impossible? It is then much better for both parties if the Expert withdraws well before Trial than that he should continue preparation under duress and with reluctance and then give weak and uncomfortable evidence which will not help the Court to reach a proper decision.

---

[20]   Francis Bacon   Essays 'Of Wisdom for a Man's Self'

Loss of faith

It follows *a fortiori* that an Expert who comes not to believe in the correctness of the overall technical case of his client should not appear for him at Trial. But the time to raise difficulties and state a 'devil's advocate' view is at one or more of the many conferences which take place during the preparation stage, not in the witness box, and all experienced trial lawyers do encourage such free exchange of views during the 'work up'. This gives opportunity to examine the darker corners of the case and, if necessary, conduct experiments to find the truest state of affairs. If this further knowledge alters the Expert's previously-favourable technical opinion, he must make this clear to his instructing solicitor and, if the matter cannot be resolved, seek release from the Action.

Early instruction

All of this preparative skirmishing will take time and provides good reason to instruct Experts at the earliest possible stage in any dispute. It may also eventually lead to a preference for the High Court procedure over that of the PCC which does occasionally seem to require too-hasty technical decisions by ill-prepared Experts who are required to advise in evenly-balanced disputes.

Genuine differences between Expert opinions

Presuming that such an honest approach is used by the Experts on each side, each being an Expert in the general field, it must still be recognised that the detailed technical field of each Expert within the general field is likely to be different. It follows that such difference will necessarily be reflected in their respective judgements of the relative importance of detailed technical aspects of the case. Moreover the differences are likely to be be further reflected in the reference work done by each Expert during preparation and in the planning of any experiments to check factual matters[21]:-

"Where there is much desire to learn, there of necessity will be much arguing, much writing, many opinions; for opinion in good men is but knowledge in the making"

---

[21]   John Milton (d. 1674) Areopagitica

42

If the Action proceeds to Trial, the Court will be faced with two or more technologists, often from significantly-different fields, who can express honestly to the Judge somewhat different approaches and view-points on the documents and other evidence before him. This wider perspective enables the Judge to develop a multi-dimensional view of the subject matter and, more often than not, prefer the evidence of one Expert on one particular topic while preferring that of another on some other. To hear a number of albeit dissentient voices, each of them truthful, presenting well-ordered and properly documented opinions on the same factual material, should and would, one may believe, be the Court's ideal. But the alternative of hearing two 'speaking Bodleians' droning away precisely the same views about the pros & cons of a pre-analysed dispute could deny the Court any flexibility in considering 'construction' and any real chance of examining the independent Experts to clarify the Judge's mind on the technical nature of the issues.

"But why don't they all say the same thing?" is therefore a question which seems to ignore the basis of scientific philosophy. For, in Science, one makes progress on the basis of arguments concerning *levels of probability* rather than by chasing a fictitious boundary between the rainbow of 'truth' and the base earth of 'falsehood'.

4   What an Expert does

Work usually comes to an experienced Expert initially by telephone (or fax) either from people who know him, whether in industry or in the legal professions, or from people to whom he has been recommended by individual solicitors, patent agents or counsel with whom he has worked in the past. But the novice Expert must be sought via publications lists, conference proceedings, committee memberships or academic departmental staff lists. One useful source is the BEST data-base[1] initiated by the author when chairman of the University Directors of Industrial Liaison (UDIL). Nowadays the larger partnerships also carry in-house data-bases listing the names of individuals Experts who have appeared in previous Actions or have been recommended to them. Despite the changes which have come about in the last decade concerning the marketing of professional services, there is still little point in selling oneself by advertisement. This is more likely to raise suspicion than elicit a positive response from potential clients or their professional advisers. Most of these know what they like and many prefer to like what they know.

Appropriate background

On being offered work, the Expert must address to himself two major questions:-

•   Is this a matter on which I can assist? (in particular: Is the technology sufficiently familiar? Do I have appropriate qualifications and/or experience?)

•   Can I take on this work without conflict of interest?

When litigation has already commenced, the first question can usually be settled quickly by perusing the briefing papers including the Pleadings, Patent-in-suit, and major Prior Art supplied by the instructing solicitor or patent agent. Before accepting, it is necessary to satisfy oneself that one has the necessary qualifications and experience to give independent evidence to the Court if the Action goes through to Trial. However a pre-litigation enquiry, whether directly from an industrial corporation or via their professional adviser, may not always be sufficiently specific to allow an

---

[1]   British Expertise in Science and Technology, Longman Cartermill Ltd, St Andrews

immediate answer. This is particularly true when the initial brief is to include focusing in on the nature of the potential dispute and suggesting avoidance measures. Sometimes it is necessary to proceed on the basis of a 'pilot contract' without commitment by either party to continue if the contentious subject matter turns out to be different from what was initially supposed.

Conflict of interest

The second question is often not difficult to answer in principle, but may prove so in practice. Briefly, Experts have two guiding rules:-

•   If the Expert is 'retained' by a client organisation, that is to say if he personally and/or a major research programme in the field in which he has an interest happen to be currently funded by the client, in no circumstances can he act *against* that organisation. Furthermore, if properly qualified and available to do so, he would usually feel morally bound to act *for* his client as an Expert. Conversely, if *not* so retained by a former client, who has no current interest in his research work, the Expert would feel free to act *either* for *or* against that client.

•   However, in common with other industrial consultants, if he has received confidential information about the subject matter and instruction by a client while acting as an Expert for that client and, within a period of say two years, he finds himself approached by a competitor organisation (or its representative) to act for the competitor *in exactly the same technical field*, then he would normally regard this as conflict of interest and have to refuse the new commission.

In order to preserve his independence, the Expert should not be bound 'to the Client' only to the limited subject matter of the particular Action. UK and European firms do seem quite happy with such as the above distinctions which are consistent with many Contracts of Employment, and so indeed do most clients in the USA. However there may be exceptions. By way of example:-

•   An Expert acted on but one single case for a large overseas corporation by whom he was never retained as consultant. After the case ended he heard nothing further from these clients. Some fourteen years later, he was asked to act *against* the same previous client in respect of quite different subject matter. They objected strongly to his retention by their opponents acting, in bringing the matter before the Court, as if the Expert had some continuing obligation to them. Given the concept of 'independence' this did seem especially unreasonable ... and so the Court found.

Settling fees

Having agreed to act, it is usual to agree a scale of 'fees and expenses'. If one can charge all clients the same hourly rates, current for at least the duration of the calendar year and recharge expenses at cost, this merely involves a statement to this effect. Approval is normally sought from the client, followed by exchange of standard letters confirming these arrangements. However different and equally viable systems are in use, including per diem rates coupled with retainer fees and so on (Chapter 13). The basis agreed must be clearly delineated and proper records of activity kept which may be important in connection with the 'taxation' of costs after a Trial many months hence.

Very rarely, difficulties with fees can arise at a later stage. An example is the so-called 'instruction' which, when accepted, is supposed to tie the Expert to represent one of the parties when in reality the client or his solicitor has no serious intention of asking him to act. Another very recent phenomenon is seriously delayed settlement of Accounts and the consequent imposition of interest charges by the Expert. These and other matters are further discussed in Chapter 13 which also reviews the retention of the Expert for the duration of Trial, a matter normally dealt with in a way not dissimilar to that used in determining Brief Fees for Counsel.

Initial briefing

Having accepted instruction, the Expert should then expect to receive a briefing bundle and to start work. At the earliest stage of a dispute, this may merely be a letter from a director of the client firm saying 'Get to the bottom of this problem and report to the Board'. At this stage one first presumes that there is a wish to attempt to settle the dispute without litigation. However if the dispute has been festering for some time and views expressed or actions taken, it is essential to be briefed fully before commencing activity. This requires not only detailed reading of reports and correspondence but usually one or more meetings with those who have been involved and who know the background. Certainly no purpose will be served in pursuing lines of enquiry or attempts at resolution which have already been fully explored by client's technical staff.

Alternatives to litigation: its avoidance

Full-blown litigation is not the only way of settling technical disputes. More and more, recourse is made to cheaper, quicker and less formal procedures: arbitration, negotiation, mediation and other types of 'alternative dispute resolution' (ADR). Besides saving costs and reducing the heavy pressure on the courts with its attendant delays to hearings, these procedures have the immense advantage that they are are all *confidential* to the parties, no published report at all entering the public domain. And ADR can often make it easier easier for individuals within a corporation to save face on the basis that[2]:-

"A peace is of the nature of a conquest;
For then both parties nobly are subdu'd,
And neither party loser"

In Expert Determination, the parties normally place themselves in the hands of the independent Expert to make a decision which they agree in advance to accept. Whereas formal arbitration involves reference to a Court, 'Expert Determination' is only subject to the Law of Contract. In fact the parties may wish to enter into a specific contract prior to a decision which makes the Expert's decision final and binding thus avoiding the cost and uncertainty of protracted Appeal procedures. The decision can then be challenged only on the grounds of fraud, partiality or mistake. However the grounds for such challenge are narrowly defined: for instance, mistakes of fact and of opinion have to stand, the only significant reason for overturning the decision being if the Expert has addressed 'the wrong question'! While it is open to the (losing) party to sue the Expert, short of establishing professional negligence, such litigation has not been effective in obtaining redress. It is usually possible to cover the 'negligence' risk by extension of a Professional Indemnity insurance.

---

[2]   William Shakespeare (d. 1616)   King Henry IV Part II iii

Unlike his more advisory role as an independent Witness, the Expert here takes on the role of 'adjudicator' which may well require exercise of wisdom and judgement beyond the immediate area of his technical expertise. Some parties are naturally reluctant to commit themselves in advance to such adjudication and it is not unusual to stop short of a final decision; rather to be required to clarify and even decide technical issues and issue a report which can be agreed by the parties and then used by them in some more formal arbitration procedure. This provides a sort of half-way house to the legal process. More common still is the ADR meeting, usually chaired by the Expert, in which he hears the submissions of the Parties, identifies common ground between them and tries to suggest compromise solutions to their differences, a form of mediation. His proposals are not binding on the parties, but are intended to offer new ways forward towards a legal settlement contract. In general, Expert Determination to give a binding decision is more appropriate in settling disputes between implacable enemies, while wholly informal 'mediation' is successful between temporarily-aggrieved corporate friends.

ADR in practice

As an independent practitioner, one is usually courteously received by one's client's potential adversaries and can in consequence first hold 'off-the-record' meetings with their scientists and engineers. This puts the Expert in the position of a sort of 'intellectual stake-holder' in which he can receive and appreciate the arguments both of his client and also the competitor, without at that stage expressing commital to either. On a number of occasions, there has been opportunity to use such meetings to dispel apprehension and to develop neutral communication lines between companies which have almost ceased to be on speaking terms. This allows both sides to consider whether the origins of the potential dispute are 'material' in the context of their global operations. If the differences seem immaterial, one can recommend the recommencement of settlement negotiations between the directors, and this is sometimes successful. And if things do not work out so well, at least no permanent harm has been done and the foundations may have been established for some higher form of arbitration.

Much of this kind of work is simply the resolution of misunderstandings between otherwise friendly organisations who for instance may have reached false conclusions as to the invasion of their markets by unlicensed competitors who, in turn, see no merit in such protection as is being claimed for the products in dispute. In such cases, the two organisations may at first *jointly* commission an independent Expert to prepare a Report setting out the issues and the technical facts gleaned from interviews with staff of both companies supported by relevant internal documentation. This Report is often supplemented by additional (published) information and the results of any agreed experiments or plant trials. If so requested, the Report can contain a chapter of conclusions as to the rights and wrongs of the dispute but more often it is simply used as a 'facts primer' by senior management engaged in eye-ball to eye-ball settlement negotiations.

Alternatively, after preparing and submitting his Report, the Expert then chairs a semi-formal meeting in which discussion of the issues takes place between the appointed representatives of the each party. After this, following due consideration, he is required to sum up the position and give his personal (i.e. non-binding) opinion regarding the several responsibilities of each of the Parties.

Decisions without documentation?

An interesting suggestion has been made to settle disputes by a 'simple' procedure which apparently involves the complete absence of any documents. This has the obvious advantage that it will be extemely cheap to set up. The Expert is left for an hour in a room together with one representative from each party whose oral presentation of the two sides of the case convinces him in favour of the one or the other.

Although perhaps ancient in origin, being redolent of champions engaged in single-handed combat, the concept is also wholly contemporary. The most obvious model is the 'TV chat-show': let us say 'Fair-play from Frost' or 'Winning with Wogan'. But ordinary Experts, needing time to learn the technical details and to think over the arguments besides avoiding being over-influenced by the better orator, must find this an impossibly tough assignment! In most industrial disputes there is no simple 'right' or 'wrong' answer but rather a gradual rapprochement can be achieved, usually during a series of meetings between parties who have usually adopted polarized positions in an otherwise evenly balanced situation. In order to resolve matters to the satisfaction of both Parties, it usually seems better to proceed very gently, if necessary over a protracted period, making it clear that due consideration has been given to every material factor which the Parties regard as significant. However painstaking the refereeing process, such disputes can seldom be settled amicably in this way unless:-

• there is some basic goodwill between the parties which extends to Board level; and

• there is no history of supposed or actual 'dirty tricks', previous attempted infringement, threats to suppliers or customers, staff poaching, and so on.

Fights to the death sometimes occur between established corporations and newly-created rival firms set up by their disaffected ex-senior staff. In such cases the intransigent attitudes of individuals can often seem to transcend the objectivity of the technical points which they should be arguing. Attempting to mediate from such a position is usually ineffectual and may be counter-productive. Each client needs to be told not to waste money on informal arbitration but rather to instruct his solicitor to commence formal proceedings.

Informal negotiation of settlements: how the Expert can assist

As an alternative to any of the foregoing procedures involving the Expert as an executive chairman or adjudicator, many firms like to keep the conduct of proceedings in the hands of their Directors and to pursue a settlement of the dispute by (friendly) negotiation. The negotiation of such settlements is a skilled job for business negotiators, with solicitors perhaps invisible though often within easy call to settle queries and, hopefully, to draw up a formal Settlement Agreement. Nevertheless it is usually worthwhile for them to have the independent Expert standing by in case, by chance, the talk turns to technology.

Experts, particularly those who have signed secrecy agreements, are usually more acceptable in attendance at such meetings than any of the parties' technical staffs who will automatically be presumed to be on a fishing trip for confidential information. Having no legal background, such Experts offer no overt or covert threat of litigation in the event of failure to resolve the dispute. In some situations, particularly those involving personal antagonisms between rival executives, they may even be able to diffidently suggest a truce from the depths of their own business naivity[3]:-

"But, children you should never let
Such angry passions rise,
Your little hands were never made
To tear each other's eyes"

Choosing an independent Expert: horses for courses

One is frequently asked to define the criteria for choosing a 'good' Expert and some infallible procedure for identifying (in advance) a 'bad' one. Taking an excessively cynical view, to the client the 'good' Expert might seem to be the one whose evidence helps to win his case for him, however weak this case may be ... but for purposes of selection this is actually an oversimplified and non-enabling disclosure. Indeed hasty appointment of an Expert who accepts readily and uncritically all the arguments developed by the client's in-house staff can obviously be a recipe for disaster when the case comes to court.

Alarming though this alternative may sometimes prove to the client, it is usually better to debate the whole matter with a thoroughly sceptical Expert who will raise every argument he can think of *against* the client's case. If these arguments can be answered, subsequent commital will be reasoned, and therefore absolute[4]:-

"If a man will begin with certainties, he shall end in doubts; but if he will be content to begin with doubts, he shall end in certainties"

Sometimes, a more experienced Expert is retained to identify, interview and advise on the appointment of novice Experts, usually in fields other than their own, on the basis that they understand the job which has to be done and can therefore recognise a potential witness more readily than others without this experience. This may well be true, and can work well in practice, but it is hoped that one future use of this book will be to assist solicitors and others to construct their own 'Good Experts Guide'. In practice the responsibility of *personal* recommendation can occasionally prove a heavy burden, as is recounted later in this Chapter.

---

[3] Isaac Watts (d. 1748)   Divine Songs for Children xvii

[4] Francis Bacon (d. 1626)   Advancement of Learning Bk 1

The shortlist of Expert qualities

Before choosing, it is certainly wise to prepare a 'short list' and then compare the perceived characteristics of each candidate with the 'job specification' insofar as it can be defined. But one must not lose sight of the fact that subject matter has a habit of developing. The technical case at Trial, in two years time, may look very different from what it seems today. It is therefore important to choose a broadly-based Expert, with a wide swathe of relevant technology at his command, rather than a narrow Expert, who may have seemed appropriate to deal with specific issues believed to be critical when the Pleadings were being drafted. In a genuine effort to assist, the narrow Expert may be tempted at a later stage to shoe-horn new developments into a limited framework of his own experience. In so-doing it is only too easy to develop misconceptions[5]:-

"But men may construe things after their own fashion,
Clean from the purpose of the things themselves"

Among the column headings of a typical check-list, though not in order of importance, are the following:-

- Depth of knowledge in the specific field;

- Breadth of knowledge in the area of subject matter;

- Appropriate qualifications/experience/independence;

- Flexibility of opinions/absence of single-mindedness;

- Industrial awareness: process and product aspects;

- Commercial awareness: impact of finance on policies;

- Genuine interest in the outcome of the dispute;

- Literacy: the rapid comprehension of "patentese";

- High quality, succinct, lucid, apposite report writing;

---

[5] William Shakespeare (d. 1616)   Julius Caesar i

- Articulacy: lucid, accurate explanations without jargon;

- Ability to teach non-specialists without condescension;

- Objectivity: keeping the eye on the ball (which, for a Patent Expert, is usually Claim 1 of the Patent-in-suit)

- Common sense and a sense of priorities;

- Quick-wittedness: response to changing circumstances;

- Ingenuity e.g. design and interpretation of experiments;

- Competence to conduct and demonstrate inspections and/or experiments;

- Tact, charm and likeability: broad external interests;

- Team experience: ability to lead or follow, as required;

- Hard working and quick reaction: as the job demands;

- Acknowledged professional competence

It would be tempting to classify various kinds of Expert, even practising individuals, on the basis of 'marks out of 10' under each of these headings. However such quantitative assessments in the field of education and all other human endeavour are fraught with difficulty. Not all of these qualities may be needed for all kinds of case; otherwise we would be perpetually seeking paragons. It is for those instructing to define the course conditions and pick their prospective winner accordingly. Though one warning sign which should normally encourage urgent deselection is the unmistakable flavour of a professional man's self-satisfaction[6]:-

"How pleasant it is, at the end of the day,
No follies to have to repent,
But reflect on the past, and be able to say,
That my time has been properly spent"

---

[6]   Jane Taylor (d. 1824) <u>Rhymes for the Nursery: The Way to be Happy</u>

53

Instead of offering a 'guide', the author has chosen to present cameos of the common groups from which Experts are drawn. He does this secure in the knowledge that such generalisations will not apply to any of his many colleagues and friends in each of these groups[7]:-

"Yet malice never was his aim;
He lash'd the vice, but spared the name;
No individual could resent,
Where thousands equally were meant"

Inventors as Experts

As a callow youth[8], Simon Cooke first introduced the author to Cooke's Rule:-

"Never call the Inventor"

His pessimism has proved itself from time to time during the past two decades. Nevertheless during this time Smith has also heard numbers of distinguished inventor-witnesses who have helped their corporate case immeasurably. The strategic idea of putting the inventor of your Patent-in-suit on the Stand is that he will descend from his Rolls-Royce to tell the Judge how he had this blindingly original idea in the bath (or better, as to 'title', in the company bicycle shed). This idea, developed into an invention and realised in a practical product or process, led to his personal elevation to head a multinational corporation whose enormous profitability is based exclusively on the novelty of the technology which he, with perhaps one or two select collaborators, had disclosed to his grateful and appreciative then-superiors. This is the ultimate evidence for 'commercial success'.

Real inventors can fall short of this functional idealisation. Usually:-

• They are interested in quietly getting on with their science and are resentful of the frequent, aggressive interrogations by droves of technically ignorant and inquisitorial lawyers.

• With few exceptions, each believes that his invention was trivial and obvious; if not, how could he have thought of it in the first place? At

---

[7]   Jonathan Swift (d. 1745)   On the Death of Dr Swift

[8]   "Me" says Smith "not Mr Cooke. I would never describe him as a 'youth'"

best, it was a minor workshop modification of what was already common knowledge in the industry, even if no one had yet written it down. And yet the legal vice-president has told him in person that, for some lawyers' reason he does not fully comprehend, *he must not say this*.

• Such a 'scientist inventor' was the late Emert Pfau of *General Tire*, subject of the following incident:-

Having apparently attempted to 'proof' him for an hour or two without getting quite what he wanted, Simon Cooke came in search of Smith who, having no paperback with him, was idling away the morning reading with incredulity and delight some of the more bizarre Examples of his client's Patent-in-suit.

"You have a go .. ," said Simon " .. and see if you can get anything out of him".

Which I did, and was thrilled to report by night-fall (or what passed for nightfall in the grim, grey Cleveland of the 1960s) that Pfau said he had:-

" .. just mixed a lot of oil with synthetic rubber".

And so, years later, the UK Court found. And, for this very good and non-obvious reason, upheld the Patent.

Despite this excessive and misplaced modesty, such inventors are often deeply resentful of the way their albeit simple idea has been exploited without proper kudos accruing to them. Still the same battered Chevy in the parking lot. They therefore see no obligation whatsoever to run round the world being uncomfortably cross-examined in various Courts just to help a parent corporation whose recently appointed Chairman (" .. he never invented anything more original than a fake expense account ..") happens to be their former lab assistant. Another inventor problem one may meet is 'premature burn-out' and thereby hangs another tale narrated subsequently in connection with US Deposition procedures. More rarely, although quite frequently enough, one encounters 'the inventor turned commercial manager' who so overloads his evidence with self-aggrandising hype that mere 'exponential sales growth' based on his novel technology is *simply not enough*. As a result, the poor Judge may be left wondering why revenue from this 'better mousetrap' has not quadrupled weekly since the date of filing.

Inventors should perhaps reflect that it is often their patent agent who has really defined their inventions and that their representation of these inventions to a Court is a conventional simplification which should properly require neither self-abasement nor self-aggrandisement. In addition to these more personal limitations, there may also be a legal problem: that is that the inventor is likely to be a key 'witness of fact' with whom the lawyers acting for a Party are not permitted to discuss the issues in the Case ... as they are with (Expert) 'witnesses of opinion'.

Academic staff as Experts

Academics can make wonderful Experts. Aside from a little gentle research, many have nothing to do all day but soak up knowledge and regurgitate it in the form of easily-understood teaching courses designed to train successors. As a breed, we are not afraid of speaking in public or of suffering critical, dare one say occasionally vicious, peer review. Modest, moral, and (of course) wholly impartial, we are happy to endorse Horace[9]:-

"Seek for truth in the groves of Academe"

However some brilliant and truthful academics do need a modicum of house-training. In particular from the outset a thoroughly commendable urge to teach the finer details of our specialisation to anybody from the janitor to Leading Counsel may have to be curbed without breaking our spirit. We have had to learn that, except in the Patent business, no technical term of more than two syllables is likely to be comprehensible in legal circles unless of course it is in Latin. And that a casual mention of 'third-order tensors' will instantly set the lawyer heads nodding wisely as the glaze spreads across their corneas like some intellectual cataract.

Despite our likely seniority as scientists, we too have a lot of learning to do about 'pleadings', 'particulars', 'injunctions', 'interlocutories' and the rest of the legal jargon of which a smattering is given in Appendix B. Or, worse, we can think that we have picked up the lawyers' jargon and actually begin to use it[10].

---

[9]   Horace (d. 8 B.C.)   Epistles II ii

[10]   "'I hate the word "intestate', my companion said. 'Why do they have to give old men's diseases such awful names?'" James Thurber (d. 1961) The Lady from the Land Hamish Hamilton

Academic Experts can score highly on 'depth of specific knowledge', though for this reason some of us do suffer from an excess of 'self-esteem':-

•   Needing an Expert in heat transfer for a Trial, his instructing Solicitor once asked the author to suggest someone and he approached an old colleague, Dr Noman, a genuine 'back-room boy'. Noman beavered away and from time-to-time produced the odd twenty or thirty pages of pencilled calculations which none of us really had the energy or intelligence to understand properly. At conferences, our team was roundly harangued[11]:-

"The method employed I would gladly explain,
While I have it so clear in my head,
If I had but the time and you had but the brain ..
But much yet remains to be said"

Each time this Expert was sent away to boil down his conclusions to the format of a 'management report' with annotated mathematical appendices. But each new sheaf he prepared was based on different assumptions and he seemed unable to decide, even in lengthy communication with the transatlantic experimentalists, which set of these assumptions was the most plausible.

Two or three days before Trial, the overseas witnesses appeared in London, heavily jet-lagged, to go into immediate full-day discussions with Counsel. After a demanding day on British time, the visitors only wanted to crawl off to bed and sleep it all off. Soon after midnight, our client's principal physicist was awakened by Noman, who had thought of some new assumptions and wished to try them out on the in-house experts. Bleary but courteous ... and anxious to do everything possible to advance his corporation's case, the American offered one or two helpful comments.

At 2 a.m., the phone rang again; Noman had tried the ideas out and come up with "a new set of equations". This time he was politely but firmly told to wait till the morning ... thus causing some offence. Much the same thing happened next night so that the solicitor had to advise this consultant politely to 'lay off' but was told peremptorily that his "work was important to the case" and he "must not be denied access to the team". The solicitor then instructed Noman that his work should *stop* because it was now too near Trial to be utilised. This was taken very badly indeed, a telephonic

---
[11]   Lewis Caroll (d. 1898)   <u>The Hunting of the Snark</u>

appeal being supported by personal supplication. After this, Dr Noman[12] was not seen around the courts again.

On a brighter note, however, Smith's Rule can usefully be applied:-

"The newer the university, the more amenable the academic".

Nowadays, it would be quite wrong to associate this tractability with the lack of any real work, such as fundamental research or its supervision, normally required of a new university's staff, who might therefore be fresher, more eager and more available to fill out the government's meagre working week with private assignments based on the helpful, supportive and wholly undemanding overhead structure of their departments. Despite, or perhaps because of, a chronic lack of funding, most academics are now at full stretch. The point is that one is usually much more likely to find practical, down-to-earth technologists with some industrial product-and-process experience in such places than may be apprehended floating amongst the dreaming spires, or even lying upon the lazy backs.

Besides the quality of their knowledge, academics have one further distinct and concrete advantage. There is no doubt of their independence. Anyone who has worked in universities for long, and discussed far into the night the importance of maintaining 'academic freedom', will appreciate that the Academic is his own man. Any with character is quite prepared to turn and bite the hand that feeds him *at any level*, whether that level be Head of Department, Vice-Chancellor, Minister for Higher Education or ...

Industrial research staff as Experts

The client's research staff might seem to be ideal witnesses but they usually know too much and, depending on their personalities, could be either too willing or too afraid to disclose it in Court. Neither are they of much value as 'independent' Experts: they usually either love their employers or they hate them and neither condition qualifies them very well as witnesses of opinion. Furthermore some may be needed as witnesses of fact so precluding them from instruction on the issues.

---
[12] The assumed name refers of course to the Hilaire Belloc character

Usually some compromise can be reached in which the truly independent Expert deals with the general field, taking the brunt of the opponent's attack (see Chapter 11) but company men are called to give evidence in depth on very specific remits so helping to protect them from fishing expeditions in cross-examination.

The Expert from another company

Technologists from neutral or friendly companies could, in theory, be useful but they have become a vanishing breed. When approached, they exhibit initial enthusiasm to help at a personal level which is often soon crushed by the dead weight of board-level authority leaning on them from above.

The concept of the truly independent corporation in free competition with its rivals is a figment of anti-trust law. It is a commercial fact of life that in any industry there is generally a network of collaborative agreements between supposed competitors, some above-board and registered, others verbal and secret, which enables the industry as a whole to function in the way it does. Disturb this at your peril!

Retired employees as Experts

On the face of it a retired employee might be considered ideal as an Expert because many patents which are litigated only become of serious value towards the end of the monopoly period. Their priority date was many years ago when current employees may have been too young to be involved in the discoveries leading to the invention. Once retired, quite possibly these days at some early age well before the traditional '65', the ex-employee is free to consult and to advise anyone who will employ him. Or is he? There are two main problems:-

•   Contract of employment

•   Pension rights

When needing Experts with production experience in the chemical industry, QMC-IRL on several occasions located 'just the right man' who had recently retired from a large chemical corporation. In each case he was delighted to discuss his experiences, to focus in on the technical problems of the litigation as we presently saw them and to offer a wealth of references to practical experience gained at his former employer's plant. On each occasion we suggested that it would be polite and prudent to refer back to the employer (who was not of course a party in the Action) to obtain agreement to use of any material which might be needed to reinforce these memories. Matters were confirmed in writing, together with brief and discreet notes indicating the type of evidence which the ex-employee would be able to vouchsafe based upon his armchair revelations.

Each case took a remarkably similar turn. A long dwell period, without any discernible reaction, followed by a polite but firm refusal on various grounds of potential stress, medical advice, and so on. When telephoned privately, each admitted that he had heard a fluttering, not of a coronary valve but rather of a former 'employment contract'. One of these fellows also admitted to us that there had followed an impromptu review leading to a modest enhancement of his retirement pension.

• However in one case the independent witness against us was retired from such a 'neutral' corporation which it later transpired was supplying under licence to our opponents. He was in his mid-70s when first required to prepare what seemed to the author to be an extremely cogent technical resumé which underscored a powerful case. My client feared the worst ... but the Action was delayed by both sides and only reactivated some seven or so years later. By his early 80s, sadly this witness had apparently become sick and enfeebled and had the Action actually fought at Trial there is little doubt that he would have had to have been replaced. Ageing is only one of the problems for Experts advising over a protracted period. Ill-health, family responsibilities and many other reasons may intervene and incapacitate.

Morality and prudence: assisting the client without partiality

As discussed at the beginning of this chapter, one of the questions which is raised most frequently is the nature of the 'independence' professed by an Expert. The extraordinary suggestion is sometimes made, or implied, that to be in receipt of fees and expenses which are ultimately paid by an industrial client is to abandon any pretence of true independence and to place oneself in a position identical to that of a retained consultant or salaried employee. In fact unthinking extremists have suggested that it could be seen as immoral to accept any payment at all, making it necessary for one to donate one's time in the cause of jurisprudence to the support of Bilkoes Washers Inc, while wife, children and too-numerous grandchildren starve in the proverbial hovel and one is left in the cheapest of digs savouring the dregs of last year's Ecuadorian Picpoul. But such sponsors of *pro bono publico*, even if they may be vociferous, are not numerous. One often wonders if, in their spare time, they are also the kind who, from the safety of middle-age, incite governments to send vulnerable youngsters into obscure foreign countries in a vain effort to keep the peace.

Attitudes of the Expert in public and in private

The Expert's true armour is his independence and this must never be compromised but can, with advantage, be demonstrated. While external appearance is no infallible guide to attitude or belief, it is nevertheless important for the Expert to *behave* in an independent manner, not simply when giving evidence in Court and out & about at plant inspections or demonstrations of experiments, but also in private conferences with solicitors, counsel and, above all, with the clients. This is not simply a question of 'avoiding fraternisation', perish the thought when one has the opportunity of working with such delightful colleagues, though close identification with one's client *in public* is not usually advisable.

Client's vary in their attitude to their Expert. Many of the more sophisticated understand and respect that some measure of detachment denotes the 'independence' which is the Expert's intrinsic value and for which they are paying his fee. Others seem to feel perturbed, if not aggrieved, if the Expert is not in there publically fighting 'the enemy' in the same way as for instance their favourite (US) Attorney might be. However in the event of some notable procedural irregularity it is really much better to place the hatchet in the solicitor's hand than rush round at demonstrations of the other side's experiments announcing that 'they' are using the wrong equipment, that this or that has not been properly calibrated, that their staff are all prize idiots and so on.

One widely-accepted view is that the Experts for each side should quietly observe everything relevant that they can, take copious notes and, where possible and appropriate, also photographs and video-tapes. This observation should be done by the Expert alone, stressing independence, unless corroboration of opinion is necessary, in which case the Expert should draw the matter to the attention of another member of his own team. In an 'away' event, the Expert should never forget that he is a guest in someone elses factory or laboratory and behave accordingly. In fact he should best avoid making any kind of 'scene' unless this proves absolutely necessary. But occasionally even as an observer one can find that[13]:-

"An event has happened, upon which it is difficult to speak, and impossible to be silent"

Such is the case in the rare event that overt cheating takes place during a plant inspection (see Chapter 7) or during litigation experiments (Chapters 8/9). In which case[14]:-

"On an occasion of this kind it becomes more than a moral duty to speak one's mind. It becomes a pleasure"

In normal circumstances though, one should be always prepared to ask questions which will help to clarify what is being demonstrated but one should try to avoid making audible comments about any of the phenomena one is observing or the competence of those actually doing the work. Some solicitors instruct their Experts otherwise. Presumably on the basis of direct instruction from their client, they insist that the Expert comment not only on his own Experiments but also on those of the other side. In the author's view, this is to be avoided.

• In some experiments at a corporate laboratory in the USA, the UK Expert for the Defendants was called upon to make public his observations of the granular appearance of the polymers which were synthesised by each side during the course of prolonged experimental programs, such appearance being a diagnostic feature of one of the prior art patents cited against our client. As the Patent happily expressed it:-

"The product appears as small balls"

Besides being received with a mixture of embarassment and derision, sporadic Expert pronouncements, thus crudely:-

---

[13]   Edmund Burke (d. 1797)   Re the Impeachment of Warren Hastings

[14]   Oscar Wilde (d. 1900)   The Importance of Being Earnest ii

"I see small balls!"

polarised the attitude of our in-house technical team who naturally insisted on hotly denying the force of the Expert's so-called 'observations' together with his rather naive conclusion based upon them. Most of these Expert statements were made on the basis of simply peering into the depths of a rather evil and murky polymerisation brew containing many and various lumps of gritty contaminating materials present in massive concentration. The end result of this joint observation was a veritable 'bear-garden' in which even the semblance of civilised behaviour was abandoned.

An immediate and tangible outcome of establishing such personal hostility was serious difficulty in attempting to reach an agreed draft of the Report on each set of the client's Experiments. This in turn greatly increased the volume of inter-party correspondence between solicitors which is a major contributor to the costs of any Action. Furthermore, had the case come to Trial, there would probably have been substantial conflict concerning the actual observations which were made[15] and there was risk of attack on the integrity of individual Experts which would doubtless have been poorly received by a Court looking to them for guidance.

But if showing open hostility is stupid, at the other extreme too-close fraternisation with the opposing barristers, solicitors, patent agents or Experts can also be ill-advised, even if some of them may be personal friends and. for instance, may come from the same department in the same college. This can be viewed askance, particularly by US clients, who are used to the aggressive stance of their own Attorneys which seems to generate deliberately the unpleasant atmosphere of suspicion and hostility in which so much US litigation is often conducted and which must presumably prove so lucrative to the law firms.

Being well aware that the personnel on the other side are just other professionals doing a job, the author feels that it does no obvious harm to veer towards the politely friendly. One can try explaining this to clients in terms of Davis Cup or other sporting teams, who play against one another according to the rules and to the best of their ability being determined to win on court or in the field but who naturally remain friends outside the arena.

---

[15]   "All I can say is ... I saw it!"
    Robert Browning (d. 1889) Natural Magic

Besides being quite understandably uneasy at any analogy, however apposite, between intercorporate litigation and a mere spectator sport, some clients really do seem more comfortable when working themselves into a frenzy of hatred for the bad guys of the opposition and all who sail with them. And if this is the naive situation in which the Expert finds himself, it is perhaps best temporarily to detach and appear to conform.

Your client might like you to show commital to his cause by growling at your opposite numbers. There is no strict obligation so to do, and it can be seriously counter-productive. On the other hand it is certainly better for you not to rush up and begin licking their faces.

The following Table 4.1 (p 65) lists matters wherein an independent Expert can assist his client. These summaries are developed in subsequent chapters.

5   Taking a Case to Court

Previous chapters explored some ways and means in which independent Experts can help to settle disputes without recourse to formal litigation procedures. However the number of patent disputes which can be settled at the outset in this way (though growing) is still relatively small, often because of the poorly defined nature of the matters in contention but also because of the initial self-righteousness and intransigence of so many corporations. The remainder of this book therefore addresses the much more frequent situation in which litigation is commencing with a view to obtaining a judgement in court, each Party being convinced that justice is on its side and that its opponent will suffer not only costs but also substantial damages for the commercial harm which it has inflicted. For instance in an Intellectual Property Action the Plaintiff sees this harm as an unwarranted infringement of his proprietary rights which have often cost him dearly, while the Defendant sees it as an attempt by the Plaintiff to claim a monopoly in the marketplace to which he is not entitled.

The starting point here is an introduction to the basic rules of the law game which the Expert will need to understand. It has already been implied that the basis of the legal Action is normally an allegation by Party 'A', the Plaintiff, that Party 'B', the Defendant, has not complied with the requirements of one or more Statutes. Common Law can also be involved, for instance in 'breach of confidence' or 'passing off' cases. The formal Defence will normally be of some such form as:-

- Defendant *has* properly complied; or

- Defendant *did not need* to comply; or

- Pleadings by Plaintiff are otherwise *incorrect*.

Thus for example in the Patent Court the basic legislation is today found in the Patents Act 1977 and the Pleadings prepared by Plaintiff's Counsel will list infringement in respect of certain specific provision's of the Act by Defendant who will deny this for stated reasons. So if the Plaintiff owns a Patent, which is often a monopoly to manufacture and sell a particular product made by a particular process, the Defendant will have to answer the proposition that he has infringed the Patent thereby reducing the profit made by the Plaintiff in exercising his monopoly.

TABLE 4.1: What the Independent Expert can do

- On the basis of available information, including the principal patents and prior art, advise client firms (often through their solicitors or their patent agents) of the likely strengths and weaknesses of their technical position prior to taking irrevocable legal action

- Collaborate with the client's laboratory and factory staffs in obtaining evidence as to the true technical position, confidentially, and for the eyes of the client's directors alone

- Give third party advice to clients already beginning to be involved in a dispute, including the preparation of independent reports on available evidence and knowledge which will be of value to a client in negotiating a settlement prior to issue of a writ

- Act as formal, or, more usually, informal referee, so as to resolve technical aspects of such disputes, involving the parties' senior technical staff on a "without prejudice" basis in the light of existing knowledge

- Assist solicitors and patent agents in the preparation of a strong tecl ⸻ ⸻ for their client

- Assist specifically in technical procedures authorised by the Court, such as the planning and execution of Process Inspections, Experiments-in-Chief, -in-Reply, and -in-Rebuttal

- Assist solicitors and counsel with the drafting of technical documents such as Process Descriptions and Notices of Experiments

- Supervise the Demonstration of Processes and/or Experiments, and witness those carried out by the opponents

- Review and edit Reports on Processes, Experiments, etc and assist generally in reaching agreement on these with opponents

- Prepare Expert Reports on information and evidence for submission to the Court

- Assist Counsel by preparing comments and criticisms of technical reports that have been prepared by the opponent's experts

- Assist Counsel by preparation of a technical tour d'horizon for use in the opening speech prior to the commencement of formal litigation

- Assist (usually) junior counsel in drafting the Particulars of Objections, Particulars of the Defence, Interrogatories, and other legal/technical documents, in the early stages of litigation

- Assist the litigation team generally in the determination of the strategy and tactics of the litigation by indicating what may be technically true or false, what may or may not be susceptible to technical proof, what was the relevant state of the industrial art, and so on

- Assist specifically in reviewing the Discovery documents disclosed by each of the parties, indicating strengths, weaknesses, inconsistencies and possible omissions

- Give technical evidence to the court

- Assist Counsel in the crossexamination of the opposing experts

- Assist Counsel with the resolution of technical issues to be addressed in the closing speech

- Review the Judgement in respect of technical decisions which will have some bearing on Appeal by the loser

- Assist with the computation of costs and damages based on production records

- Coordinate the work of other experts

Basically, the Defendant can say in reply:-

* that he has not infringed the monopoly; and/or

* that the Patent is/was invalid and so the granted monopoly should be revoked.

However the wording of any Act is necessarily terse yet wide-ranging and, even if it has been drafted with care (which is not always true of some recent legislation), cannot be tailored to specific cases. The Court is therefore convened to interpret the Act or Acts, or to interpret the Common Law, in their application to a specific process or product in a specific industry in specific jurisdictions (usually countries) as at specific dates. In order to do this fairly and consistently, the Court takes note of the arguments used in previous judgements which form the body of Case Law relevant to the Court's jurisdiction.

Where there is no previous case law, or the Court deems the existing Case Law inapplicable to the case he has just heard, the Judge or Judges create new Law. The Court does this by writing a Judgement which sets out fully the pros and cons of the arguments advanced by both Plaintiffs and Defendants together with the detailed Evidence on which they are based and, after weighing these, reaches a balanced conclusion in favour of one or other of the parties, the reasoning for which is disclosed. However Courts have to proceed with care in creating such Law because, at least in large cases involving corporations with substantial resources, there is a considerable likelihood that the losing party will instruct its solicitors to appeal against the verdict of the lower Court. At the Appeal the case is argued anew on the basis of the transcripts of Evidence given at the Trial in the lower court and the loser's Counsel will seek to persuade the Appeal Court that the lower-court Judge wrongly interpreted or failed to take into proper account material evidence which, when properly weighed, should have led to a different decision. The Appeal Court not infrequently accepts such argument and the lower-court Judgement is overturned, returning the now considerable costs to the debit of the original winner. Again, detailed reasoning will be given in the Appeal Judgement which also adds to the basic Case Law[1] :-

"And diff'ring judgements serve but to declare
That truth lies somewhere, if we know but where"

---
[1] William Cowper (d. 1800): 'Hope'

<u>English Court Procedures: the adversarial system</u>

Two litigation teams prepare to do battle: that of the Plaintiff who seeks 'relief', usually in the form of money but also with the more important object of interfering by means of an injunction with the production of his competitor; and that of the Defendant who usually wishes to establish a level commercial playing field wherein to compete with the Plaintiff by destroying his monopoly position with regard to some designated process or product both wish to employ, make and/or market. In the English High Court, each of these teams is led by a senior barrister ('Leader'), usually a 'silk'... that is to say a Queen's Counsel (QC). In a typical Patent Action, in addition to the Leader each team comprises junior counsel, solicitors, patent agents, independent Experts, in-house experts (employed by the client), various witnesses of fact (who may also be technically qualified), often factory operatives or supervisors, service or installation engineers, and sales staff. It was formerly not uncommon, in a large High Court Action, for each Party to call as many as ten or twelve witnesses (of whom six or seven might be witnesses of fact), although the more who take the stand the greater is the cost of the Trial and the higher the risk of self-contradiction arising in the evidence. To reduce this risk, and in an attempt to shorten trials and reduce both cost and the delay in hearing an Action, the limit for Experts is coming down towards the idealised biblical number[2]:-

"In the mouth of two or three witnesses shall every word be established"

At present in an average trial it is common to field five or six witnesses on each side, of whom at most two or three on each side will be independent Experts. The list of independent Experts to be called has now to be agreed with the Judge before Trial. Very often, particularly if the client is from a foreign country such as the USA, the team is strengthened by secondment of one or more in-house patent counsel who may have followed the litigation round the world. Such help is often invaluable in anticipating arguments and citations which need to be considered during the preparation of the case. However, these visitors are unlikely to have any formal role in court proceedings.

British litigation usually involves a splitting of legal responsibilities of the team between Solicitors, whose prime duty is to prepare the case, and Counsel, the barristers who are employed to present it to the Court and

---

[2]   Holy Bible   I Corinthians xiii

'plead' on behalf of their clients. In large actions, often involving global multinationals, at which millions of dollars are at stake, it is usual for the instructing solicitors to field a team of one or more partners and several assistants, who 'instruct' two or three Counsel, typically a silk assisted by one or more juniors. Whereas formerly barristers were all career lawyers who knew little more of the relevant science and engineering than they were taught by their Experts, the new breed of silk and *a fortiori* his juniors is a highly qualified scientist who can develop a real understanding of the technology that is being debated. It is therefore most unwise for a novice Expert to presume that he can necessarily outgun a barrister in a cross-examination duel simply by moving the argument further into the arcane recesses of his own expertise. The juniors may act as assistants of the silks, finding references, preparing arguments and so on. They also act as deputies in addressing the Court and in examining certain of the witnesses. It is particularly common in the patent court for say a 'physicist' or 'engineer' silk to delegate the examination of a chemist or chemical engineer witness to his junior who is qualified in these subjects. Whereas the rôles described above are clearly differentiated in function, in practice the preparation for trial is usually carried out by a task force, the 'litigation team', of which all the foregoing lawyers are members together with the Patent Agents and the independent Expert(s).

Crucial rôle of the instructing solicitor

As we have seen, the organiser of the team, its legal guru and its godfather, is usually the instructing solicitor (or, very occasionally ... for instance sometimes in the PCC, the patent agent[3]). He will use his experience and judgement in parcelling out the work that needs to be done, checking that it is properly done, ensuring coordination between the members, sorting out any serious differences of opinion and setting the agenda and recording the conclusions of meetings. He will also act as commanding officer, leading his team during process inspections, demonstrations of experiments, and so on, when the team takes the field publically. The independent Expert will have no difficulty in distinguishing the well-led and inspired team in which he is invited to serve from the dull and barely competent. There is no room

---

[3] There are as yet very few Patent Agents with experience of successful pleading in court, as opposed to the simpler task of conducting opposition proceedings in the Patent Office.

in the litigation business for a 'Duke of Plaza Toro'[4]. During preparation of a case not every member of the team will need to be be present at each of its meetings but the best performance will require both detailed meetings of those involved in special aspects at the working level and also higher-level 'review and coordination' meetings, usually attended by client representatives and often also by representatives from parallel litigations abroad. The conduct and function of these meetings is further particularised in Chapter 6.

Experience of this 'dual support' adversarial system and the teams which operate it is that it all works rather well. Far from 'doubling up on cost', the clear role differentiation between solicitor and counsel enables each to excel in the client's interest. At trial, the atmosphere is not unlike backstage on a first night when the production team does a well-drilled support job for the actors out on the boards. By way of contrast, though the author has worked with US attorneys who can both prepare *and* deliver a brilliant case, the majority seem to fulfil one of these functions rather better than the other. Furthermore, being the boss both on and off stage has its disadvantages. During the Attorney's addresses to the Court, there may be no one of sufficient seniority such as the instructing Solicitor to prepare documents in readiness for the next phase of the Action. Indeed the British solicitor is no better example[5] of:-

"Reading maketh a full man; conference a ready man; and writing an exact man"

Hence, most US Attorneys work with one or more partners, this giving some of the advantages of the British system.

Finding out how best to help

It usually takes the novice Expert some time to get used to what his litigation team is actually supposed to be doing. He knows of course that there is a general and sincere desire to 'win' for the generous client who is picking up the tab but it is very unlikely that anyone will spend time instructing him as to the rules of procedure which are already so familiar to

---

[4]   "He led his regiment from behind ..
      He found it less exciting"
      Sir William S. Gilbert (d. 1911)   The Gondoliers

[5]   Francis Bacon (d. 1626)   Essay 'Of Studies'

everyone else he seems to meet. A few instructing solicitors even seem to feel that the Expert should not be encouraged to learn too much about what goes on in the engine room of litigation, perhaps in case his transparent innocence is in some way compromised. If the Experts have to worry their pretty little heads about the 'rules of the game' then they can't so easily tell the whole truth and nothing but the truth can they? This is like being invited to play draughts without being told the moves or given any pieces! Such a restrictive attitude can waste valuable preparation time because from conversations and documentation the Expert quickly gathers half-truths and misconceptions about the legal precedents and procedures which he appreciates are obviously important and which naturally, to him, are shrouded in intellectual mists. In fact it can take some months, if not years, as an Expert Witness to risk scorn and derision by exposure of one's fundamental ignorance of the Law and its administration. In this Book there is an attempt to save non-legal readers such unnecessary embarrassment by offering explanations in lay terms of what a litigation team needs to achieve and how, under the leadership of its senior lawyers, it sets out to do so.

Planning ahead for a possible Appeal

We have seen that the 'lower court' decision can be subject to Appeal based on arguments that the Judge was wrong in some material respect in his interpretation of what was put before him. It is important to have this possibility firmly in mind at an early stage, even during early preparations for the initial, lower-court Trial. Appeals are heard by the Appeal Court consisting of three Judges sitting together who hear further argument by the barristers *but no new evidence*. The Appeal decision is final, except on points of Law concerning which a further appeal may sometimes be made to the House of Lords. In the USA, there is an equivalent route for appeal to the Supreme Court. Reference has already been made to the disquietingly high rate of reversal of certain lower court judgements. There are cynical sayings which circulate in the corridors of the courts, recently summarised in a speech by the present Master of the Rolls[6]:-

"It seems that a Judgement of First Instance should be 'short, simple .. and wrong' ... and, as one judge was overheard to say: 'I was upheld on Appeal yesterday .. but I still think I was right!'"

---

[6]   The Rt Hon Sir Thomas Bingham, M.R.: Speech on being awarded the Fellowship of
       Queen Mary & Westfield College on 16 March 1993

- In similar vein, there is a another saying that[7]:-

"For the first seven years a Judge is worried about getting it wrong; for the next seven he knows he is right; and after that he doesn't give a damn either way"

- Retained to appear in front of a Judge who had recently suffered some reversals, an Expert friend was instructed:-

"Don't mind what you say ... so long as you make sure we lose at first instance"

Despite such self-deprecatory 'lawyers' humour', most judge's do not particularly like having their judgements overturned and if it happens repeatedly they may worry that it can be seen in the corridors of legal power, however unfairly, as a slur on their ability which could have a deleterious effect on their subsequent careers. Where there is a choice, many therefore might reasonably prefer to base their judgements prudently on established precedent rather than, perhaps more contentiously, choose to plough some lone furrow of jurisprudence which will have a good chance of being promptly back-filled elsewhere. Just as some judges have a long record of reversals, others have a remarkable record of being upheld on the vast majority of appeals.

Understanding Counsel's strategy

Leading counsel may play on this sense of judicial caution. The Expert needs to know that his Leader has always in mind the provision for the less-forthright Judge of a series of stepping stones across the tide of the litigation, each one of which is firmly based on established case law which has stood the test of an Appeal.

This ubiquitous approach to advocacy has given rise to the dignification of a relatively small number of (usually) elegant and pertinent judgements which are quoted by Counsel repeatedly and *in extenso* in his efforts to head the Judge off from any more original approach to resolution of the matter in hand. If the Expert is to understand his Leader and assist him in his endeavour, far from remaining ignorant of the Law he will be wise to become familiar with the more important of these basic judgements so that he can make intelligent comparisons between their underlying science and

---

[7]   Current at least in the vicinity of Lincoln's Inn.

technology and the subject matter on which his team is currently working.

Introduction to Case Law

Certain earlier judgements have become particularly popular in defining the specific ground rules for decisions in Patent actions and, being most familiar with these, they are used as examples. So often have these Cases been cited, and so effective have they been in influencing the decisions of the Patent Courts, that they have begun gradually to assume the authority of the Commandments. The relevant passages have become known to all practitioners, including established Experts, and the preparation of Evidence can often include the shoe-horning of technical facts into the footwear of these judicial decrees.

The 'construction' of a Claim

The Patents Act 1977 states the principles to be applied in its section 125 which makes reference to Article 69 of the European Patent Convention. However the Protocol on the Interpretation of Article 69 which is referred to in Section 125 (3) states:-

"Article 69 should not be interpreted in the sense that the extent of the protection conferred by a European patent is to be understood as that defined by the strict, literal meaning of the wording used in the claims, the description and drawings being employed only for the purpose of resolving an ambiguity found in the claims. Neither should it be interpreted in the sense that the claims serve only as a guideline and that the actual protection conferred may extend to what, from a consideration of the description and drawings by a person skilled in the art, the patentee has contemplated. On the contrary, it is to be interpreted as defining a position between these extremes which combines a fair protection for the patentee with a reasonable degree of certainty for third parties".

Such a delphic pronouncement, despite the elegance of its drafting, might seem to lesser mortals as begging the whole question on construction of the claims and, in practice, interpretation of the scope of each claim would always have to be decided by the Trial Judge. This is what actually happens. By way only of illustration, and without offering any opinion on the quality of the judgement (which has been appealed), a useful collection of relevant case material was cited by Mr Justice Morritt ('Morritt J.') in a recent lower court decision dealing with a matter of adhesion of the tabs on disposable diapers. As is so often the position, the Trial Judge had to make a decision on the 'construction', the true meaning of the wording of the claims of the Patent-in-suit, which, in this particular instance, the Defendants had wished to interpret rather literally. Like many before him, Morritt J. cited Lord Diplock ('Diplock L.J.') in *Catnic Components v Hill & Smith* [1982], known familiarly as *Catnic*, whose judgement contains this definition:-

"A patent specification should be given a purposive construction rather than a purely literal one derived from applying to it the kind of meticulous verbal analysis in which lawyers are too often tempted by their training to indulge. The question in each case is: whether persons with practical knowledge and experience of the kind of work in which the invention was intended to be used, would understand that strict compliance with a particular descriptive word or phrase appearing in a claim was intended by the patentee to be an essential requirement of the invention so that any variant would fall outside the monopoly claimed, even though it could have no material effect on the way the invention worked"

On this basis the Court had found that the term "vertical" in Catnic included any angle less than 8 degrees distant from '90 degrees to the horizontal', because such an angular variation decreased only slightly the load-bearing capacity of the structure which was the subject of the Claim. In other words the deviation from true vertical did not affect significantly the purpose for which the invention could be applied. In applying this approach, now called "purposive construction", Morritt J, stated:-

"The question of construction is one of law for the court. The function of the evidence is to explain the meaning of technical terms and to educate the judge so that he can read the patent through the eyes of those most likely to have a practical interest in the subject matter of the patent, namely those skilled in the art (cf. *American Cyanamid v Ethicon* [1979]). But that is not to say that the skilled addressee does not know the usual meaning of non-technical terms or normal English usage. He must be assumed to have such knowledge as well otherwise the court will quickly find itself adopting the second approach referred to in the Protocol"

On this basis, in construing the phrase:-

" .. the tear strength (of a plastic sheet) is less than the adhesive strength of the tape tab adhesive"

... the Judge found that this could properly be evidenced by a high probability of tearing of the sheet when peeling off the tape tab. He rejected the Defendant's submission that, in order to satisfy the wording, such tearing should be inevitable. He accepted that a high risk of damage during normal use was the real-life situation addressed by the patentee to the amelioration of which his invention was directed.

As a result of this kind of approach, the interest of the Court in Expert evidence relating to construction has been enhanced. The question the Expert has to answer is no longer "What exactly do the words mean to you?" but rather "What is the significance of the words in the (industrial) context of the invention?". In responding to such a question, it is not usually sufficient for the Expert Witness to state a belief. Rather, the belief must be backed up by facts and reasoning, as exemplified in the practical definition of "vertical" for the purposes of *Catnic* quoted above.

Obviousness

The contesting of the validity of a patent is also subject to interpretation of the Act. As discussed in Chapter 1, in order to qualify for grant of a patent the invention must involve "an inventive step". This is defined in section 3 of the 1977 Patents Act as follows:-

"An invention shall be taken to involve an inventive step if it is not obvious to a person skilled in the art, having regard to any matter which forms part of the state of the art by virtue only of section 2 (2) above ..."

Section 2 (2) states:-

"The state of the art in the case of an invention shall be taken to comprise all matter (whether a product, a process, information about either, or anything else) which has at any time before the priority date of that invention been made available to the public (whether in the United Kingdom or elsewhere) by written or oral description, by use or in any other way"

Morritt J. analysed this teaching of the Act quite conventionally in the form of four "relevant propositions", as follows:-

1:     The person to whom the invention must appear obvious is the hypothetical man skilled in the relevant art but incapable of invention.

2:     The question is one of fact, as of the relevant date.

In *Technograph Printed Circuits v Mills & Rockley Electronics [1972]* *"Technograph"*, Lord Reid's judgement includes:-

"To whom must the invention be obvious? It is not disputed that the hypothetical addressee is a skilled technician who is well acquainted with workshop technique and who has carefully read the relevant literature. He is supposed to have an unlimited capacity to assimilate the contents of, it may be, scores of specifications but to be incapable of a scintilla of invention. When dealing with obviousness, unlike novelty, it is permissible to make a 'mosaic' out of the relevant documents, but it must be a mosaic which can be put together by an unimaginative man with no inventive capacity" "Whether or not it was obvious to take a particular step is a question of fact; it was formerly left to a jury. But the question is not whether it is now obvious to the court (or to the jury) but whether at the relevant date it would have been obvious to the unimaginative skilled technician. A thing which now seems obvious to anyone may at that date have been far from obvious to him. In this case he would have been faced with a large variety of different methods, none of which had proved commercially useful. He would have had no assurance that any successful solution was possible, still less would he have known in what direction to look for it. He would be expected to try out all obvious modifications or combinations of these methods which seemed to him worth trying"

3:     The question is whether the advance over the prior art was technically obvious not whether it was obvious in the sense of being worthwhile commercially (cf. *Windsurfing International v Tabur Marine (GB) [1985]* henceforth *"Windsurfing"*; and *Hallen v Brabantia [1991]*).

4:     But manufacturing or commercial problems may explain why, if the advance over the prior art was obvious, it was not previously adopted (cf. *Parks Cramer v Thornton [1969]*). In contrast, if the invention has supplied a want and been a commercial success, that is some indication that it was not obvious (cf. *Non-Drip Measure Company v Stranges [1943]*).

In *Windsurfing*, Oliver L.J. analysed the steps to be taken in answering the question of 'fact' in a series of tests as follows:-

"There are, we think, four steps which require to be taken in answering the jury question. The first is to identify the inventive concept embodied in the patent-in-suit. Thereafter, the court has to assume the mantle of the normally skilled but unimaginative addressee in the art at the priority date and to impute to him what was, at that date, common general knowledge in the art in question. The third step is to identify what, if any, differences exist between the matter cited as being 'known and used' and the alleged invention. Finally, the court has to ask itself whether, viewed without any knowledge of the alleged invention, those differences constitute steps which would have been obvious to the skilled man or whether they require any degree of invention"

This last citation is of special importance and the 'four steps' are almost always taken by present-day judges in considering the question of obviousness. So if 'obviousness' is a major issue, the Expert will be very helpful to his team if he can assemble his evidence, both 'pro' and 'con', for their consideration in such a way that it can be discussed under these headings. If he does *not* all is not lost but, just as if he were to write his opinions in a foreign language, some translation will be necessary and something of his argument may thereby be lost.

Commonsense reading of the Claims

In his Judgement of *3M v Rennicks (Seibu) [1991]* , Aldous J., the senior UK Patent Judge, also referred to *Catnic* on 'purposive construction' and extended this to a situation where it had been argued against the Patentee that:-

" ... it was not possible to decide whether infringement had occurred in all circumstances contemplated by the Patentee".

The Judge took a robust view of this criticism which he based on Lord Russell in *EMI v Lissen [1939]* :-

".... if possible, a specification should be construed so as not to lead to a foolish result or one which the patentee could not have contemplated"

This is encouraging to the Expert who is thereby expected to take a commonsense view of a patent claim, not having to extend it to its literal frontiers and eschewing the more twisted and garbled readings occasionally put to him in conference or in cross-examination by desperate counsel. In his judgement on *Monsanto v Maxwell Hart [1981]*, Graham J. supported a purposive approach to the claim. In this case, the material of a synthetic playing field called was described as 'grass-like' which, it had been argued, meant a particular shade of green rather than the bluish colour actually obtained by performing the Examples in the Patent. However crucial evidence by a user, a distinguished soccer player, was that the actual shade of green was immaterial to the players, particularly when games took place under flood-lights as was frequently the case.

In *Gillette v Anglo-American Trading Co [1913] "Gillette"*, the Defendant successfully pleaded that he had, in effect, been producing by a certain method prior to the date of Plaintiff's patent and was merely continuing to make in the same way. This judgement[8] puts the onus on to a Plaintiff of showing that the Defendant has changed (i.e. improved) his method of manufacture and product after, and as a result of, learning from the Patent disclosure. For a Defendant who sincerely believes that he has not adopted the teaching of the Patent, such a 'proof of non-infringement' sounds reasonably straightforward. However in practice manufacturing of a product is a continuously evolving operation in which every week, month, or year, a myriad of minor 'workshop improvements' are introduced in the factory process to increase production or to reduce costs. Workshop improvements usually have a small but measurable effect on product quality and performance. They are by definition not inventive and therefore not patentable. Nevertheless as a result of their introduction the process and product both change over a period of time. It is then a matter for Expert evidence to establish:-

• whether or not the product now is effectively the same as the product before publication of the Patent, that is to say that such changes as have occurred were not 'material';

• whether there was a significant increase in quality and/or reduction in manufacturing cost following publication of the Patent;

• if so, whether or not this increase could relate to use of the teaching of the Patent.

In a recent Action involving an 'old Act' patent (see Chapter 2), Aldous J. reviewed case law in respect of (unsuccessful) pleas of insufficiency; false

---

[8] cited by Aldous J in Judgement in *Merrell Dow v Norton, Penn and Generics [1993]*

suggestion; inutility; fair basis; and ambiguity. He relied particularly on:-

• *Valensi v British Radio Corporation [1973]* *"Valensi"*, which judgement teaches that the specification is sufficient if the 'skilled man' can use the instructions given to make the invention work. In the Court of Appeal, this position was both endorsed and significantly extended:-

"To prove inutility it is, in our view, necessary to show that an invention, so far as claimed, will not work as described or with any modification which the skilled addressee can properly be expected to make"

In *Valensi*, the Appeal Court also found that any 'false suggestion' in the Patent must be 'material' for the patent to be found invalid, 'material' meaning that:-

" ... the Crown was misled into granting a patent".

• *Intalite International v Cellular Ceilings (no 2) [1987]* *"Intalite"* in which Whitford J. endorsed the Valensi judgement with respect to false suggestion and applied its test to a pleaded passage in the case concluding that:-

"Even if the passage might be misleading, in the sense that it postulates, in substance, a non-existent advantage, it is a matter of such insignificance that it cannot form the basis of an attack on validity. It cannot sensibly be suggested that this passage could have misled the Comptroller into granting the patent"

• *C. Van der Lely v Ruston's Engineering [1984]* *"Van der Lely"*, in which May L.J. found:-

"We were also referred to *Therm-a-Stor v Weatherseal Windows [1984] FSR 323*, and on this issue I would gratefully adopt a short dictum from the judgement of Dillon L.J. at page 339 to this effect .. 'the claim in a patent must not go beyond the disclosure of the specification'. In my opinion on the authorities, the question on the 'fair basis' issue is purely one of construction. One must read and construe the specification in the purposive way to which Lord Diplock referred in the *Catnic* case and with the knowledge and experience of the skilled addressee to whom it is directed. Having done so, one must ask oneself whether the claims are fairly based, that is to say whether the material in the specification so construed provides a fair ground or base for the claims then made ... fair, that is, as between the patentee and the public."

These authorities, and the manner in which the Courts are endorsing them, make it much less than likely that weakish pleas of 'insufficiency' (comprising the former false suggestion, inutility, or fair basis) will succeed in seriously challenging the validity of any patent which has been exploited commercially and against which infringement has been proved. As for 'ambiguity', in *3M v Rennicks (Seibu) [1991]* Aldous J. took a firm, even blunt, approach in dismissing the Defendants' plea:-

"I have been able to give Claim 1 a sensible meaning and therefore this allegation has not been established"

In this view he was supported by independent Expert evidence. It would therefore appear that there has been a steady swing of the judgement pendulum away from the nit-picking legalistic analysis of the precise words used by an inventor in claiming his monopoly towards more practical criteria. In that it accords with the author's experience, training and beliefs, this should be welcome to independent Experts. However it necessarily places upon Expert Witnesses a greater onus of responsibility in explaining to the Court exactly what the sense of a less-adequately drafted patent actually means in terms of applicable technology.

What the Expert may learn from Case Law

The foregoing gives only a very general indication of how the Courts interpreted the 1949 Act and gives some guidance as to how they will approach similar problems under the 1977 Act. It is included merely to give a feel to the novice of how judges and counsel are constrained within their working system. These constraints can with advantage be studied in greater detail and properly understood by Experts if they are really to fulfil the function of helping the Court. Such study will also save their client's time and money during the preparation stage. It is especially unprofitable for the novice Expert to try to rewrite the rules of litigation in an attempt to bring the legal 'model system' into closer accord with his personal knowledge of the technical and commercial scene. The law business really is a different world. If one wishes to to play chess with professionals, one must accept the artificiality of the knight's L-shaped leap and the curious 'taking of pawns' *en passant.*[9] For instance having said that the Oliver judgement in

---
[9] Simon Cooke comments "Patent actions are much like three-dimensional chess, in which a wrong move on one facet can cause a lot of trouble in another"

Windsurfing is generally accepted as the authentic legal case law on 'obviousness', it follows that the concepts and definitions therein introduced also constitute part of the *lingua franca* of the Courts. It is a part of the Expert's self-training to try to understand these constraints and, if necessary, adapt his thinking to conform to them. If he wishes to study more deeply this aspect of his craft, he should dip into some of the standard law books on the subject ... such as 'Terrell'[10].

A rather artificial concept: 'the skilled man'

If he is put forward as the unimaginative 'skilled man', it is particularly unhelpful for a professional impersonating this kind of expert to protest that in the real world of industrial technology every technician worth his salt, who assiduously studies even a part of the published literature of his subject, is usually brimming over with original ideas (which may or may not be welcome to his employer). The Law assumes that there *is* a kind of man who can follow every direction given in a Patent, interpret these directions in the light of, and actually using, his 'common general knowledge' (or that of the industry in which he is working) .. and not add 'one scintilla', presumably less than one neurone's worth, of original thought[11] to assist the efficient discharge of his responsibility.

The nature and capacity of 'the skilled man' is defined in this well-established Case Law and there is as little hope of substituting some other concept as there is of allowing pawns to move backwards or sideways. In this situation the Expert or indeed any industrial technologist or technician, must needs answer *as if he really were* 'totally uninventive'. This can be done only by consciously subtracting one's naturally inventive streak from the remainder of one's knowledge to produce a passive result[12]. This in no way compromises the integrity of an Expert's evidence; it does nothing more than mould it into a form in which the lawyers, who have established and now control the rules of legal procedure, can readily use it. However the law in this area still seems to be rather confused. For instance, the Court of Appeal in *Genentech* (a case under the 1977 Act) seems to have found that

---

[10]   W Aldous, D Young, A Watson and S Thorley Terrell on the Law of Patents 13th edn. 1982

[11]   "How can he get wisdom ... whose talk is of bullocks?" Holy Bible Ecclesisasticus xxxviii

[12]   Their strength is to sit still" Holy Bible Isiah v

all PhD scientists were inherently 'inventive', presumably because of their research training. This is seen by some to lead to the absurd proposition that no patentable invention can ever be made by a team of PhDs because the invention must necessarily be obvious to them!

Answering within a particular time frame

It is of the greatest importance to establish one's pattern of answers in exactly the right time-frame and particularly to avoid tainting one's Evidence with any whiff of hindsight. In some matters, where the technology is static or develops rather slowly, this is not a difficult constraint but in fast-developing fields, such as electronics or biotechnology, it is sometimes necessary to locate one's response accurately, even to the nearest month. This can be supported by relevant publications as well as contemporaneous notes and internal reports.

Common general knowledge ('cgk')

Perhaps the least realistic aspect of the legal model portrayed in the Act involves the *de facto* proposition that a skilled man, or indeed any other person, might have read or heard a significant proportion of published or uttered information about the topic from anywhere in the world as at some specific date, usually the priority date of the patent-in-suit. In truth it is the besetting sin of modern science that, so great is the flood of published work in the majority of hot subjects, most of us read on a regular basis a smaller and smaller proportion of the references pertaining to studies at the fringe of our own special research, design or production interests, let alone the broader reviews of applications in a wider context.

'State-of-the-Art = All that is published world-wide' is a statutory rule which is easy to define and to administer. It is difficult to think of any alternative which would accommodate the many real technologists, like myself, who read a number of tried and trusted journals in their field and then wait for anything else to emerge, months ... sometimes years, later in the various Abstracts. With the continuing development and availability of on-line databases, there is a faint possibility that a few well-heeled corporations will be able to put at least some of their staff in approximately the position which the Law envisages. But, for the private or academic inventor, or the innovator in a smaller company, it is likely that occasional recourse will have to be made to professional information bureaux. Even this may have to be limited to searches concerning a handful of their most promising creations. It naturally troubles the novice Expert that he may be encouraged to assemble the 'common general knowledge' of the subject by assiduous *post hoc* reference to publications world-wide in any language rather than rely on that small portion of available knowledge that he, himself, actually had at the relevant time. But the Law knows that 'cgk' is an artificial concept, as evidenced by the use of the word 'impute' in Lord Oliver's *Windsurfing* judgement (loc.cit.).

Technically, and so lawyers tell us, properly, cgk should be limited to that body of knowledge with was 'well-known' in the industry as of the relevant date. The difficulty is that what was well-known varies widely as between individuals and corporations active in the industry. An Expert, perhaps from a small firm, who simply confesses to a limited hands-on knowledge may find himself out-countenanced by another, from a Du Pont or I.C.I., who truly had access to every data-base on earth in his particular field. Some practitioners have suggested that cgk should be limited to what can be found in student textbooks but, at the time of writing, there is no convincing sign that this practical limitation is acceptable to the courts. They should say what they want, so that the Experts can provide it.

A brief summary of Trial procedure

In an English Patent Action in the High Court, the Court normally consists of a technically competent judge sitting alone. This is the position in the UK, in Canada and in Australia, but in the USA it is common for the Parties to appear before an elected judge, usually a good lawyer but often without any scientific background ... or even, in many instances, to experience the dubious lottery of a trial by jury. In continental Europe, it is not uncommon to meet a panel of judges in the 'court of first instance' who reach their decision on a majority vote after receiving advice from their own independent Court Expert(s).

The order of appearance ('batting order') in a UK Patent Action is that the Patentee, as Plaintiff, appears first ('opens'), explaining how his monopoly has been invaded. The Defendant usually denies this invasion (by pleading 'non-infringement'); he then attempts to deny the Plaintiff's monopoly by pleading 'invalidity'.

As we have seen, statements by a witness are called 'Evidence' (or 'Testimony' in the USA) and may be 'Evidence of Fact' or 'Expert Opinion'. The in-court procedure is generally as follows:-

• Leader 'A' defines the issues and then puts to the Court the best case he can for the Party 'A' who has briefed him. He then calls evidence to support this case.

• His opposite number, acting for Party 'B', then attempts to throw doubt on the value of this Evidence by cross-examination of A's witnesses, putting his own case to them.

• Leader B may then address the Court in an attempt to denigrate Leader A's argument, with the intention of substituting this alternative case more favourable to his client.

• He too calls Evidence, which is cross-examined by Counsel 'A' with a view to its being weakened or destroyed.

• Finally, each Leader then addresses the Court pleading for a decision favourable to his client. During these closing speeches, each Counsel tries to summarise the technical evidence he has adduced and presented via those of his witnesses who have to a sufficient degree survived cross-examination. Counsel rams the points home and supports his assertions by quotation from the Evidence as it has been recorded in the verbatim Transcript. In summing up, it is also not unknown for certain more inspired and imaginative counsel themselves to improvise bridges over technical lacunae in order the better to assert their case[13]:-

"And summed it so well that it came to far more
Than the Witnesses ever had said!"

The Judge, with his eye on the clock (or, during some speeches, on the calendar), tries to limit Mr Brook's peroration[14] to the matters *he* sees being

---

[13] Lewis Carroll (d. 1898)   The Hunting of the Snark

[14] "For men may come and men may go,
But I go on for ever"
Alfred, Lord Tennyson (d. 1892)   The Brook

at issue, interrupting and probing the arguments put to him in what to a casual onlooker would often seem to be an aggressive, even a (politely) hostile, manner. This is the period of the Action when inexperienced clients sometimes need the most support, being convinced from the Judge's critical, even aggressive, demeanour that "all is lost". However this may be far from the true position, for a Judge who is becoming determined to find 'for' a Party must needs investigate and dispose of every argument 'against' that Party, both in pursuit of the just decision and lest his failure to do so gives grounds for a subsequent appeal to a higher court. He therefore puts firmly what he sees as the most damaging points to that Party's Counsel to see if he can dispose of them by reference to the Evidence. Any such References will almost certainly find their way into his Judgement .

The above summary is typical of procedure, but the rules allow minor variation, for instance in freedom of Counsel not to interpolate an opening Speech for the Defence but rather to call evidence in rebuttal of the Plaintiff's case as soon the latter is concluded.

Disposition of the witnesses

A 'witness of fact' is not supposed to hear Court proceedings before he enters the Witness-Box (.. 'take the Stand', in the USA), though many Courts seem to relax this rule, particularly in the US. Presumably in Britain he is thought of as a weaker vessel than the Expert and so inherently more susceptible to the influence of Counsel and the evidence of other witnesses. Perhaps the experience of hearing these authorities might[15]:-

"Charge his mind with meanings that he never had"

Expert witnesses, presumably being less pervious, can remain in court throughout the Trial both prior to and after giving their Evidence. Despite their independence, and assumed impartiality, they are expected to advise their solicitors and counsel, often quite openly from the front of the court (see Chapter 11). Such advice is normally restricted to interpretation and clarification of what other technical witnesses have said in evidence. The exception to this is that a witness currently himself under cross-examination, which is to continue after a recess, must not communicate with his clients or their legal advisers. He must remain 'in purdah' until

---

[15]   William Cowper (d. 1800)   The Task bk iii: 'The Garden'

released from the witness box by the Court.

As an independent Expert Witness in a complex technical Action, one may expect to be 'in the Box' for perhaps between one and four days, usually two to three days, that is to say in all for about nine to twelve hours. The survival strategy which this implies is reviewed in Chapter 11. For the rest of the Trial, the Expert serves his side in an advisory capacity.

Arguments put by counsel to the Court are called 'Speeches' and conventionally put a fairly high gloss on their client's position while dealing at least adequately with arguments put against them. The Court, often as we have seen in a technical case a High Court Judge sitting alone, listens carefully to evidence and argument and may himself question each barrister either to elucidate their arguments or to put points to them which he feels are important and have not been adequately supported or refuted. As a result of the instruction he receives from Counsel, his hearing of the Evidence and his careful reading of the cited Documents, the Judge compiles a 'decision' or 'judgement' *for* one of the Parties and *against* the other[16] . At a further hearing, he usually goes on to make a number of Orders, particularly as regards the liability of the Parties for the Costs of the Action (US: 'Attorney's Fees').

Forms of address

Law Court etiquette demands certain forms of address which are no doubt intended to depersonalise the confrontational aspects of the procedure. The High Court Judge is addressed in Britain as 'M'Lud' ('My Lord'), because he is one, or in the USA as 'Y'r'onner' ('Your honour') because he isn't. The latter appelation is also used in the UK Patents County Court ('the PCC'). The British High Court Judge is referred to deferentially by everybody as 'His Lordship'. British barristers address and refer to one another in Court as 'My learned friend', 'Learned counsel' or occasionally as simply 'My friend' ... not only because it is conventional so to do, but also because they probably are good friends in the real world outside.

American attorneys, at least during the deposition proceedings the author has

---

[16] There is also the possibility of a split decision e.g. a Patent may be held valid but not infringed, as in *3M v J & J (Micropore case)* ... or the Patent held partially valid and its valid claims infringed or not, as the case may be.

attended, seem to address one another by such affectionate soubriquets as 'Turkey', which one must presume derives from the same root as 'turnkey' (probably indicating a facilitator of justice), or 'Creep', which must supposedly refer to the slow but sure road to a just verdict.

The Court timetable

The English High Court normally sits five days a week in two sessions per day from 1030-1300 and from 1400-1600 hrs. These may sound quite short daily hours but the actual period in court is frequently prefaced with urgent conferences starting as early as 8 a.m. and may be followed by further meetings, the writing of notes, the making of calculations, and the perusal of citations, together with scanning of the day's Transcript, from (traditional) four o'clock 'tea' up to a lateish dinner at 8 or 9 p.m. Even at dinner, the minds and the talk never stray far from the job in hand. In truth there can be nothing more boring for the unwary 'outsider' than to accept an invitation to dine with a litigation team in full cry. Alas, this is the fate of many of our consorts.

The total amount of court time on a per diem basis is found to be about right, except that a lunch break of only one hour in London in the neighbourhood of the Law Courts which, allowing for strolling time, can dwindle to forty minutes 'in & out'. Because this is an important opportunity for discussion between Counsel, Solicitors and Experts on the morning's play, the brevity of this period can present major logistical problems unless 'quiet' tables have been booked at some establishment which specialises in speed of service ... often to the detriment of quality of cuisine. Seclusion is usually necessary anyway in order to stay isolated from the flapping ears of one's opponents. But an extra quarter-of-an-hour would help.

Fortunately, the quality of the food is really of little significance because, save for the blessed period of 'purdah' during the Expert's cross-examination, the lunch recess is spent replying to a seemingly endless series of technical questions from Counsel arising from the morning's proceedings. These, he will suggest, require instant and precise one-line answers, preferably without showering him with partially-consumed, lager-impregnated roast beef-and-yorkshire pudding.

How we used to do it

Things were more leisurely in the byegone age of *General Tire;* the author remembers Sir Lionel Heald QC asking him late one Friday lunchtime in a private room at the Devereux pub, a particularly difficult but key technical question of which Smith needed notice (and indeed consultation of several publications) before answering:-

"Never mind," said Counsel amiably, "I shall spend this afternoon giving the Judge his ration of the Law".

Which he did, to the undisguised glee of the short-hand writers, ... simply reading lengthy tracts from old Judgements which they could mark up from the printed pages.

About a quarter-to-four there began to be faint but definite signs of revolt from the bench (the late Mr Justice Lloyd-Jacob) which provoked an instant change of tactic by Counsel. As the author recalls the occasion, the transcript would have continued something like this:-

"Returning to my argument of this morning, M'Lud, my further submission depends on a rather lengthy technical explanation ... if your Lordship wishes ..." (dramatic pause) ...

"Ahah! Would that be a suitable point for me to rise, Sir Lionel? We can hear that on Monday morning at 1030".

"If it please your Lordship" said Lionel sadly ... looking suitably aggrieved and winking at his team at one-and-the-same time, upon which the Court thankfully rose.

The short-hand writers collected up the bundle of marked-up Law Reports and our team was left with the whole of the weekend to get our technology in order for the new attack.

Today's judges will not usually countenance this sort of delaying tactic. At a present-day (sandwich, ugh!) lunch, the independent Expert now has to rely on the material he has prepared, rather than on what he could (or might) prepare given more time.

An Irish interlude

Some other jurisdictions still seem to be as relaxed and pleasant as was formerly the British Court. The author remembers an agreeable Action in the Irish High Court in Dublin during which the sun seemed to shine on that normally wet, quintessentially Georgian city almost every day during the several weeks that his team inhabited the Shelbourne hotel. Smith was victualled at negligible cost by excellent steaks, draught Guinness, old Jamieson's and one-or-three well-chosen bottles[17] of Chateau Palmer 1967 which had remained on their wine list probably since purchase *en primeur*, having even by then risen in price only to a mere 7 punts. He has still not quite forgiven his instructing solicitor for returning to Dublin on some procedural matter after the case had been won ... either for polishing off the cellar's last two bottles or for telling him about it.

• The case concerned some plastic drainage pipes. The technology was not particularly advanced or difficult. The team was technically and legally well prepared. In the event despite cross-examining, perhaps a little ... a little ..., the other side's case was moderately underwhelming so that the Action collapsed without a significant fight. One splendid independent Irish manufacturer, complete with authentic lilting brogue, was called to give evidence. His charm and honesty (at least under oath) blossomed out to sweep the dust of intrigue from the furthermost recesses of the dingy court-room:-

"What did you do when you saw the design of the device in the Patent?" intoned cross-examining counsel ... "I .. er.. copied it .."

... then after uneasy glances at our rows of aghast faces:-

"... I mean .. I ..er .. used it as the baaysis of my own design".

Strolling in the City on another morning, with the intention of buying some theatre tickets, we asked a bystander the way, who (truly) replied:-

"To be sure, the Abbey Theatre ...oi wouldn't start from here if oi were you!"

---

[17] "Drink no longer water, but use a little wine for thy stomach's sake and thine often infirmities" Holy Bible The First Epistle of Paul to Timothy iv

A very different schedule in the USA

Trial procedure in the USA is of a rather less relaxed but generally quite efficient system. But the procedure seems to vary quite a bit from State to State and from court-room to court-room. The presiding judge presumably has considerable latitude in deciding how to conduct proceedings. In the Phoenix Court, the Judge usually had everyone in there working by 0800 and then ran straight through to 1300 when the Court rose for the day. Aside from a short recess mid-morning at some suitable point, this is effectively a five-hour continuous session when people are at their brightest. After a very light lunch, the Experts then worked with the Attorneys on material needed for the next day until early evening which always gave ample time for a long, relaxing dinner and early bed. This 'early bird' plan works well, particularly when outside temperatures are high enough to fry an egg on the side-walk and the two-block stroll from the courtroom to the parking lot at noon is a recipe for instant heat stroke.

One of the procedural quirks of the US courts which one can find difficult is the interpolation of witnesses according to their availability. This lack of formality prevents any sort of logical unfolding of a case through the presentation of evidence and often becomes really disjointed, one witness often being recalled three or four times in the course of a Trial lasting a couple of months[18]. This can be on the same subject matter, so that one quickly loses track of who said what when and to whom.

Record keeping

Everything that is said in the UK Court is noted and written down. By contrast, in the USA, each Attorney seems to be able approach the Judge and whisper in his ear[19] after first requesting a "Side-bar, yrhnr". The author has not, at the time of writing, discovered exactly what 'Side-bar' is ... for instance whether or not it is drinkable ... but in US Trials it seems to happen quite frequently, even during examination of a witness.

---

[18] Recall and interpolation of witnesses can also occur in the UK courts but strenuous attempts are made to avoid it

[19] "I said it very loud and clear;
I went and shouted in his ear.
But he was very stiff and proud,
He said: 'You needn't shout so loud!"
Lewis Carroll (d. 1898) Through the Looking Glass

It is clearly not an opportunity to slip a backhander to the judge as is said to happen in less respectable jurisdictions! Such frequent enforced rests can be helpful to a witness in avoiding tiredness but also somewhat distracting because of the resulting lack of continuity. To the alert witness, held in alternate suspended animation and frenzied mental activity, it is not unlike trying to concentrate on the argument of an Arthur Miller play in the company of a marginally incontinent three-year old.

Types of Action

So far we have only considered the grand end-product of legal preparation: Trial of the Action. But the Expert will find that there may be a number of intermediate appearances in court prior to this at which his attendance may or may not be required. These are short hearings before the Judge intended to obtain quick tactical advantage or to resolve legal wrangles about procedure. Some examples are:-

•   The Interlocutory Injunction: an attempt to persuade the Court that so much financial damage is being caused by the continued flooding of the market by Defendant's products that he should be ordered to take his product off the market forthwith pending Trial at which the Order may be continued permanently or, if the Defendant is successful, lifted ... when there may be heavy financial penalties for the Plaintiff under his cross-undertaking given to secure the interlocutory injunction in the first place.

•   Striking Out a frivolous defence: a sudden death play-off, in which the Plaintiff asserts that no proper answer has been given in response to the Pleading served, so that the delay to Trial, together with its ultimate cost, impose an unjustified hardship on the Plaintiff. He therefore pleads for Summary Judgement in his favour.

•   Matters of timetable: the strategy and tactics of acceleration or delay in bringing forward an Action to Trial usually influenced by extra-legal considerations such as the wish to defer a competitors decision to build a new production plant on your patch.

•   Complaints concerning the witholding of information, particularly Discovery of documents, but also Process Descriptions, Test Reports, and so on.

- Leave to conduct Experiments, inspect Processes and so on.

- Leave to administer Interrogatories

- Leave to amend the Pleaded Case

Technical evidence at these intermediate hearings is usually submitted in the form of Affidavits, relatively short summaries of technical opinions, supported by a few key publications or test results which together form the Exhibits to the Affidavit. Particular care needs to be taken in the drafting of Affidavits, a topic which is covered elsewhere in this book.

Such are the mechanisms by which a formal judgement can be reached. Succeeding Chapters assume that "the die is cast", a writ has been issued, and the parties have formally engaged in legal combat. At this point, before proceeding to Trial, in the manner of Woody Allen or even more earnestly, the would-be litigant should necessarily ask himself and his advisers:-

"Do I sincerely wish to proceed with this Action?"

In helping the client to answer this question, an independent Expert can usually assist by giving an overall if albeit preliminary appraisal of the perceived strengths and weaknesses of his client's technical position. Having no prior history of involvement in the client's technology, it is easier for the Expert to be objective since his future livelihood does not depend on showing that an earlier technical policy in which he was implicated was 'right', as is often the unfortunate position of the in-house adviser.

Counting the cost

It is possible at the outset to construct a balance sheet for litigation which takes in both worst case (WC) and best case (BC) scenarios. These differ in detail but, by way of example, a WC scenario might involve extensive and complex experimentation, say on a manufacturing plant, with an inconclusive outcome, losses in the High Court, at Appeal, and in the House of Lords, and a generous award of damages against our client. At the other extreme, a BC scenario might involve either a generous settlement in client's favour before Trial or such a decisive win in the lower court that it defies appeal. In a case which goes to trial, even for the BC scenario the winner will not be able to recover his full costs from the other side; 50-60% recovery is a realistic figure. But the poor WC is 160% down the drain. Since expense of going to Trial is often much higher than that of mere 'preparation', there should obviously be a strong financial incentive to negotiate a settlement prior to a formal locking of horns in the courtroom. However the cost of winning will almost always be more than counterbalanced by the commercial advantage of laming a competitor in the marketplace. The real-life question which has to be addressed by the client is therefore 'how to bear the cost of losing'. It is difficult to assess the probability of winning but it is usual first to ask one's Leader for his estimate. This may give little comfort. A well-known Patent silk of the old school used always to reply (helpfully) to his clients:-

"Fifty-fifty, with a margin of error of one hundred percent!"

Whatever the decision, for or against, it is highly desirable for a client to be in control of the dispute, either by deciding to sue or by being prepared to live with a pre-assessed risk of receiving a writ from his competitor. But it is altogether less satisfactory, though not by any means uncommon, to find one's company involved in litigation 'by accident', usually through ignorance of legal rights ... by way of example through inadvertent but convenient infringement.

A naive approach to 'infringement'

There is sometimes a naivety among potential defendant managements in regarding as 'workshop improvements' techniques or materials which have become widely known in the industry as a result of patented disclosures. For instance Licensee 'X' may employ garrulous workmen or consultants who know virtually nothing at all about patents and know-how but who move round the industrial circuit telling competitors how 'we' make it cheaper or more efficiently. But that a thing is now 'well known' and may well have been introduced to your factory by such a new employee from another part of the industry, which is using it without payment of royalties, is no indication that it is not subject to proprietary rights. This is a matter for a skilled patent agent or solicitor to sort out. It is generally no defence against a charge of patent infringement that your new process fell off the back of someone else's lorry!

Regrettably, process infringement within industry is not uncommon and this persuades many industrialists to protect their processes by 'secrecy' rather than by registering relevant IP. In the factories of unscrupulous manufacturers such secrecy may occasionally be extended to cover a manufacturer's deliberate use of other peoples inventions without paying for them. But he will often be found out when a disaffected employee leaves and decides to 'spill the beans'.

The following Chapter proceeds beyond this appraisal stage assuming that the joint opinion of lawyers and Experts sees a reasonably good chance of winning and that, on the basis of this advice, the client has now given instructions to his solicitors or attorneys to start the legal Action. The novice Expert will now need to understand in much greater detail the procedural moves which are about to take place and how he may best contribute his expertise. No apology is made for frequently, in this book, likening the litigation process to that oldest and most deadly of war simulations: chess[20]. And continuing this theme of litigation as an aspect of western culture, parallels will be drawn with the opening, middle game, and end game. The first and last of these involves recognised formal procedures but the middle game is subject to considerable variation.

In summary, in this Chapter the reader has been shown the 'instruments of torture' and how they will be deployed. If a potential litigant, he has been invited to recant. In reading further we must assume that our Client remains "steadfast in his belief" that the dispute is to be resolved through litigation.

A novice Expert should know that at this stage there is a not better than a 1-in-10 chance of a case which starts preparation ever coming to Trial, the greater likelihood being settlement of the Action at some intermediate point. On the other hand the Parties may decide to fight it to a finish in which case the Expert must prepare himself as fully as possible to give his Evidence to the Court. Because of this possibility and because his advice to his client may be material during any settlement negotiations, the Expert must therefore give his full attention to preparation of the detailed technical case from the moment that the writ is served.

---

[20] " Tis all a Chequer-board of Nights and Days
Where Destiny with Men for Pieces plays:
Hither and thither moves, and mates, and slays
And one by one back in the Closet lays"
Omar Khayyám (d. ?) Rubáiyát (transl. E. Fitzgerald first version 1859)

6   Preparing for Action

The previous chapters introduced events which may lead to litigation and the general court procedures which constitute 'Trial'. While individuals may sue for a variety of reasons (such as loss of reputation, desire for vengeance and so on), corporate bodies should be, and nearly always are, concerned only with financial gain or loss.

Starting an Action

As shown in Table 6.1 (p 129), the first shot is usually the issue of a writ followed by serving of the Statement of Claim of one party, called the Plaintiff, against its adversary, the Defendant. This and other court procedures are firmly controlled both as to format and to timetable and it is important to the Expert to remain aware of this timetable throughout the preparation of the case. The Expert should therefore be kept fully informed about any Orders made by the Judge which may accelerate or retard the approach to trial. The second party now replies stating a Defence against the allegations made in the Claim and often counter-claiming for alleged irregularity on the part of the Plaintiff: the Reply & Defence to Counterclaim. In modern actions it is quite common to find a string of Plaintiffs suing a string of Defendants, some of whom may be cited as suppliers or providers of an infringing design and so on. Even if effectively 'the same company', the law requires the separate naming of each corporate body throughout the world. This is important with regard to Discovery of documents which is normally limited by territorial considerations and which for technical cases, so some believe, should now be world-wide by corporate identity (vide infra). The whole procedure is now exemplified for the special case of the High Court Patent Action.

The Patent Action

In a typical Patent infringement action:-

•   a product is bought in the shops, identified as to source and named as the infringing article made by a particular process. This is usually accepted by the Court as typical of a group or class of all such articles made by similar processes.

- it is established by Plaintiff's in-house technologists, supported by commercial intelligence, that this product and/or its method of production infringes Plaintiff's Patent(s)

- a Writ is drafted and served with a Statement of Claim and Particulars of Infringement stating these facts.

- a Defence is received denying infringement and asking for further particulars

- if the Defendant challenges validity, he serves detailed Particulars of Objections summarising the case for non-infringement and/or denying the validity of the Plaintiff's Patent(s) for a variety of (usually, at this stage, formal) reasons.

These basic Pleadings are often supplemented by Further and Better Particulars i.e. more technical detail concerning the alleged infringement and/or the defence. A variation of this format is when the potential Defendant in such an action indulges in a pre-emptive strike by applying for revocation of the Patent(s) which it runs the risk of infringing.

Pleadings

The 'Pleadings' constitute important documents with which the Expert should be fully conversant, particularly as they are amended from time to time on the way to trial. The Pleadings define with legal, but not usually technical, precision the issues in the case, which may be narrowed down by Admissions. Pleadings are usually prepared by the respective Junior Counsel on instructions from each solicitor. As regards the technical side of the case, best results are obtained if the Expert is involved both in the original drafting and also in the wording of any subsequent amendments. These technical issues are the wicket on which the Expert has to bat and he needs to be happy about its preparation and maintenance. For this reason it is best to try to serve well-drafted Pleadings at the outset because any amendments incur fees, make the amending party seem indecisive and may sometimes delay the Trial to give more time for the other party to react to the new case. Good drafting can be facilitated through direct collaboration between Junior Counsel, who is responsible for the legal drafting, and the Expert, who will explain the technological implications.

Formal opening tactics

Litigation involves set moves according to established rules. In this respect it is not unlike 'chess'. It certainly has its chess equivalents of the 'giuoco piano', the 'Ruy Lopez' and the 'Knight's gambit'! As described earlier, there is a strong tendency to try to channel the opening moves and responses of litigation along formal lines, moving among the squares defined by the Statutes in a familiar way in the light of experience of historical judgements which have survived Appeal just as the chess master relies on his knowledge of previous winning games. The quotation of certain favourite judgements was mentioned and exemplified in Chapter 5.

Requests for Admissions and Further & Better Particulars: valuable clarification or pointless sparring?

Following the settling and serving of the Pleadings, there is usually a period of formal silence during which each party tries, with its independent and in-house experts, to re-assess the strengths and weaknesses of its case. Any attempt to do this before serving the writ is bound to be one-sided, unless there is independent knowledge of the likely defence. However relevant knowledge may be readily forthcoming from, for example, a foreign judgement or an Opposition Decision in a Patent Office. After this, both sides formulate, with their counsel, a series of written questions, often with a group of suggested alternative answers, which are intended to clarify the issues. This is in order to avoid wasting time on preparation of elaborate dossiers of evidence on matters which the parties are prepared to admit and agree as 'common ground'. Experts are almost always involved with junior counsel in the drafting of these Requests and in the interpretation of the replies. Everyone is not equally convinced of the value of this exercise. To draft precisely requires an early degree of commital to a particular technical viewpoint prior to gathering together much of the detailed information which will influence that viewpoint. The 'cart is before the horse' with a vengeance. And to draft 'precisely' ... but incorrectly as to technical issues, will encourage one's Opponent to believe that there is a lack of grasp of the relevant technology in the home camp. As a result Requests for Admissions may begin with reasonable precision about points which both sides already know will not really be in contention but they can quickly degenerate into broadly expressed generalities concerning what each side believes to be the main areas of dispute. Even these can be revealing in alerting the opponent to matters which have hitherto not surfaced in his own preparation. So there is much to lose even in serving the usual imperfect set of Requests. Because of the imprecise nature of the 'questions', it is very easy for one side to reply with a series of 'don't knows' or requests for 'further and better particulars' in the hope of getting its opponents to show their hand more clearly early in the run up to trial. Moreover there is no legal compulsion to answer at all! A 'don't know' can sometimes be countered with a 'you must know because ...' but this again reveals the state of knowledge one Party has of its opponent's processes and may risk compromising valuable information sources. In truth the drafting of Requests for Admissions and Further & Better Particulars is an exercise requiring great skill and sensitivity. Perhaps the relevant game model here is 'poker' rather than 'chess'.

Drafting of Affidavits

As was mentioned in Chapter 5, there are often preliminary hearings in court which require the submission of Affidavit evidence from the Expert sworn under oath. The preparation of Affidavits requires no less care than the drafting of a full Expert Report, which is discussed in detail in Chapter 10. So far as the Expert is concerned, the principles which apply remain the same, namely:-

•   Draft it initially in your own words and then discuss with those instructing what amendments may be made in the interests of expediency, particularly the avoidance of over-commital to a particular line of argument;

•   Do not allow yourself to be bullied into including any material which, however helpful it may seem to your client's case, causes uncertainty in your mind as to its technical correctness.

These points may seem to the novice Expert to be elementary and to go without saying but the speed of preparation necessary in putting together the Evidence for an intermediate hearing does encourage a few solicitors, and not a few patent agents, to send the Expert a ready-cooked chicken for his sampling and instant approval. If you receive one of these, look at it carefully and you may find that some intellectual giblets have been left inside producing a pretty stinking document. Or there has been an overenthusiastic injection of legal botulism by, dare it be suggested, the junior counsel who is to appear for your clients at the Hearing. It is as well to remember that:-

• Affidavits may, in certain circumstances, be subject to cross-examination; and

• If, as is quite likely, the Action goes forward to Trial, these same Affidavits are likely to be put to the Expert in cross-examination, particularly if their content differs from his more recent Trial Evidence.

An Expert's opinion usually does develop and change during preparation for Trial as this involves a much deeper involvement in the subject matter including: detailed study of the common general knowledge, analysis of both side's Discovery documents, design of Experiments (and attendance at those of the Opposition) and so on. It is therefore unsurprising that a crude and trenchant Opinion, perhaps originally drafted by others as a 'quick fix' in the early stages of a dispute, can come back in the form of a historic Affidavit to haunt the Witness after he has finally sorted out a balanced view for presentation to the Court. If despite all the warnings given here this does happen, there are a number of (truthful) ways of dealing with the problem. For instance one can say that one has changed one's mind in the light of new information which has become available. But this could suggest:-

• your lack of Expert judgement, and possible (inadvertent) misleading of the Court, at an earlier stage;

• the possibility that, as an Expert in the field, you should already have known the 'new facts' which have influenced you.

Or, as one has heard given in Evidence on more than one occasion, the Expert can say that he approved and signed on oath as 'true', a draft Affidavit prepared by solicitor or patent agent which he "had not properly considered". But this suggests:-

• willingness of those instructing to put words into the mouth of the Expert, rather than requiring his scientific opinion;

• weakness of the Expert in not resisting this pressure, a weakness which the Court may suspect could carry over into the rest of the Expert's Evidence.

In any event, your credibility as an Expert and the value of your opinion to your client's case could have been seriously undermined purely as a result of sloppy, even irresponsible, instruction, abetted by your own lack of forethought and too-ready compliance. A better way of proceeding is based on a specially prepared document called the 'Proof of Evidence', as follows.

The Proof of Evidence

Early in the dispute, preferably soon after his appointment and before there is any pressure of a 'court dead-line', the Expert should always be provided with a full set of historical documents including all technical references and reports, patent office decisions and so on. After reading these, he should be further instructed to carry out his own searches to an extent necessary to fill the gaps in his understanding and so form a preliminary opinion. Traditionally this first opinion forms the draft 'Proof of Evidence', which is sometimes elicited orally by the instructing solicitor from the Expert in a series of interviews the transcripts of which are fed back to the potential witness for scrutiny, correction and amendment. This is still the best way of proceeding with many witnesses but more experienced Experts can usually provide their own first-draft Proof based on a check list of points to be covered agreed in dialogue with the instructing solicitor, helpfully on a floppy disk which can be read by the law firm's WP equipment so saving solicitor's time and making subsequent amendments mutually compatible.

This first draft is then considered at a conference, usually also involving junior counsel and patent agents, after which hopefully there is good mutual understanding both of the strengths and limitations of scientific 'proof' which can be fairly adduced and of the peculiar constraints of the legal procedure. As a result the first draft Proof is revised by the Expert and if necessary put into the Expert's own words. Modified, updated versions, are issued by him each and every time new information comes to light. If this is done properly, that is to say it is always kept up-to-date, then, when there is a sudden demand for an Affidavit, a marked up copy of the latest 'Proof print-out' can be sent to the Expert indicating exactly the areas wherein his evidence will be required. Indeed because the Proof is now already in the Expert's own words and is known to enshrine his latest views which take into account all the most recently available information, it will certainly be justified for the Solicitor to supply the Expert with a 'draft Affidavit' containing a selection of sentences taken from the Proof. The Solicitor should then instruct the Expert to check carefully that the act of selection of these certain passages and the omission of others has not in any way biased the Expert's view, as now expressed in the Affidavit, about the relevant technical matters. Such checking is not onerous and most Experts would be prepared to respond to this by returning their edited version quickly. Of course, Expert opinion may still develop as preparation for Trial continues and so a record should be kept each time further modification of the Proof takes place as a result of new information input. If this new information is properly catalogued, it will be a simple matter to 'defuse' an injudicious early affidavit. This can be done in the Expert's Report, for instance by his indicating exactly which inputs have led to each change of opinion during the intervening months or years.

It goes without saying that the Proof of Evidence should be a wide-ranging document dealing eventually, so far as is possible, with every conceivable aspect of the dispute which involves technology. It will usually form the basis of the Expert Report to be put in evidence. For instance, rather jumping ahead, the section headings of a mature Proof in a typical Patent Action might comprise:-

- Brief description of the invention

- The relevant industrial art (i.e. the science/technology)

- Commercial use of the invention

- Alternative solutions to the same problem

- Who is the nearest equivalent to the 'skilled man'

- The teaching of the Patent-in-suit

- What the Claims mean to you as Expert, and why[1]

- Common general knowledge, as of the filing date

- The teaching of prior publications: Do they anticipate the invention or make it obvious?

---

[1] Without attempting to construe the Claims. One must avoid trying to teach the Judge what they mean; he will form his own opinion!

- The technical teaching of (a) Plaintiff's and (b) Defendant's Discovery documents

- Results of litigation Experiments: what they establish

- Process description, in relation to Process Inspection

- Preliminary view on 'infringement'

- Preliminary view on 'validity'

- Detailed Appendices, summarising reasons for views

Discovery: a crucial role of the Expert in analysing the history of the invention

An important phase in the work of of the independent Expert is the receipt of the lists of Discovery documents. It is a requirement of UK and other common law countries that all relevant documentation tracing the history of the technology in dispute is made available to the other Party. This is not always as simple as it seems. It has been known apocryphally for Discovery to consist of half-a-dozen inocuous copy letters together with a note saying that it is company policy to shred every document more than a month old. Likewise stories abound of fleets of dumper trucks emptying tons of documents into the gutter outside the offices of the instructing solicitors on the basis:-

'We didn't know what you would think was relevant, so we have taken care to send you everything we have'.

In UK and Irish litigation, a commonsense approach is used by a junior solicitor or patent agent in assisting the client to trawl his firm's records for the major documents which could have some relevance, particularly Reports, Reviews and commercial production documents. In a large Action such Discovery could amount to perhaps a quite manageable 100 000 - 200 000 A4 sheets. However, if there is a parallel action in the USA, the sky seems to be the limit. In a recent Action, a team of US lawyers and para-legals worked for several months in our UK client's works, providing a welcome return to profitability of local gourmet restaurants during a severe recession.

Their fees (plus necessary subsistence expenses) could hardly have been less than £80 000. The Discovery reputedly totalled more than five million pages which, had the case gone ahead, would have had to have been photocopied at let us say 3p per page, and so likely to cost about £150 000 plus listing, packaging and postal costs. Presumably this selected material would then have had to be read again by at least one junior lawyer per document from each of the Parties, taking say an average of one-quarter minute per page to read 2000 sheets per day for a total of 2500 man-days (i.e. some 11 man years) costing say a further £250 000. This preliminary expenditure of say half-a-million pounds by one of the Parties would then yield a short-list of documents, say a mere half-million sheets of 'special relevance', which might require to be further duplicated for detailed perusal by more senior solicitors, counsel and Experts on both sides followed by necessary meetings to coordinate their work. At this point the documents would have had to be fed to some filing/retrieval system and probably key-word indexed, a job usually undertaken by efficient but expensive specialists who nevertheless may miss things through not being fully briefed on the issues. Thus such a complete Discovery procedure, so beloved in the USA in the interests of a fairer Trial, might well have burned the best part of one million pounds sterling simply to establish some sort of documentary starting line.

Rather than use this admirably comprehensive approach, one may well favour the 'cheap-and-cheerful' UK method which encourages a more thorough examination of more narrowly selected initial material that may indicate, for instance by cross-references, the existence of other specific Discovery documents which are missing. These further documents can then be identified either by class of document or by specific title/subject matter and requested as 'further and better Discovery'. Often they can be identified as Trial Exhibits from other litigation in various parts of the world.

The rules of Discovery

The Expert needs to know a little about the formal rules of Discovery. As a crude summary of these, under English Law disclosure is required by each party to the other of **all** documents relevant to issues in the Action which are or have at any time been in the possession, custody, or power of the parties. This is done in two stages: firstly the provision of a 'list' of the documents and secondly an 'inspection' of those which are neither 'privileged' nor 'lost'. The privileged group of documents consists mainly of correspondence between lawyers (or patent agents) with their clients intended to give or obtain legal advice or documents such as reports on laboratory experiments or factory tests conducted for the purposes of litigation.

The word 'document' encompasses not only reports, accounts, letters, notebooks and so on but also any other form of retained information, including films, tapes and discs. The intention of the Order for Discovery made by the Court is that either side can find out more about the opponents case, both its strengths and its weaknesses, which, in theory at least, should level the playing field and may encourage settlement of the Action before it proceeds to Trial. Initial inspection is often carried out by a junior lawyer such as a trainee solicitor, who may or may not do a good job in relation to the technical subject matter of the Action. Such documents as are selected on inspection are then copied and codified, for which as we have seen a substantial cost may be incurred. In some instances, parties or their legal advisers have gone out of their way to interpret the Court's Order for Discovery as narrowly as they feel able, even if this may be known or believed to deprive the Opposition of material which will facilitate the preparation of its case. This lack of free disclosure has likewise been a major problem in criminal trials when the Crown occasionally tends to withold forensic evidence which would assist the Defence (see Chapter 14). Thus every help short of actual assistance is usually offered in Discovery, documents being arbitrarily deselected for disclosure on the basis of 'lack of relevance' or 'privilege' so causing irritation and suspicion. A variant of this game is to 'mask' certain paragraphs in the disclosed documents, usually on the grounds of commercial confidentiality, so making the sense of the document difficult or impossible to understand. Alternatively or additionally, whereas a party may find it difficult to deny the existence of documentation actually in its possession, the concepts of 'custody' and 'power' are open to various interpretations which can lead to loss, mislaying, non-availability, lack of access and so on. The existence of 'missing' documents may sometimes be inferred or proved from references to them in those documents which have been disclosed from their appearance as Trial Exhibits in other jurisdictions, notably in the USA. Occasionally they may be confidently requested on the basis of Expert opinions that such documents, particularly design documents, must necessarily have existed before a product went through development into production.

The persistent witholding of relevant documents is a major cause of skirmishes before the Court prior to Trial, where either or both parties fight rear-guard actions designed to give their opponents the minimum possible time to inspect the missing material. Even after several Orders of the Court, it is rare to see anything approaching the volume or quality of disclosure apparently envisaged in the generous Discovery process as originally conceived when this procedure was instituted. However even if they often seem to find it hard to actually achieve the high degree of disclosure they are after, courts can nowadays become angry with legal advisers who play games in the patch they have marked 'Discovery'. As US District Judge Wayne E. Alley wrote in an order in the District Court for the Western District of Oklahoma on 24 February 1989:-

"If there is a hell to which disputatious, uncivil, vituperative lawyers go, let it be one in which the damned are eternally locked in discovery disputes with other lawyers of equally repugnant attributes"

• But his Honour begs the question of exactly where in his Hell the lawyers should be accommodated. We can only suggest that a small private circle between the Sixth and the Seventh might have sufficient vacancies[2]:-

"There are three smaller circles, one below
The other like the circles you have left.
They are all full of spirits of the damned ...
The end is an injustice; and such ends
are either brought about by force or fraud.
But fraud, since it's peculiar to man,
Is hated more by God; the fraudulent
Are therefore lower down and suffer more."

This would allow Smith and some of his fellow-Experts to keep a watchful eye on certain of their erstwhile instructing solicitors (and the latter's -- by now -- permanently-retained counsel) from a face-down position-of-vantage on the Fifth Terrace of Purgatory!

A major problem always arises when a litigant is in one jurisdiction, but his Discovery documents are effectively in another. A typical situation is the US company, which keeps all its technical information in the USA but markets its products through a UK company which discloses little more

---

[2] Dante Alighieri   The Divine Comedy   transl. K. Mackenzie,   Folio Society, London 1979, Canto XI

than a few 'customer response' reports. Even if manufacture were here in the UK, the discovery position would be little better. For instance, in considering the obviousness of a patent, the crucial research & development records leading to the patent would not be available to a UK court unless the US company were to be joined in liability on the basis of 'common design'. This was formerly difficult in law but is now quite often achieved. This limitation on Discovery was recently castigated by Lord Justice Hoffmann[3] in the Appeal Court who suggested that there should be a legislative change to require multinational corporations to disclose R & D records on a *group* rather than on an individual company basis. This would be of considerable assistance.

Enforced Discovery

In extreme cases, particularly where there is a risk that relevant evidence will be destroyed by one of the parties prior to Trial, special Orders can be obtained requiring the Defendant to permit the Plaintiff's solicitor to enter a factory, office or laboratory and seize any material believed to be of relevance. This has long been the practice in Latin countries where, in France for instance, the legal procedure called *Saisie,* usually at weekends with the help of an armed guard (or at least a couple of beefy mechanics with their heaviest spanners), may often engage the Expert at short notice in his first 'hands on' encounter with the other side. In English Law the equivalent is called the 'Anton Piller Order' in which a similar summary inspection takes place.

• A solicitor of the author's acquaintance with a rich operational experience in this field relates how, during such an inspection, he approached the Defendant's factory through a rear entrance to find the Managing Director in his shirt-sleeves energetically flushing the firm's copy invoices down the lavatory.

Expert's analysis of the Discovery documents

Even though disclosure may not be complete, assistance with Discovery is one of the most important ways in which an Expert can contribute to the effectiveness of the litigation team. Some instructing solicitors understand

---
[3]   Law Report <u>The Times</u>   29 March 1993

this very well and take pains to bring the Expert into contact with all of the available documentation at the earliest possible opportunity. However, a few do regard it as in their gift to first sort through the selected and copied documents themselves, in order to choose a smaller bundle for the Expert's subsequent scrutiny. This care is often misplaced. Not only does such filtration run a major risk of witholding material of major technical importance in preparation of the case, it can also put the Expert into the invidious position of later being cross-examined on fundamental documents, such as those picked out freely from the whole pack by his opposite number, which he has to confess have not previously been shown to him. Besides the implication of slip-shod instruction that this suggests, there is a limit to the 'thinking on his feet' that an Expert can do when faced with new material in the witness box. Perhaps it is as well that seamless dictation on to the Transcript of an instant 'considered Expert opinion' is not an easy skill to acquire.

Having a set of lever-arch files containing all the Discovery documents, the Expert is normally required to read them and report to solicitors and counsel on the interpretation of any with a technical content and their likely relevance to the substance of the Action. To be cost-effective, this task is best performed in a structured way:-

• One method which can be used is to pick out obvious key documents, such as Annual Reviews of Progress, and construct from them headings under which Discovery information can be assembled.

• A second method, often used in conjunction with the first, is to formulate a series of key technical questions, closely related to the Pleadings, and assemble document references under each of these questions as sub-heading.

The files thereby created are basic material for subsequent preparation of the Expert Report (see Chapter 10). Indeed after completing his notes on the Discovery and reviewing the position on 'common general knowledge' (of his own subject), an experienced Expert should already have a pretty good idea of the form and content of his future Report. All that is missing now is information on the Process and the results of Experiments but, quite soon, even these will often be available in draft.

Keeping track of the documents

The question always arises as to how the Discovery documents should be identified and the contents listed for immediate search purposes during later preparation and the trial itself. It is persuasive to think in terms of a personal computer (PC) with hard disks supported by data-base software with free text search facilities. However, experience of this approach suggests that it may have limitations particularly for use at Trial. Certain documents, such as Trial transcripts, may already be available on disk, in which case the search programme will be a boon and a blessing. Many junior counsel now maintain these systems as a matter of routine. However the other documents, including formulae, diagrams, graphs and tables, will have to be entered manually, by scanner, and this is a skilled yet tedious job. For the present, better by far to enter in the PC only the electronic equivalent of a short abstract/keyword list plus title, authors and date.

The author generally marks up his Discovery documents (from each Party) with a Michelin star system of 1 - 3 rosettes for 'help' and 1 - 3 daggers for possible 'hindrance' of his client's case ... as he then sees it. This classification is also entered in his PC files. Most of the unmarked documents can then be relegated to an addendum file which will contain the now less-relevant, perhaps 70 - 80% of the total sheets, and from which references can be withdrawn if some new technical slant is perceived during preparation. As a result of this exercise one may be left with but a single, relatively slim, set of 'active' Discovery files containing on average not more than say 30 000 - 70 000 sheets each of which relates to a specific 'pro' or 'con' of the dispute. These need to be fully marked up and known well at an early stage of preparation. They should also be reviewed in the light of common general knowledge and their significance made known to solicitors and counsel.

The importance of the Expert doing this job thoroughly cannot be over-emphasised:-

• In an action in the late 80s, in keeping with the impeccable record-keeping tradition of that corporation, a US major's Discovery documents as Defendant were of the highest quality, the more so in comparison with the Plaintiff's discovery which was of a standard industrial grade. However detailed comparison with Trial Exhibits in the parallel US action showed that Defendant's Discovery was not quite complete, a matter which was partially rectified on request after targetting on specifics. The full Discovery included details of the searches and experimental work prior to application for a patent not greatly different in scope from Plaintiff's patent-in-suit but filed some months later, powerful evidence of 'non-obviousness'. Moreover earlier Defendant's documents described a great number of theoretical and experimental approaches to solution of the problem (economic synthesis of a polyarylene) which had not been adopted commercially. Much of Plaintiff's preparation work for Trial went into drawing up a "Simkin's list"[4], following a celebrated case wherein non-obviousness of an invention was established by citing the large number of different approaches which had earlier been tried by a Defendant and others in attempting to solve the problem successfully addressed by the invention-in-suit. The diligence with which this list was produced reflected the energy and dedication of the Patent Agent acting for Plaintiff during preparation of the case.

As a result of this work, the Court was not disposed to accept the Defendant's pleas that the Plaintiff's patent was either 'obvious' or a 'solution to a non-problem', as suggested by the Defendants. In fact this case could be said to have been largely won on the basis of the other side's Discovery.

What to look for in reviewing Discovery documents

There can be many different objectives in trawling the other side's Discovery files. By way of example, in considering a Defendant's Discovery one might seek answers to the questions:-

- 'Who was who' in the Opponent's hierarchy?

- How was the problem, that eventually solved by the Invention, perceived? Was it chronic or acute?

- What was the size of research team and the scope of program(s)?

- What theoretical background was brought to bear?

---

[4] Named after Dr Simkin, an industrial librarian. The relevant case reference is *Olin Matheson v Biorex*

- Was the Plaintiff's technology thought of, tried out, found wanting? If so, why did Defendant miss the boat?

- Or was the Plaintiff's eventual solution considered, and rejected as 'impossible' by hide-bound in-house theoreticians?

- What contact was there with between Plaintiff's and Defendant's representatives, formally and informally?

- Was there any indication of leakage of technological confidences? For example, by migration of staff?

- What was the standing of the research team in comparison with the norm for the industry?

- How did Defendant's clients react to the various solutions suggested to them? Did they gossip information?

A similar and equally useful trawl can be carried out through the Discovery documents of the Plaintiff which might contain, for example, the detailed history of the invention or discovery which is the subject of the Patent-in-suit or other IP. In general the Expert should trawl not only the other side's Discovery but also that of his own client although, in this instance, sign-posts will usually be provided by the Client to the principal disclosures. Even so, it is best to be thorough and look at the lot.

The dubious value of lab notebooks

A feature of US inspired litigation during the 70s, perhaps now a little on the wane, was the widespread disclosure of every supposedly-relevant page of every technician's every laboratory notebook concerned with work in the area of the patented art, usually to establish priority in patenting. A special technology was presumably developed by the in-house legal departments to produce the least legible of xerox copies, which were pored over endlessly by patent attorneys to decipher exactly the figures relevant to say, the routine standardisation of a sodium borate solution. But there is, in general, insufficient time in a UK Trial to develop detailed arguments which require assiduous sleuthing from page to page, cross-referencing with the books of others who may have taken over the work during holiday periods and finally ending up triumphantly with the conclusion that Example XXVI of the Patent-in-suit seems to have used a 0.0137M buffer rather than the 0.0135M actually published in the text.

Notebook pages seem to fall into the same category as video-tapes of Experiments, for use in quickly checking specific points. They can be invaluable for such specific purpose but they are of little value *en masse* in presenting a case to the Court.

Technology leakage

Discovery can be entertaining, as well as instructive. All scientific employees of large corporations ought to be made aware of how many friendly chats at the airport bar after the rave-up conference have acted as starting blocks for a great technical leap forward in the receptor company.

The disclosure routine in Discovery can uncover indiscretions long buried, such as the notorious 'Malaga Memo', a tangible product of an 'old Spanish custom': the corrupt private sale of your firm's technology to a competitor.

• The seminar had been a success: good food, sangria, sun and sea, if not more, and the Research Manager of West Nebraska Fur Mines was in a receptive mood when approached in a dark corner with a bulging envelope containing Blue Vinney Corp's latest process description. But back at base his Vice-President showed commendably greater moral fortitude and a week later the envelope was received back by its rightful owners under cover of a short note which explained that it had found its way to WNFM illegally and was forthwith being returned unread.

When litigation between BVC and WNFM began, a diligent Discovery trawl yielded material enough to make the fur fly. Not only did WNFM disclose nine file copies of the Blue Vinney document, but one contained within its pages the infamous 'Malaga Memo', addressed to the photocopying section, requesting distribution of 26 copies to everyone of importance within WNFM from its Chairman down to its factory managers in Hawaii!

This made for a rather poor start to WNFM's case from which it never quite recovered, particularly since the signatory of the Memo had been designated to the Court as their leading in-house technical witness.

Confidentiality: Care with Discovery material

In the UK, documents disclosed on Discovery can only be used for the UK proceedings. There is an implied undertaking that they will be used for no other purpose. In the USA, disclosure is often subject to a Protective Order restricting the use of discovered documents. All Experts must be careful to ascertain the position and observe the rules, especially when acting for clients involved in international litigation. It goes without saying that everything they read must be kept confidential and only used for the purposes of the Action but extra-special care must be taken with all Discovery designated 'confidential'.

The in-house Expert should take some care concerning the photocopying of any privileged material lest, by so doing, the privilege be lost. It is important to take advice from the corporate legal or patent department about this at the earliest opportunity. After the writ has been served, any Expert should technically direct his reports and correspondence to the external legal advisers to avoid the accumulation of any material in the client's files which could later prove an embarrassment. However, in practice, failure to do so rarely causes problems in the UK though it may do so in the USA

Experiments: Planning; Execution; Documentation

There are now several tasks in which the Expert will be involved concurrently or at least with a considerable risk of overlap in time. These may include Process Inspection, in the case of a 'process patent', and the design, rehearsal, execution and demonstration of Litigation Experiments. Experiments are usually only conducted by the Parties if they feel unable to prove some aspect of their case through use of Admissions and disclosures in the Discovery documentation, supported by oral evidence of 'fact' together with Expert Opinion. More positively, Courts normally decide technical cases on the balance of probability so that any weight added to this by tangible, demonstrable measurements can have a bearing on the decision.

The Litigation Experiment is designed to establish a high probability that a technical 'fact' in the case is as described in the Pleadings. It is therefore

usually associated closely with the wording of the Pleadings. .
soundly based, give unequivocal results and allow of fault-free demo
to the 'other side'. Typical is the experimental Proof of Infringement
by a Patentee against an alleged infringer, which involves demonsi
that the alleged infringing product or process falls within the scope of o.
more Claims of the Patent. Experiments are frequently designed oy
independent Experts to provide a firm basis for their opinions:-

"Don't just accept what I say; look at what we have actually done"

But it must first be decided whether Experiments are needed or not.

Are Experiments really necessary?

Depending on their past experiences and conditioning, non-scientists
(including even some skilled and experienced litigation lawyers) may
sometimes take an exaggerated view of the importance and value of
experimentation. Alternatively, they may denigrate all experiments and
experimenters alike. As a novice Expert you will be surprised that probably
your first meeting with your Leader will begin with his forceful and often
extreme opinion on *either* the 'need' *or* the 'non-need' for experimentation in
support of the litigation. This polarisation is unfortunate, because over-
reliance can raise false hopes ... or excision lead to missed opportunities.
One should not make these decisions on a 'hunch'. Failure of
experimentation happens not infrequently because insufficient technical
planning and evaluation takes place prior to the drafting of a Notice of
Experiments and its notification to the Opposition. Ensuing prejudice of
many counsel (and judges) against experiments may well be just the result
of historical bad management in a crucial area of litigation.

Whatever their expressed views on experiments, Courts are often impressed
by such tangible 'proofs' which support expert opinion. While this remains
the situation, litigation experiments will remain important and it will be
necessary to design them reliably and to demonstrate them with aplomb[5].
What is needed at the present time is a marked improvement in their quality,
particularly their *reliability upon demonstration* to the opposing litigants.

---

[5] presuming that you have one with you and are not swinging the lead.

The Notice of Experiments

Not infrequently, the first serious inkling of how the Parties' experts view the technical content of the case is included in their respective 'Notices of Experiments'.

Up to this stage, the only technical documentation submitted has usually been the Pleadings, including 'Particulars of Objection' which as previously indicated is a rather formal legal document not always very specific in technical terms and with a built-in flexibility to allow subsequent argument. On receipt of the opponent's Notice is therefore a time for further substantial conferences involving a full interchange of views between the technical and the legal members of the team. In particular the novice Expert may find that, after a full reappraisal of the opponent's case, the lawyers decide not to rely on one or more of *his* Experiments drafted in his Notice. This may be disappointing to the architect of the experimentation, particularly the keen independent Expert who is naturally anxious to make a special contribution to the cause, but he will realise in time that experienced counsel often do have a nose for which experimentation is likely to succeed. As with the early 'dirty' nuclear weapons, just using technology "because it's there" can prove a fairly mindless exercise with long-term deleterious consequences. The experience of counsel must be relied upon to guard against rushing in with the wrong weapon at the wrong time.

Because of a wish not to give the game away, or because the client's technical case is in disarray, there has grown up another pernicious lawyers' art in drafting a Notice so that it will 'get by' ... that is to say persuade the Court that it is a serious description of experiments purporting to support certain facts ... while giving little or no inkling to the other side of what actual practical work was carried out and is to be offered for demonstration. Not infrequently Notices are served which differ fundamentally from what has actually been done, certainly from what is actually demonstrated when the bluff is called and it appears that this unhelpful, even deceptive, approach can be used by either party with some impunity. In a serious legal process with considerable money, reputations and livelihoods at stake, such misleading tactics may seem reprehensible and readers may be surprised at the extent to which they are tolerated by the Courts. As mentioned later in this Chapter, there certainly seems to be a strong case for the root-and-branch overhaul of regulations for the proper conduct of litigation experiments.

The disastrous results of bad experimentation

In the late 60s, Charlie Merriam of the former Chicago partnership Merriam, Shapiro & Close used to boast to the author that he won many of his cases on the basis of the other side's experiments. It is certainly true that the 'wrong experiment', or worse, the 'wrong' results from the right experiment, can have a devastating effect on a Party's credibility. The 'wrong', particularly the 'opposite', result is the legal equivalent of the prematurely released grenade picked up by the enemy and lobbed back into one's own trench. The eventual detonation can intellectually hospitalise an entire litigation team. Only Leading Counsel seems adept at striding unscathed from the ensuing wreckage. When faced with an overly-enthusiastic demand for an experimental program, it is an important function of the external Expert to try to guard against such disaster even if, as related later, this can risk putting him temporarily at odds with his counsel, his solicitor and the whole of the client's in-house laboratory.

Strengths and limitations of experimentation

There is a regrettable tendency in conference for even the most distinguished scientists who have been retained to advise to eagerly offer 'experimental proof' of 'facts' which, in the event, they find themselves unable to deliver. As we have seen, one of the sources of misunderstanding between lawyers and scientists is that those commissioning the experimental work do not always appreciate that science cannot prove 'true' or 'false' but can only indicate the *level of probability* of obtaining a particular result by means of a defined and, hopefully, appropriate experimental procedure. Although as scientists they must all understand this, novice Experts, anxious to show that they are helpful, clever and good[6], and harangued by their formidable Leading Counsel in the imposing surroundings of the Inns of Court, sometimes fail to communicate this limitation. Instead they throw out their chests and try to rise to the occasion. They do not seem to properly contemplate the possibility of 'failing to deliver' in their laboratories or, if they do indulge in such contemplation, they elect to keep such musings to themselves.

---

[6] "If all the good people were clever,
And all clever people were good,
The world would be nicer than ever,
We thought that it possibly could"
Elizabeth Wordsworth (d. 1932) St Christopher and other Poems

This failure may sometimes result from a too-assiduous faith of the Expert in the results of his own work. In terms of an earlier discussion, a probability of perhaps 90% is too readily claimed or represented as 99%+. Such failure, which only too often will take place for the first time at a Demonstration of the Notice in the presence of the opposing Experts, cannot but suggest to the Court the conclusion that the true facts are other than those which were represented in the Notice, so both weakening or even destroying the technical arguments they were designed to support and discrediting the Expert at one and the same time.

Courts are not usually much impressed by experiments which 'should have worked' but 'went wrong', and which consequently require to be explained away in the witness box. Novice Experts should at least reflect at the outset that many hundreds of thousands of their clients pounds sterling (or, at the present time, rather more of their dollars) together with the credibility of their own reputations may well hang on the initial advice they give. There follow some examples of failures, necessarily without attribution:-

• Our team inherited over fifty brilliant heat-transfer Experiments from a previous US Action. We ran many of them in chief (i.e. as our first line of attack) but the results were less than compelling and our client's armada was substantially outgunned by Drake's 'cheap and cheerful' practical tests.

• Certain basic measurements were conducted by our opponents by two quite different, but apparently equally appropriate, techniques which gave different results ... enabling a fatal 'unreliability wedge' to be driven between them.

• A galaxy of poorly planned and virtually unrehearsed Experiments-in-chief, relying on doubtful Expert advice, was offered by the Opposition as an opening salvo, several of which went lame during the race, others being savaged by well-targetted Experiments-in-reply.

• Opponents offered impeccable Experiments-in-chief to which, on Counsel's advice, our side made no reply, effectively conceding the results. But our client subsequently went on to win the case, largely on the basis of the opposing Discovery.

Simple experiments, fully rehearsed

To reiterate, a well-designed litigation experiment is usually required only to disturb the balance of probability in the Party's favour and is not generally required to demonstrate a fundamental truth of nature. Such modest experimentation can often be set up on a relatively simple basis. Moreover it can be frequently repeated which gives a much improved chance of its being "alright on the night".

Of course it goes without saying that if the science and technology is not as the Expert believed (and presumably advised his client) at the outset, it is far better to establish this quickly by pilot experiments in private on the basis of which the client's legal advisers can be told at the earliest possible time that an erstwhile 'water-tight case' has unfortunately sprung a leak. In such an event the Expert has a duty to man the pumps and execute such running repairs as are feasible to get his vessel into port. Experts who are unable or unwilling to do this must needs be replaced, at whatever inconvenience and risk, even if this occurs late in the run-up to Trial.

Drafting and Serving the Notice of Experiments

After completion of the design and proving of suitable experiments and now at the point of drafting of our Notice, we have reached an important stage in the Action. By now, the Pleadings, Counterclaims, Interrogatories and so on have been served, replies have been received, correspondence has been exchanged between solicitors in an attempt to clarify key issues; there may have been unsuccessful discussions between the Parties regarding terms of settlement and also various preliminary skirmishes in Court. There is therefore now a fair idea of the technical nature of the dispute and both sides, being prudent, will in addition to experimentation for the Notice most probably have conducted a series of private tests on the relevant products, processes, etc. to establish to their own satisfaction that the facts of the matter support their case. These tests will include those directed to establishing the fundamental factual evidence required by Counsel. In US litigation, such private work will be 'discoverable' to the opposition but in the UK and in Europe it can often remain hidden behind the wall of legal privilege. Counsel now advises that the matter is not likely to 'settle', but is more likely to proceed to Trial. He therefore requires preparation of a formal Notice of Experiments which purports to establish, with high probability, some of the key facts on which he proposes to rely.

We have already seen in earlier Chapters that the key battle lines in a Patent action are drawn up as follows:-

- Plaintiff (the Patentee or a Licensee) alleges infringement of a monopoly defined by their Patent

- Defendant denies infringement and/or alleges invalidity of the Patent

The Plaintiff's and the Defendant's Notices of Experiments-in-chief are usually exchanged i.e they are served at the same time. That of the Plaintiff is particularly concerned with 'proof of infringement'. In fact if infringement is *not* established at this stage it is open to the Defendant to apply for a Declaration of Non-Infringement which, if granted by the Court, could terminate the Action. The form of the Notice is not rigid, indeed as discussed later it does not seem to be rigid enough, but it is supposed to set out both the facts which it is alleged will be proved by experiment and the methodology of the experiments themselves. There is, at present, flexibility in two important respects:-

- the degree of detail concerning the experimental techniques which are to be used and the actual observations to be relied upon;

- the inclusion or omission of typical results, average results, or a complete set of results of the tests carried out for the purposes of preparing the Notice and/or in in rehearsal for a possible Demonstration of the Notice.

One can see no good reason why the Courts should not set down their fairly detailed requirements in these two respects, at least in the form of 'guidelines for drafting'.

Towards better Notices of Experiments

As we have mentioned, at present the Experts sometimes have to attend and observe several weeks of the other side's experiments on the basis of a three- or four-page formal document which gives no scientific or engineering detail as to the equipment or techniques which are to be employed. As a result, on arrival, often without essential observation equipment, they have to spend valuable time requesting details of proprietary test instruments or materials which could well have been appended to the Notice. As to inclusion of previous results, there seems to be an unholy fear among instructing solicitors that disclosure of any previous results in the Notice will draw attention to inexplicable differences which may occur during the demonstration. As it was once put to the author by a lawyer during a (serious?) discussion of 'reproducibility' :-

"If you only have one reading, you don't have to worry about variability!"

But you do have to worry, you really do! A single result from a test procedure is almost as useless as[7] :-

"A man's tits, a heifer's balls and a viola part of the 'Messiah'".

However if the work leading up to the Notice of Experiments has been carried out properly, there will already exist a corpus of results which can be analysed statistically to determine a reliable value for the given test parameter. Presumably this 'true' value must necessarily support the Client's case or the Notice would not have been drafted to contain it (though the author has seen even this rather fundamental assumption cave in under the peer pressure of a Demonstration). This being so, why not disclose the mean value of each parameter, its standard deviation and the number of measurements in the Notice, so that, in the event of obtaining an atypical 'outlying value' during the Demonstration, this can be properly and scientifically combined with the earlier results as an additional reading to further increase the precision of the mean value?

This procedure would admittedly cool the jolly Casino atmosphere of so many Demonstrations, which might disappoint the bystanders, but it would also limit clashes between Expert testimony at trial, so saving much time and money and helping the Court reach a properly based decision. If this were to become required practice and all such previous results were to be presented as part of the Sworn Affidavit of the independent Expert, there would also be fewer requests for Demonstrations, thus substantially reducing the costs of litigation to the benefit of the clients. Productivity does not, at present, seem to be one of the strong points of our court procedures.

---

[7]   Anon. "The three most useless things in the World" - A rather colourful saying in the British music business of the genre "viola joke".

Experimental results without substantiation

It is notable that Experiments may be cited in US litigation but they are not normally required to be demonstrated. Without the safeguards here outlined, or the opportunity for a witnessed Repeat in front of the Opposition, this practice is open to abuse and would seem to be inadequate as a litigation support procedure. Worse than this, it invites the retention of bogus scientists as witnesses quoting bogus experimental evidence which the Court necessarily finds it extremely difficult to probe. The temptation to proceed in this corrupt way will be even stronger when the decision is to be left in the hands of a lay jury. This topic is further discussed in Chapter 14.

Strategy and the design of litigation experiments

The practical requirement to relate any proposed experimentation to the Pleadings is not always as easy as it sounds. The early preparation of a case usually involves the crystallisation from a rather murky commercial brew of a few pristine crystals, 'the technical issues'. Moreover this is a kinetic problem. These issues do not necessarily materialize at once and indeed, as preparation proceeds, other important issues may co-crystallise which were little suspected to be crucial at the outset. Knowing how this can happen, Junior Counsel who normally is responsible for drawing up the Pleadings will wisely have tried to make these rather formal, drafting them in wide terms which seem (and often are) utterly unspecific, appealing little if at all to the attendant scientists and technologists. Indeed so flexible do counsel sometimes remain up to the date of Trial that it can sometimes be quite difficult for the Expert to find out from them what certain passages in the legal documents actually mean. A good example of this is obtaining advice on "construction" of the Claims of a delphically-drafted Patent, where Counsel frequently feels a need to second-guess the Judge and wants to be able to float a selection of alternative flies over his lordship's nose during the opening speech in the hope of obtaining an appropriate 'rise' (see Chapter 11). However unless it is explained to them by the Expert, Counsel do not always fully understand that by taking a particular approach in the design and execution of its Experiments, the Party may in fact already have boxed itself in to a particular construction. The consequences of this therefore need full discussion with the Expert prior to drafting and serving of the Notice of Experiments.

Defendants' experiments

During the period of presentation of the Notice, Demonstration, and preparation and agreement of this Report on the Experiments-in-chief (Chapter 8), Experts acting for each side having perfected their own Experiments-in-chief will be working on their draft Experiments-in-reply (Chapter 9). The Defendant experimentation differs from that of the side which bats first (the Plaintiff, as Patentee) for the following reason:-

•   The 'first side in' needs only to establish its basic winning propositions. Whereas theoretically no Experiments-in-chief have to be offered by the Defendant as alleged infringer, in practice such a course of action would normally leave the first team in sole possession of the field.

•   The Defendant would then have to depend only on the arguments of its Counsel and evidence of Experts that the Plaintiff's results which have by now been publically demonstrated are for some reason false, irrelevant or unfairly based. This could prove an uphill task.

Unless the Plaintiff's first innings is beset by unforeseen disasters, it is virtually certain that the Defendant will conduct some Experiments-in-chief of its own in order to redress the balance and these will have been indicated in its Notice. According to the rules, this will allow the Plaintiff to have a second shot at experiments, called Experiments-in-reply, which are discussed fully in the next Chapter. The important point here is that when planning its Experiments-in-chief, the Plaintiff knows that it is likely to be able to supplement these Experiments at a later date when it is clearer about the detailed facts of the Defendant's case. The Defendant, on the other hand, would like to rebut the results already obtained by the Plaintiff, while simultaneously or concurrently establishing contrary results of its own:-

•   If the Defendant carries out very little experimental work, more particularly if the results are less than conclusive, the Plaintiff may subsequently elect *not* to offer the Experiments-in-reply to which it is entitled. That is then the *end of all experimentation*, possibly leaving the Defendant disadvantaged.

•   Alternatively if the Defendant carries out a comprehensive experimental programme, not only does it expose the technological strength or weakness of its case but it also presents a very broad target to the

Plaintiff in the planning of comprehensive Reply experimentation directed principally, if not exclusively, at rubbishing the results as permitted under the regulations.

True, the Defendant will have a further opportunity for its own Reply Experiments but, by then, Trial dates will be pressing and considerable impatience may be shown by the Court to see all Experiments by both parties completed and written up. This is a form of built-in bias in favour of Patentees. It is an advantage to start from the position of injured innocence.

For the Defendant's Expert adviser, the right decision here is crucial. It is vital for the Expert to limit the Opposition's programme to what will work and work well, rather than agree much of what clients and counsel think would be nice and then later be forced to withdraw test after test because of unexpected, particularly variable, results obtained during rehearsal and/or lack of time to develop a fool-proof procedure. There is some sub-section of Murphy's Law which states[8]:-

"The frequency of a given event is in inverse ratio to its desirability"

In other words, the more experiments you do, the more things are bound to go wrong.

Be prepared

Often, when a member of the team batting second, one is conscious of a 'wait and see what they will do' attitude within one's own corridors of power. But this apparently statesmanlike calm can be followed by blind panic after their successful Demonstration, in which a brace of divinely-inspired sure-fire Reply experiments is expected to emerge from the Expert like a stream of ectoplasm in the space of a few weeks.

Lawyers can turn ugly when it is explained that good litigation experiments 'don't grow on trees'. Experts be warned! You and your side need to begin thinking of, and testing, a wide range of experiments, even before the Pleadings fall on your mat.

---

[8]   Anon. Commonly stated 'principle' in engineering management

The US Deposition: what happens and how witnesses prepare

In the USA, it is common to depose all technical and commercial witnesses during the months before trial. The objective of the Deposition is to obtain evidence in advance of Trial on all or most of the issues which are expected to be contentious. It is an opportunity to clarify the provenance of documents and the meanings of certain passages therein, to find who was who in an industrial hierarchy and so on. A record of the proceedings is taken by a court stenographer and the Transcript is part of the formal evidence which may be submitted to the Court at Trial. From the Court's point of view, Depositions are seen as valuable opportunities for the Attornies to save trial time by getting answers to questions in advance so that they can focus their examination of the Witnesses at Trial with greater accuracy. From the Attorneys and the Witnesses points of view, it will lock in the Witness to a particular sequence of answers which may be further explored on the Stand during the Trial using additional, often contradictory, documentation which has arisen from a further trawl through the Discovery documents.

While the purpose of Deposition seems admirable, the execution is generally woefully inadequate. In the absence of a judge, the main criticism is the lack of any referee or chairman to keep the examination procedure on the rails. Moreover the rules seem to allow for a bewildering array of procedural handicaps which can be applied by the 'home' Attorney to gag his own witnesses. The applicability of these restrictions is hotly debated throughout each session by the unrestrained and personally aggressive Attorneys who often engage in long battles during which the Witness remains unproductively silent. On these occasions he is apt to think[9] :-

"The noblest answer unto such,
Is kindly silence while they brawl"

Often when the Witness does speak it is only to affirm that he "does not recall" the contents or origin of a document which is being put to him. Since there seems to be little or no restriction on the number of times that a Witness can be recalled to give further evidence, attendance at Deposition hearings must account for a fair proportion of the high Attorney fees which are such a distinguishing feature of US litigation.

---

[9]   Alfred, Lord Tennyson (d. 1892) <u>After-Thought v</u>

Witnesses seldom seem to give of their best at Deposition hearings, for the purposes of which they have to suddenly switch off from their regular work for perhaps a day or two at most. In contrast, a Trial witness will usually be seconded to the litigation team for several week before Trial and have his facts and arguments clearly in his mind by the date of his examination. One should have particular sympathy with the inventors of patented products or processes who are popular Deposition victims. Many bear their crosses patiently as they are paraded on an international circuit like victims at some latter-day Auto da Fé acknowledging, before they are scorched, that:-

"The Law is not tainted with blood"

•   A rather shell-shocked inventor of a large corporation had been doing the rounds of the jurisdictions for some months, even years, now readily convincing many who spoke with him that, as a distinguished substance-survivor he now knew little about his invention and so was quite safe to be deposed. At the time he was currently engaged in a gruelling series of Depositions prior to yet another Trial. And some of these had apparently not gone as well as those instructing him had hoped[10]. He had certainly had enough, in several senses, and this led inadvertently to the shortest Deposition session the author has ever had the good fortune to attend.

The scene was set in a Manhattan hotel room, replete with a too-large shiny lacquered table, too many telephones, too much iced water and cawfee and too many cans of soft drinks ... not to say too many lawyers, stenogs, attendant Experts and other hangers-on. As to the Witness's demeanour, one recalled[11]:-

"I went out to Charing Cross to see Major-general Harrison hanged, drawn, and quartered; which was done there, he looking as cheerful as any man could do in that condition"

Attorney for the Defendants opened the Deposition with a formal question in the usual elegant, succinct manner of these affairs:-

---

[10]   "There was things which he stretched, but mainly he told the truth"
Mark Twain (S. L. Clemens) The Adventures of Huckleberry Finn ch 1

[11]   Samuel Pepys (d. 1703)   Diary: 13 October 1660

"Are you the same Blurb Weinkart[12] who testified in these Proceeedings in San Francisco on January 3, in Cleveland on March 17 & 18, in Cincinatti on April 12, in Miami on May 14 & 15, in Wilmington, Delaware on June 5, ..."

Eventually he exhausted his mini-gazeteer, ending on an interrogatory note. The Witness looked helplessly at his own Attorney who could not give him any immediate attention because he was vainly trying to insert a new cartridge in his ballpoint prior, as he saw it, to the start of play. One of the hangers-on pulled a ring-opener on a 7-Up. Above the lambent whoosh of the conditioner came the distant rumble of traffic on Columbus Circle. Somebody drummed his fingers irritatingly on the table ... After perhaps a minute of deep consideration, Blurb pronouced the long-awaited evidence:-

"I dunno", he said.

The session was thereupon adjourned and the worthy UK Expert returned to England, whence he had travelled specially, at client's expense, to hear the advertised revelations.

For the time and money expended, the evidential results of the deposition procedure seem meagre. Would not the desired result be better secured by pre-exchanging compulsory Affidavits of the Experts, covering issues agreed beforehand with the Court in a short preliminary hearing?

Getting close to Trial

By now, the date of Trial has been fixed for some months, if not years, and the count-down to it is in progress. Jumping ahead in time, the reader is now asked to assume that:-

•   The Process Inspection has been completed and an Agreed Report issued (see Chapter 7)

•   Experiments-in-chief have been completed and likewise reported by both Parties (see Chapter 8)

•   Experiments-in-reply and or -in-rebuttal are either completed or immediately pending (see Chapter 9)

---

[12]   The author has, of course, disguised his name to avoid any possible offence.

- Expert Reports have recently been exchanged between the Parties and a 'primer' document has been produced to instruct the Court in the basic technology of the Art, so far as this is 'common ground between the Parties' (see Chapter 10)

These major set-pieces are dealt with in separate chapters because each can be treated as a self-contained project in which the Expert has a well-defined, starring role.

We are now about six to eight weeks away from 'opening' and the Expert must assist in putting the show on the road. At least at this time, if not much earlier, a 'war room' is set up at the offices of the instructing solicitors.

This conference room doubles as a specialist library, the shelves of which are furnished with all the relevant papers and citations in the case except possibly a few confidential bundles such as those dealing with the 'commercial success' of the invention which are unlikely to require consultation by the (technical) Expert. There is a conference table equipped with the traditional nonsenses of professional people: paper pads, clips, pencils-to-be-stolen (with the law firm's telephone number hopefully prominent as a genuaflection to the God of marketing) and so on. There are telephones, fax and video-TV units (best chained to the walls).

What from the Expert's point of view may well be missing are the PCs on which we do all our work and which could act as a much more convenient data-base for us than the shelves full of paper. One wonders if PCs are seldom provided because those instructing, possessing secretaries and other status symbols which surround them, have, unlike the more practical barristers, never fully got to grips with the wonders of these fantastic machines[13]. Or is it simply that they fear that we impecunious academic Experts may leave with them 'under the arm'. No matter! The answer is to import your own lap-top machine, together with a small ink-jet printer.

Looking ahead, it would be a shame to also be denied a CD-ROM reader for the next twenty-five years, while those instructing debate if it is 'here to stay'. Please let the twentieth century commence.

---

[13] The PCs, ... not the barristers or the secretaries!

Clearing the decks for Action

The main technical task for the Expert is now to fully understand the technical case against one's own client, as evidenced by the Opposition Expert's Report, together with the results of the Opposition Experiments. Each Report may well be illustrated by numbers of Exhibits, many of them references to citations which have hitherto not featured in the Case and which will have to be studied for relevance and impact. Such study may lead to the conclusion that the opponent's Report is in some way flawed, in which case it is usual for the Expert to draft a Supplementary Report which draws attention to this which will include appropriate reasoning and, usually, further Exhibits.

Supplementary Reports do not have to be exchanged contemporaneously, as do the main Expert Reports and, with leave of the Court they can be served at any time, even well into the Trial itself. During this period, there are increasing opportunities to work with Solicitors and Counsel, both in explaining the pros and cons of the technical case as it is developing under the impact of the new documentation and in assisting with diagrammatic and other aids which Counsel will need to teach the specialised technology to the Judge.

When there are several Experts on one side, and also possibly a number of witnesses of fact, it is important to study the preliminary submissions of all of these. Conventionally, Expert opinions are presented in Expert Reports although witnesses of fact produce only Witness Statements. These will have been intelligently vetted by the solicitors and counsel prior to service but there may be technical implications arising from overlap of Evidence which the lawyers did not appreciate but which the Expert might be called upon to explain under cross-examination. If the fields of the Experts overlap, as is often the case, there will be a risk of conflict of opinion in the areas of overlap. Whereas a purist might suggest that such conflicts should be presented, warts'n all, before the Court, this is actually a waste of the Court's time if a short discussion between the Experts prior to the Trial can resolve the matter. This is not to suggest the establishment of a technical 'party line' but, rather, the resolution of a complexity in the technology by means of the normal working practice of scientists i.e. 'consultation' (as was explained in Chapter 3).

During the last week or two before Trial, the Expert will have to spend a substantial time with Leading Counsel, who will be writing his opening speech. Your Leader will have read your Reports and other documentation and may be expected to raise many points which seem to require simply further explanation but often one or two new points which require re-thinking, even under-pinning with new citations. He will not mince his words; if something is unclear, or simply wrong, he will want it clarified or rectified. These conferences or, more properly 'consultations' ("cons"), often take place in his Chambers, administered by his business-manager 'Clerk', away from any helpful technical library in rather cramped conditions and sometimes heavily diluted by the rest of the litigation team plus a posse from the client corporation which, besides paying the bills, is by now showing commendable solidarity with the cause. The result is usually temporary bedlam, Counsel maintaining an unruffled calm throughout, apparently not letting any interruption or the inevitable depletion of oxygen interfere with his concentration. (There is usually at least one 'smoker' present ... usually a director who is too senior to be disciplined[14]).

Such a meeting can prove a tough assignment for a novice Expert. He must take the flak in front of the audience and keep his cool. If answers can be given then and there, all well and good. If not, they must be found with all possible speed. All in all this is an excellent preparation for his future sojourn in the Witness Box.

Some Counsel conduct occasional 'public' séances roughly to the above pattern but supplement them with quieter discussions-in-depth in the relative privacy of the war-room. This solves the problem of communication in a civilised way.

---

[14]   One great advantage in working for US corporations is that by and large their senior officers have given up smoking

TABLE 6.1: STAGES OF PROGRESS OF TYPICAL PATENT LITIGATION

Plaintiff's Patent Agent draws attention to subsisting Patent(s) believed to be infringed by Defendant Client or Solicitor may write to Defendant inviting discussion (without threat of legal action)

HIGH COURT	PATENTS COUNTY COURT
Plaintiff's Solicitor issues Writ, Statement of Claim, and (formal) Particulars of Infringement	Plaintiff's Patent Agent (or Solicitor) issues Summons, together with (technically detailed) Statement of Case
Defendant's Solicitor issues Acknowledgment of Service, (formal) Defence, Counterclaim for revocation, and Particulars of Objection (technical outline)	Defendant's Solicitor or Patent Agent acknowledges Service, (formal) Defence, Counterclaim and Particulars of Defence (some technical detail)
Notice requesting Admissions	Notice requesting Admissions
Discovery: disclosure of all relevant documentation, together with a list of any documents lost or destroyed together with Inspection of Documents; and of Process (if relevant)	(Limited Discovery)
	(Inspection of Documents, in special cases only)
Devise Experiments-in-chief: Plaintiff's re infringement; Defendant's re non-infringement and/or invalidity	
Exchange names of Expert Witnesses to appear at Trial Preparation, but not exchange, of Draft Witness Statements and Expert Reports	Exchange names of Expert Witnesses to appear at Trial Preparation, and exchange, of preliminary Witness Statements and Expert Reports
• Summons for Directions, before the Court, to fix further timetable including Trial dates	• **Preliminary consideration and review by the Court of technical aspects of the case**
Demonstrate Experiments-in-chief to opposing parties	
Prepare agreed Reports on the Experiments, listing any differences in measurement/interpretation	
Devise & demonstrate Experiments-in-reply to prove inadequacy of the Experiments-in-chief	
Prepare agreed Reports on the Reply Experiments listing any differences in measurement/interpretation	
Prepare Evidence of Experts	Prepare final Evidence of Experts
Exchange Witness Statements and Expert Reports	Exchange finalised Witness Statements/Expert Reports
Drafting & exchange of Supplementary Expert Reports re matters arising from the main Reports	Drafting & exchange of Supplementary Expert Reports re matters arising from the main Reports
• **TRIAL before a Judge sitting alone**	• **TRIAL before a Judge sitting alone**
Pleaded by one or more barristers: "(Learned) Counsel"	*Pleaded by barrister, solicitor, or chartered patent agent*
• JUDGEMENT, incldg. order for costs & damages	• JUDGEMENT, incldg. order for costs & damages
• **APPEAL in the Court of Appeal**, pleaded on the basis of evidence given in the Lower Court, occasionally followed by a further appeal to the House of Lords	
• **APPEAL to the House of Lords** on a point of Law	
• **DAMAGES ENQUIRY** in the High Court, requiring evidence about profits of an unsuccessful Defendant or lost by a successful Plaintiff, interest on profits foregone, etc.	
• APPEAL of the "Damages" decision, usually to alter the Lower Court's assessment	

NOTE: Shaded stages are those in which the principal technical evidence is given to the Court

129

7 Process Inspection

In Patent Actions involving disputes over proprietary processes and sometimes over products allegedly made by such processes, it is usual for the independent Expert to be asked to attend a Process Inspection. This necessarily involves the detailed tracing of the conversion of properly authenticated raw materials through each stage of the process to produce the finished goods together with the quality control testing of these products by the normal factory tests.

Confidentiality and disclosure

Such an inspection is best carried out under guarantee of confidentiality and the Expert should always be prepared to sign a detailed undertaking to this effect. In recognition of this, the Expert should certainly be shown what he feels it is necessary for him to see. Otherwise he will not be able to offer a fully informed opinion to help the Court. If he is prevented from seeing what he believes to be key parts of a process, it is important that he should remonstrate at the time, note any explanations which may be given to him and record the existence of any lacunae in his observations in his Report and their possible consequences. But this happens rarely; normally the party undergoing inspection is anxious to demonstrate its righteousness to the Expert so that he can inform the Court accordingly.

The Process Description and other Defendant documentation

In order properly to survey a novel process in an unfamiliar factory, the Expert requires in advance some detailed descriptive documentation. This is conventionally provided in the form of a Process Description which first sets out the main steps in the Process in outline and then fills in the relevant details of each step to a sufficient extent to enable observation to be carried out with the minimum of hassle. The advantages of doing this properly lie with the owner of the process, usually the Defendant. Typically the Process is that of a Defendant who is pleading non-infringement of the Plaintiff's patent or patents ... or of a Defendant who is explaining to the Court that the process in question can be and is normally operated with complete safety so that injury to the Plaintiff results from his own negligence and so on.

The Process Description is a future Court document and, with the help of the Defendant's Expert, should be drafted as such. It can and should be set out in such a way as to establish the clear innocence and responsible behaviour of the factory owner. This is not achieved by special pleading but rather by clear and simple technical descriptions often illustrated by block diagrams, line drawings, and photographs of any special equipment which may be unusual in the Industry and so unfamiliar to the Expert. The Description should also include the main process parameters: times, temperatures, flow rates, etc. which determine the nature and quality of the product.

•   One of the clearest Process Descriptions this author has seen was provided by his opponents in *Phillips v Mitsui [1990]* Houston, USA (settled). This was followed by a generally well-conducted process inpection organised by the Defendant at its plant near Hiroshima. The action was concerned with the mechanism of polymerisation of 4-methyl pent-1-ene and required the inspectors, some like himself of advancing years and fuller figure, to climb about the heights of fractionating columns and peer into the depths of reactors running at elevated temperatures. Despite the ambient temperature, which averaged 36 deg C and humidity of 90-100%, both the home and away teams completed the inspection in good humour having developed considerable mutual respect.

This happy outcome was not wholly attributable to lack of a common language. Although there were occasions when Smith felt that sudden death in Hiroshima would be a fitting and, in the climatic circumstances, a welcome reward for his earlier service with the Atomic Energy Authority, his survival was assisted by the provision of a climatised conference room and other civilised facilities. The organisation and discipline of the host staff was impressive. Although no time was wasted, they could not have been more informative and considerate ... and so it was a pity for them that the result of this inspection was to confirm the Expert's views on the validity of his client's case.

Prior to such a well-ordered Inspection, the Plaintiff's Experts will study the Process Description and if necessary request further information. Such information may reasonably include copies of instrument handbooks or schedules of procedures which will enable the Experts the better to prepare themselves for making meaningful observations. Given common sense, this is the way a process inspection should be conducted every time.

When all the required information is forthcoming, the Experts will indicate to their instructing solicitors the approximate duration of an Inspection which they believe will be required to satisfy them that the Description is accurate and complete.

If a Process Description is not submitted, or such Description is inadequate, or even misleading, the Expert is in a quandary. Whereas his capacity to inspect is seriously undermined, those instructing him may not wish to trouble the Court with a request for an Order for further and better Process discovery. Even if they do, and the Court obliges, the result is usually further prevarication. In such circumstances the Expert may have to proceed without the necessary map to guide him. The only procedure then is to scan the Discovery documents for 'process' references and, from these, put together the best speculative account of the process that is possible, correcting misapprehensions and filling in gaps in the Description at the Inspection itself. This is very much a second best approach which, if not followed up meticulously, can be subject to all kinds of uncertainties and errors. One would be happy to see the Courts penalise severely, through costs and damages, those litigants who interfere with the dispensing of justice by making such machinations necessary.

Sampling

When agreeing the duration of an Inspection, the solicitors, advised by their Experts, will also indicate at what stage or stages of the process they believe that samples should be taken, the quantum of such samples and their physical condition, together with any special precautions necessary to prevent subsequent loss or deterioration of the samples. The purpose of taking samples is three-fold:-

- to confirm the process parameters given in the Description, or obtained by testing during Inspection in the Factory

- to obtain technical data additional to that obtained in the Factory tests, for instance by means of additional informal laboratory experiments

- to use in subsequent formal litigation Experiments.

As in other litigation work, sampling should be properly witnessed and the sealed sample containers signed across the seals, preferably by the Experts and by one of each legal team acting as "Officers of the Court". It is also quite usual for each side to take contiguous samples together with a third sample left sealed "for use by the Court". This can add up to a substantial weight of materials and the quantities to be taken need to agreed in advance to allow for this. Some further detail about sampling is given later in this chapter.

What to look for

In an Inspection it is obviously desirable to see the conversion of (sampled) raw materials into (sampled) final product, tracing every intermediate stage of manufacture. However rather than run from "cradle to grave", factory practice often makes provision for storage of intermediates in a process. This may be for the convenience of converting several days worth of production on a special machine at one particular time but also perhaps because it is known that such storage has a beneficial effect on product quality. While it is usually open to the Experts to witness the conversion of intermediates made some days before, they will not have seen the earlier stages of their production or inspected and sampled the raw materials from which these intermediates were formed. They must therefore form an opinion as to whether this loss of information could in any way prejudice the quality of their subsequent evidence. If there is any doubt, it is better to see everything even if this involves 'waiting time' between periods of observation. While such apparently unproductive waiting periods may seem irksome and costly to the client, they do offer opportunities for immediate drafting of an Inspection Report from one's notes which may trigger thoughts for further critical observations on return to the Factory.

Reasonable attitudes of the Plaintiff and of the Defendant

Much of the foregoing presumes a normal, co-operative attitude between Plaintiff and Defendant or at least between their legal representatives who realise that they are all doing a professional job which is most efficiently and expeditiously completed in an atmosphere of tolerance and good-humour. The lawyers are also aware that a helpful attitude will underline to the Court that they believe their case to be just and that they have nothing to hide.

Occasionally, because of specific instruction from aggressive clients or because of clashes of personality amongst some of the professionals involved, such a co-operative atmosphere cannot be generated or maintained. Non-cooperation can occasionally arise when there is a clash of cultures, for instance between a Western Plaintiff and a rather less than scrutable Oriental Defendant or where there is a long history of squabbling between international corporations. And it is not above a very few attorneys to engender unnecessary antagonism, hopefully in the pursuit of genuine tactical advantage for their clients rather than mere enhancement of their fees. Such in-fighting can sometimes make the Expert's life difficult.

Witholding process information

The author's own experience has usually been felicitous in that he has been able to attend the Factory fully briefed and see what he had been expecting to see. However on one occasion he was required to attend an overseas Inspection without provision of any significant documentation other than sparse details provided in a 'partial' Discovery. This was written in a language which he could not read, let alone understand. There had also been a pointblank refusal to provide any proper Process Description, even in the inscrutable native language of the country concerned. Here the reason was probably tactical, an attempt to delay the progress of the case through the Courts.

• The initial proposal from Defendants, endorsed by their own independent Expert and communicated to the Plaintiff's solicitors in his name, was that Professor Smith should be capable of completing his 'inspection' of a multi-stage process (including lengthy dwell periods) 'within two hours'. By degrees, this was grudgingly extended to 'within three days'. When the author arrived at the Factory with the British lawyers, he was told that the plant was being run in a special way to make a number of demonstration batches. No diagram, even a block layout, of the plant was available. And when the team reached the first-stage venue, raw materials had already been selected and mixed so that the first test-batch was under way!

Protest after protest was formally lodged to no avail and it gradually became apparent that the Defendant's English-speaking advisers seemed to know as little about the process we had all come to see as we did. The Defendant's home team and its English lawyers were unusually nervous and this, probably exacerbated by jet lag, translated into civil unrest. In one angry exchange, our solicitors were told that we did not need to be given any information; Smith was the 'Expert' and he should know 'where to look' and 'what to look for' ... in an unfamiliar plant, inscrutably labelled, run in some special way by a hostile team, without any documentation, even a diagram of the plant layout. However thanks to painstaking preliminary work by one of our brilliant young solicitors, some of these problems had been anticipated and we had put together in advance our own hypothetical process description based on the fragmentary Discovery documents. This proved more than sufficient, in fact surprisingly accurate, and we did succeed in completing the job within the allotted time span. We actually received a bonus in the form of an (unscheduled) plant experiment offered, perhaps thoughtlessly, in answer to a question, the observation of which was later helpful to us in dismissing certain contrived laboratory experimentation by the Defendants that had been inadequately designed to 'simulate' plant conditions.

This incident has been described at some length to warn the novice Expert that every encounter may not be plain sailing and to illustrate that some tightening seems to be necessary of the formal regulations controlling such occasions.

Towards court regulations for inspection

The author believes that there is a need for a properly recognised procedure fully endorsed by the Judiciary to regulate the conduct of Process Inspections. The protocol should certainly particularise the pre-documentation to be supplied and could also include notes for guidance on the minimum level of cooperation between the parties expected by the Courts during the Inspection visit. Such guidance, in this instance not merely advisory but rather mandatory, would make the Court's work much easier during the Trial because the relevant facts would also be assembled in a prescribed format which would vary only in detail from trial to trial. It is a parallel point to that made with regard to the formal Notice of Experiments (see Chapter 6) and no apology need be made for stating it again in the context of Process Inspection.

It is a matter of common sense that the scope of an Inspection should be limited to those aspects of the technology which are or may become contentious. Inspection is not an excuse for a 'fishing trip' for confidential information by Experts interested in novel solutions to their own clients' production problems. In any event it is essential that an Expert privileged to enter the Factory adheres to the letter of the confidentiality agreement that he has signed. Experts are well aware of these privileges and responsibilities and the author has never heard of any instance of leakage of confidential information resulting from an Inspection. This being so, it seems logical that the Experts should be given, as of right, every possible assistance to prepare Evidence which will help the Court to reach the right decision.

The independent Process Audit

In US litigation it appears to be common practice for an independent Expert to audit and report upon his own client's process. The author carried out this task for Defendants in Phoenix, USA, in the early 1980s and produced an Affidavit which was, of course, subject to cross-examination. Had there still been points of uncertainty or criticism concerning the process following the Court hearing, there is no doubt provision for further (direct) inspection by the Plaintiffs but was not required in this case. In most similar cases this will prove unnecessary.

• In this particular Action the independent process audit became necessary at a relatively late stage in the preparation for trial because of a major tactical disaster which had occurred during earlier (client) experimentation in connection with a parallel UK action. As we have seen, UK procedure allows for witnessing of a demonstration of the Experiments which unusually, and as it turned out ill-advisedly, had taken place in the USA at the client's manufacturing plant before the Expert was retained to advise. During the Demonstration of these in front of the Plaintiff's advisers, to the chagrin of the client a parameter which was specifically adjusted to be non-infringing was shown in client's own experiments to be (marginally) infringing. The author therefore started his Expert assignment with an unwelcome inherited 'own goal' ... though it was quite seriously suggested to him by some of those involved that, because the infringement was marginal, 'the baby was only a little one'.

It later became apparent that an unauthorised adjustment of the processing equipment had been made just prior to the Demonstration by an in-house engineer, who had recently been offered permanent leave of absence (on zero pay) for enjoying too physically the favours of one of the physical-testing assistants in the adjoining (temperature- & humidity-controlled) laboratory.

This unfortunate UK infringement result was seized upon by the Plaintiff's US Attorneys, who (predictably) used it to allege fraud in the earlier Process Description which had been put before the US Court. Smith was thereupon wheeled in to vet the process and produce a detailed report vouching for all the plant and test parameters being used in production of a particular range of allegedly-infringing products. This independent technical audit procedure seemed to be perfectly acceptable to the parties and one can see no obvious reason why it should not be used in UK litigation. It is obviously cost-effective. It has the great advantage of avoiding the sensitive issue of admission of 'outsiders' to what the owners believe is a uniquely well-equipped and highly-competitive production unit. The factory owners will also provide substantial assistance to their friendly Expert, which they are often less willing to do for an Expert from the other side, freely answering all his questions and providing back-up documentation all of which is invaluable in fleshing out the Audit Report. Such additional information is commonly denied to an inspecting Expert for the Plaintiffs on the grounds that it is marginal to the substance of the dispute.

If it be argued that the inspector has more chance of being 'bent' if he is (indirectly) in the pay of the factory owner, one might answer that few if any litigants have won their cases by employing bent independent Experts. And if for whatever reason the Expert is subsequently discredited in Court, which would be likely in such circumstances, his process evidence (say of non-infringement) will also be devalued, a risk which is simply not worth running in a multi-million dollar suit. Furthermore no Expert who ever wants to work again would even contemplate the possibility of drafting a mendacious process report, one which would be the subject of an Affidavit.

What it is reasonable to observe

Coming now to the act of observation, what can the Expert expect to see in the other side's Factory and how can he record his observations? He will have arrived with preconceived ideas as to the crucial observations which he must make but needs to remain moderately flexible as to both their feasibility and their importance. As discussed later in this Chapter, it is

137

suggested that:-

•   the best kind of observation is wholly non-invasive; and

•   an inflexible, dogmatic attitude to the gathering of data, whatever the cost in terms of inconvenience, is likely to prove counterproductive.

Also, a closed mind will miss opportunities for observation of subtleties not revealed in the Process Description which neither party may yet have realised could be of significance in determining a resolution of the dispute.

<u>Recording observations</u>

One should therefore approach the task of observation with a clearly delineated but flexible framework in mind which will require to be reinforced at a few fixed points by 'key observations'. It is not an easy matter to write coherent notes under factory conditions which are often hot, humid and extremely noisy, if not worse. For instance in a recent overseas case, the author's team had to make observations for many hours in the solvent-enhanced atmosphere of a mixing room in which the mixing operation simply involved the pouring of chemicals into the stirrer vortex in an open drum. So much for Health & Safety regulations in the particular country where this was carried out.

The recording of observations is best carried out by the time-honoured student method of scribbling on an A4 pad on a clip-board. The main draw-back of this method is the necessity of transcribing one's own rough notes on to the word processor prior to editing. 'Long-hand' is well-recognised by the Courts as an acceptable form of 'contemporaneous note' and as such can readily be admitted as Evidence. For such possible future use it is important to file the pages carefully or (if you are as wayward as Smith is) keep photocopies for your own use and arrange for your instructing solicitor to look after the originals until they may be needed at Trial. The best format for such a hand-written record of observations is undoubtedly in the form of a 'log' in which each observation is preceded by a time check. To aid subsequent reconciliation in the form of an agreed Report (see Chapter 8) it is best for all present to synchronise their watches, ideally to agree with the Factory clocks.

Many of us have tried to use dictating machines but find them inconvenient for two main reasons:-

- every 'note' is heard by the representatives of the other side and, in a tense and non-collaborative situation, dictation of even the mildest criticism of equipment or technique may spark off aggression;

- the Expert's own notes need to include recording of numbers, description and free-hand sketches which cannot be easily combined in any current electronic format.

There are also important secondary drawbacks such as the intrusion of factory noise (steam, hydraulics, machinery, and so on) which is picked up and magnified by the microphone, sometimes obscuring speech. Perhaps a stylus-on-tablet computer will solve the problem but would the Courts accept the record thereby created as 'contemporaneous'?

Photographic records

The use of cameras or video-recorders in a Factory is a vexed question. The author does regard such aids, particularly the 35 mm TTC equipped with a date-recording back, as an essential part of normal observation equipment. The pictures obtained are invaluable *aides memoire* when preparing evidence on an 'Inspection', perhaps a year or eighteen months hence. However many production directors have an inflexible rule that no cameras can be brought into the factory and it is difficult to negotiate a relaxation of this rule except through a distant and inaccessible Board of Directors.

- In a factory inspection visit to I.C.I. on Tees-side in the late 70s, the author wanted to use a camera during a process inspection. Counsel, who was present at the Inspection, put the point that his Expert only wished to use the camera 'as a notebook', which accurately described the position. But 'a rule was a rule' and they had to refuse.

If as Expert you are permitted to use a camera, be appreciative and take care that the negatives are handed over to your instructing solicitor to retain as material solely for use in the Action. On that basis, one may hope that the granting of permissions will become more widespread.

The unilateral photographic record

What amounts to an abuse of privilege is a Factory embargo on the use of cameras imposed *unilaterally* on the visiting inspection team while the home Expert and in-house staff are allowed to flash away regardless. This is sometimes in an attempt to obtain material which may discredit the manner in which the Inspection was carried out so running the risk of prejudicing the home Expert's own independence. In such cases it is often best to note exactly who was taking pictures of what part of the process and then request copies of all these pictures which, if obtained, can often be as revealing as those one might have taken oneself. However to avoid this kind of unnecessarily aggressive situation, the courts' draft regulations for the conduct of a Process Inspection might contain guide-lines which would provide a basis for dealing with the matter.

Abuse of photography

Occasionally one can meet the "faked" photograph which an unscrupulous litigant attempts to use in evidence.

• A dreadful old reprobate trial attorney the author knew in his early days in the USA told of him of his appearance for a carbon black company in one of those southern states with a pan-handle in the late 1950's. The Judge had suddenly become interested in Expert evidence about 'structure', the formation of chains of the near-spherical black particles, but the Attorney's Expert had not brought with him the promised electron micrographs which were supposed to show this. And so this Attorney had a problem. Ever resourceful, during the morning recess he went outside ... :-

"Thin ah saw some sheep-shit there on the sahd-walk, so ah got mah Leica down on close-up, called in at the local processing store, and .. soon after noon .. the Jurdge had his pictures".

It is not suggested that this crude sort of trick would work in a modern court-room but it is a reminder that it is extremely important to check the provenance of each photograph put in evidence against one and particularly the angle and lighting conditions which were used. As indicated in the next chapter, the taking of photographs is often a crucial part of the formal experimentation and it should be witnessed with care by an independent

Expert with some experience in relevant techniques such as photomicrography.

Process Inspection by the Court

In the days before adequate videotapes, it was not uncommon to arrange factory visits for leading counsel and sometimes even for the judge.

• For instance this was done in *General Tire v Firestone*, Smith remembers one such trip during the late 1960s to the former Firestone factory on the Great West Road in West London with a great retinue of counsel and solicitors, including the fastidious and impeccably-dressed Mr Jack Whitford QC acting for Firestone, later the distinguished Mr Justice Whitford. Already one suspects thoroughly disgusted by the Dickensian conditions of the rubber industry at that time, he unhappily contrived to be the nearest when a bag of carbon black was dumped into the feed throat of a Banbury mixer, whereupon the operator lowered the ram with excessive enthusiasm blowing back a goodly quantity of finely-powdered soot all over the assembled observers. No one spoke ... the expression told all. And I often wonder if he went on many more such factory visits. Perhaps he should have heeded the teaching[1]:-

"He that toucheth pitch shall be defiled therewith"

Today such retinue visits are rare, being correctly regarded as at best marginally informative and also a quite unnecessary expense. In an English High Court action as recently as 1992, strenuous efforts were made to persuade the Trial Judge to visit a nappy-making plant. In his wisdom he felt that the videotape would teach him as much as he would need to know about the technology of the process. Nevertheless exceptions are still made where the equipment is specialised and difficult to portray on film.

A sequence for inspection

In materials work, with which the author is most familiar, one nearly always starts by inspecting the raw materials; not only the materials themselves but their packaging, identification of source and batch number,

---
[1] Holy Bible Ecclesiasticus xiii

141

and documentation confirming the source and date of supply. Experts may ask for any suppliers documentation describing the materials and their recommended method of use. It is helpful here to be shown a generous amount of supply documentation which will confirm that the particular batch of material is a random selection from the many batches which are bought into the Factory and processed day-in, day-out. Any indications of a "special" batch e.g. marks on packages or documents such as "ordered by Research", "reserved for Inspection", "keep for litigation work", etc. can reasonably be questioned and the explanations duly noted. There should be no possible objection to taking photographs of such external labelling or in asking for them to be taken on your behalf by the factory photographer.

Putting questions firmly without causing offence

Questions or requests should be put in a neutral way, and usually through the Expert's own legal representative which both depersonalises the questions and also confirms that they are part of a Court proceeding, which the Inspection is. They will not always be expected and may cause consternation. In the nervous atmosphere, they can be resisted quite unreasonably. However if as Expert you need to know the answers, it is necessary to dig in and continue to repeat the request for as long as it takes to obtain cooperation. Such apparent prevarication is seldom an indication of 'guilt' ... it simply shows the unfamiliarity of factory personnel with the peculiarly detailed requirements of those who have to give technical evidence. If the answers are not available at once but can be obtained, the question should be noted and an answer requested later in the day or, at latest, next morning while the Inspection is still in progress. However the main point is to establish a practical timetable for answering and not be fobbed off with excuses.

What samples to take

It is usual and expected at this point to take samples of the raw materials in the pre-agreed quantities. This is unlikely to cause surprise or offence but it can more readily be done for say rock-salt or even iron brackets than for butane gas or gold ingots. In other words there are questions relating to the nature and containment of the samples and to their intrinsic value. Experts need to be able to advise on what is feasible. Matters of this sort can usually be sorted out by the solicitors well before Inspection; also the question of who is to provide the sample containers and who to arrange for the shipment of perhaps inflammable, explosive or toxic materials over thousands of miles by air freight.

In the best circles a quite detailed schedule for sampling is established in advance of inspection but this again presupposes the provision of full documentation about operation of the process well before the Expert is required to make his inspection visit which, as we have seen, is not always forthcoming. More usually, an approximate schedule with generous time allowance for sampling and the recording of 'samples taken' by solicitors from both sides together with formal sealing and packing of containers, is then agreed between solicitors when dates are fixed for the Experts to attend at the Factory.

Taking samples

The matter of physically taking samples involves certain skills in order to ensure that they are 'random' and therefore, over all, 'representative'. Their immediate storage must be in non-reactive containers, suitably sealed against the ingress of moisture and, in some cases, oxygen. For most chemicals, screw-top jars and/or glass-stoppered bottles are regarded as satisfactory but biologically-active samples may require more elaborate packaging. The factory under inspection will often offer to provide what are believed to be suitable sample containers and, subject to Expert agreement, such offers are usually accepted. However where spiteful squabbles are in progress, this useful offer may not be made and it will be necessary to arrive on the morning of the Inspection with a full load of clean and shining 'empties'. It is common practice to affix a wide tape over bottle and jar closures, mark on them identifying codes, and have the tapes signed, with date and time, by a legal representative from each side, so keeping the supernumeries alert and usefully employed during the *longueurs* of inspection.

Quality Control records

It is usual also to inspect the Quality Control (QC) Laboratory which tests and releases batches of raw material for use in the Process.

If possible the Expert should see the QC tests performed during the Inspection on any batch(es) forming part of the Demonstration but, if not, it should be possible to see *representative* tests and to obtain copies of all the actual test results (signed by the responsible QC manager) and also the standard control limits routinely used for rejection of any batch 'out of specification'. One may request, and is usually given, copies of the QC sheets extending back a few days, so establishing that the batches being processed have 'typical' production properties.

To inspect a process plant properly, it is of course necessary first to note all the operating parameters being logged by the plant operatives and then request a full set of copies of all the control sheets they have to complete.

• In one overseas inspection, Smith was told that this was impossible because all data were automatically entered into the process control computer. After a battle royal, all in laborious translation involving frequent denial of the existence of any paper archives, together with his Chicago attorney he was admitted to the computer room and asked what he wanted to know. He asked again for today's print-outs:-

"No print-outs exist or are ever taken" said the translator "What do you want to know?"

During a baffled pause for thought, a temporarily unemployed Attorney accidentally leaned on a cupboard door which slowly swung open to reveal ... the last full month's print-outs of all the plant operating parameters up to today's morning shift, all in familiar 'computer english':-

"Ah, so zat is what you need ...!"

We had no further trouble in obtaining the relevant information.

Sampling a Batch Process

The Process itself may have a number of self-contained stages in which batches of material are processed to form successive intermediates which are eventually formed into products. Such 'batch processes' are usually relatively easy to inspect, a natural point for sampling being provided at the point of isolation of each intermediate whether it be a material or a form of construction. The same applies when a number of separate components are produced which are assembled to form the product. In each case it is not difficult to identify the intermediate or component with respect to its starting materials.

Sampling a Continuous Process

Many industrial processes are 'continuous', in which raw materials are fed into one end of a conveyor system and product emerges at the other. Besides difficulties of access to individual parts of the process (vide infra), there exists a conceptual difficulty in that at any given instant the materials entering the process are not directly reflected in the composition of the emerging product. It is of course true that there will be a defined overall duration of process for flow of materials to occur from entrance to exit but, such is the design of processing equipment which may involve considerable blending and even reverse flow, that in practice this may be little guide. It is usual to deal with such a process on a statistical basis. Indeed the process control parameters used to set up and operate the production line will normally take this into account. Yet other processes are 'semi-continuous' containing batch elements and continuous elements. In general the plant operators will have to make measurements and take regular samples during the Inspection as part of their ordinary process control activities and so, if at all possible, it is best to make use of these measurements and samples for inspection purposes.

Special sampling: problems of cost and of safety

Occasionally conventional sampling, which has not been designed with the requirements of the litigation in mind, is not good enough and arrangements will have to be made to measure and sample the plant in unconventional places where the plant designer has not thought fit to provide inspection ports. This inevitably causes difficulties which are far better resolved well in advance of the Inspection proper, firstly by inter-party correspondence between solicitors and then usually by informal contact between the Experts and the Plant Manager.

When inspecting processes where the Defendant's have nothing to hide one is always impressed by the willingness of their engineers to open up (or even instal) remote sampling ports, special piping, pressure and temperature sensors and so on to help provide the data and materials which are requested. The companies are usually glad to authorise this because they believe that it will help to establish the rightness of their case. On the other hand, a production plant is subject to the most stringent safety regulations and it is not always possible to achieve what the Expert feels he needs with adequate safety. In such cases, flexibility of approach is again important. The sympathetic Expert will usually concede any such difficulty and devise other routes and techniques to obtaining the data he requires.

Making independent measurements

It is worth recording all available data, even if the use to which it may be put in evidence is not immediately apparent. Rather than rely completely on the readings of plant instruments, it is often useful to make a few approximate measurements of one's own to confirm the plausibility of what is being indicated. It is also a good idea to estimate dimensions of equipment, distances between units in a continuous process and make free-hand sketches of lay-outs, as well as checking key temperatures, pressures and so on, on a rough & ready basis. For this purpose, the Expert may choose to carry to the inspection a crude 'tool-kit' of what he expects to need: perhaps pre-calibrated temperature-measuring equipment, hand lens and pocket microscope, steel rule, crash helmet, bullet-proof anorak and so on ... depending on the plant, the subject matter and the attitudes of the Parties. For independent measurements to carry legal weight, it is of course necessary to calibrate the equipment in front of a witness and preferably to demonstrate the calibration to the Other Side. Occasionally one does meet with unnecessary obstruction in making independent measurements or sampling at unusual places. If, as is sometimes clear, the objections are doctrinaire and technically baseless, it is best to reiterate one's request with gentle insistence on its feasibility until resistance crumbles. It is quite amazing to a certain type of manager that any measurement can be made differently from the way it is normally done in his plant.

Attempted fraud

It is certainly not a matter of regret to him that the author himself has never actually met (or, at least, detected) outright fraud during the demonstration of

146

a process. However, he has heard some pretty terrifying stories many emanating from the old-time 'oilies' in the US refineries:-

• As an example, one platforming process plant was modified, at dead of night just before an inspection, by the plant manager who inserted a length of solid rod internally in a catalyst-slurry feed line and opened a hidden valve at the back of the reactor to siphon off the flow of catalyst. Of course the feed pumps and input flow gauges continued to register 'normally' as if catalyst were still feeding into the reaction. Not surprisingly, since as a result of the subterfuge none of the catalyst was being introduced, subsequent chemical analysis of the product confirmed its absence. This in turn seemed to indicate its 100% consumption in the reaction, so differentiating the process from some other. This other was a more truly catalytic, proprietary method, in which the (true) catalyst was regenerated rather than consumed.

The fraud was detected by a robust and suspicious independent Expert who climbed up a ladder and belted the feed pipes with a monkey wrench until, at the solid section, he heard a different ringing sound. One can just imagine the scene when he called for the line to be disconnected there to check the volume of the outflow! Very occasionally, in such exceptional circumstances, one simply has no choice other than to 'make a scene'.

Shipping of (labile) samples after completion of the inspection

Not infrequently arrangements have to be made to ship reactive samples over large distances and across several frontiers, each with different customs regulations. This can raise difficulties, many of which we are told only prove soluble in the world's major lubricant, hard cash.

• Towards the end of 1990 the author's team took a number of such samples during an inspection at a factory north of Tokyo, both as liquid reactants and as semi-finished sheetings prior to a prescribed low-temperature 'curing' process. Both Parties acknowledged that the materials would change in structure if stored at room temperature but we had reached agreement that such change would be *de minimis* for litigation purposes if storage of all actually or potentially labile samples were to be carried out in solid carbon dioxide, called 'dry ice' (at a nominal temperature of about -70 deg C). During the inspection the team wandered about the Defendant's factory with a number of 'cold boxes' in which were placed the various factory samples with the intention of shipping them to England and to the USA for detailed testing, both before and after cure. These caskets were loaded with samples sealed, opened for further additions, re-sealed and so on, all with formal witnessing and signatures on the seals. Our main container was dark-coloured and about the size of a child's coffin. It was draped with a dark-coloured cloth to provide additional (external) insulation. Being heavy with solid coolant, it required two 'bearers', front and rear.

On the last day of the Inspection, we all left the Defendant's factory at about noon and repaired to the local hotel for a bite to eat prior to driving back to down-town Tokyo. Being tired after some very early starts followed by long days in the Factory, we entered the hotel lounge silently, looking drawn and sombre in our dark suits and sober 'litigation' ties, bearing our 'coffin' aloft and setting it down on a long table near the door. Only then did we notice that the other occupants were a charming wedding party who had been utterly non-plussed by our unheralded arrival. The gorgeous young bride decked in blossom eyed the container like a frightened rabbit, her husband and the guests attempting to maintain a jovial exterior while we tried to recall what Confucius had said about such a situation, scrabbling the while in our Japanese phrase-books for:-

"Have no fear! This casket does not contain a small dead body ... simply y'r ord'n'ry 'reflective traffic sheeting' ... temporarily immersed in dry ice"

For obvious safety reasons the boxes were not gas-tight, so that they leaked carbon dioxide continuously. For this reason the samples themselves were also stored within the boxes in individual signed & sealed packages. This enabled the cold boxes to be topped up with refrigerant as and when this became necessary without breaking into the sample packages. Although one of our more robust US Experts had no compunction in flying his steaming box back to his base in the mid-West as 'hand baggage' in Business Class, so no doubt ensuring the deep (if not healthful) sleep of his fellow-passengers, we had instructed a Japanese shipping agent to guide our larger boxes through the Customs and see them safely loaded for London Heathrow. There the British solicitors would officiate at the unloading and check for the presence of residual refrigerant surrounding the sample packages to confirm that the temperature had not risen *en route*.

All this worked well except for a scare at the start when some unexpected public holiday threatened to interfere with supplies of dry ice to our hotel. Moreover, there was further confusion over the precise date for flying out the samples which resulted in the need for one of our younger solicitors having to volunteer to remain in the Palace Hotel for a few days after we left as 'cooling expert and thermometer watcher'. As luck would have it, our Hotel was by then fully booked and he had to seek another such as would have no objection to a single man keeping a bubbling coffin under his bed and demanding repeated packages of special refrigerant from room service. Fortunately, whatever the management really thought of the whole affair legendary courtesy prevailed and the necessary services were readily provided, no doubt appearing on the bill and inflated by exorbitant additions for tax. But just try that lark at the Waldorf Astoria!

In the event the box provided good insulation, so that the loss of dry ice was minimal; the sitter-in duties were reduced to one check per day so that our worthy representative was able to enjoy his temporary incarceration without, so one understands, experiencing an over-irksome burden of monasticism.

One of the author's petroleum clients has worked out a completely safe method for the shipment of volatile hydrocarbon samples, involving stainless-steel pressure vessels in reinforced containers under the supervision of an expert shipping company who presumably knew how to arrange for their so-called 'inspection' by the various customs officers. The client was also in touch with specialist firms who could provide, at moderate charge, containers and documentation for freighting almost any known aggressive material between any countries. Instead of a 'do-it-yourself' approach, this may be the most sensible way to proceed.

Duration of the Inspection

The duration of an Inspection should be as short as is consistent with proper observation of the process parameters relevant to the Action. The per diem cost of Inspection is substantial, not only in terms of fees of those assembled but also in the inevitable disruption of the normal functioning of the Factory. Nevertheless it is the one and only opportunity for the Experts to satisfy themselves as to the real-world nature of the processes or products in dispute. They must resist any pressure to pre-agree time scales which are likely to prove unrealistically short. A simple Inspection by experienced Experts on the basis of impeccable preliminary documentation can often be completed in one working day but absence of information, apparent conflict between Description and practice, difficulty of sampling, and a host of other problems may easily extend the visit to several days. The General Rule is:-

"Don't stay longer than you have to, but remember this is your only chance, so observe anything and everything of importance in the Action"

The borderline between observation and intervention

It is not uncommon for an Expert Inspector to be unhappy at the lack of definition of the process he is required to report upon. For those who have experience of similar plant, that is to say the majority of Experts who are likely to be called to give evidence on its function, there arises an almost irresistable desire either to 'put things right' or, at least, to initiate an experimental investigation designed to measure crucial parameters prior to bringing them under control. These impulses must be suppressed! The Expert has been hired to 'observe' the plant *not*, as is often more usual for him, *to improve its operation*. If observation indicates that a number of key variables are not being measured, he must content himself with noting this in adequate detail. The core value of the inspection operation is in the quality of the Inspector's contemporaneous factual notes[2] not in his hasty on-the-spot opinions of a production unit he has only just encountered for the first time. Later, in evidence, the Expert will no doubt have opportunity to use this knowledge to cast doubt upon the Opponent's description of its production process. This is the right time for legitimate and considered criticism relevant to the Issues in the Action.

A border-line situation occurs wherein the Expert wishes to make an observation of a variable which, though apparently neglected in normal production control, can be measured with very little extra effort by the plant operatives. As we have seen, it may then be in order to request through the solicitors that this extra measurement be carried out. However the request itself, let alone accession or refusal by the Opposition, can be double-edged. By drawing attention to the need for data in a particular area of process control, the observing Expert is committing himself to the importance of these data and perhaps as a result acknowledging in advance an aspect of subsequent criticism of his own work:-

---

[2] "'The horror of that moment,' the King went on, 'I shall never, *never* forget!' 'You will, though,' the Queen said, 'if you don't make a memorandum of it'".
Lewis Carroll   (d. 1898)   Through the Looking-Glass

• If he is right in his approach, the Opposition is alerted to the potential attack and may take steps to adjust matters so as to de-fuse it.

• If he is wrong, he will be cross-examined on the use he has actually made of the additional process data and, if the answer is 'none', he may be accused either of dissembling or of incompetence.

Likewise, if the request is made, the solicitor for the Opposition has to make a quick decision, which he will no doubt do after conferring with his own Expert and with the Plant Manager:-

• If the measurement is indeed easy to make and important, but he refuses, this suggests that there is something to hide.

• If he accedes ... and the data obtained show that the plant is running in some way other than his clients had believed, then he may have 'given away' a crucial 'own goal'.

Unless he can be assured of an unequivocal outcome, the Solicitor's usual, and probably sensible, response is a refusal.

As a result, an occasional variant met in the less respectable litigation circles is the offer to 'consider the request overnight, and let you know in the morning'. Next day the wan and hollow appearance of the plant operatives tells its own story: they had carried out a dummy run in the evening, and possibly into the night, so as to be in a position to let their leader know whether it was safe to permit the irregular observation. This may seem a great way to proceed until one of the operatives leaves to take a job with the other side, carrying his knowledge of the 'inspection fraud' with him to his new employers.

If the Expert is denied his observations, his own position is also equivocal:-

• If he really needed them in order to draw firm conclusions, of what value is his evidence without them?

• But if on the contrary he can draw conclusions without them, why was he suggesting an unnecessary and expensive disruption of the Opponent's plant demonstration?

The author would recommend wherever possible trying to manage with a set of observations which can be made without too much disturbance of the protocol offered for inspection. If this seems to be inadequate, one must note this ... but try to remain flexible and remember[3]:-

"Life is the art of drawing sufficient conclusions from insufficient premises"

Tiredness and irritability

Fatigue can be a real problem during a process inspection. Not only is it important to try to keep alert under difficult conditions through many hours and extended days, it is equally important to avoid becoming angry, eith with the intransigence of the opposition's technical staff or their attorneys. Both sides will usually start the inspection with a high moral tone, expressing a wish to seek the truth and advance the art of jurisprudence by presiding at a 'model' process inspection. However in the company of nervous clients, present in force in their own factory, this facade can often break down at the first hurdle, perhaps because the Inspector is showing a more detailed interest than was anticipated and the Defendant's solicitor then feels that it incumbent upon him to show some fight.

After a day or two, rows can develop about almost anything. Typically annoying to the lone Expert inspector is the situation when two key parts of the process are to be demonstrated concurrently in different buildings, this having not been disclosed in the process description. One can try to guard against this by taking along a co-Expert or an assistant ... but this is not always permitted on grounds of 'process confidentiality'. Bitter experience shows that the more primitive the process, the greater the bally-hoo on confidentiality. If as Expert you really are prevented from observing something which you regard as crucially important, convey this through your solicitor to the other side. Explain politely what seems to be the nature of the obstruction and ask for it to be removed so that observation can continue. If you do not do this, in considering your Report at some later stage the Court may rightly wish to know why you did not maximise the potential for observation while you were there on site.

If, as is rare, the going gets really tough .. you really want to finish your work and go home ... and the way forward is strewn with silly procedural

---

[3] Samuel Butler (d. 1902)   Notebooks Life ix

obstructions, it is essential not to lose your cool. Note everything which is said and everything which is done to obstruct you. Make sure that your own solicitor is quite clear about your position ... namely that you are being prevented by the Defendants from doing the job you came for. There is a time and place set for telling this story and it does not involve shouting in the factory of the Opposition.

Position of the Defendant's Expert

It is common practice during an Inspection for the Expert for the Opponent to attend. As one who should by now be thoroughly familiar with his client's plant and process about which he is soon to give Evidence-in-chief, he should in general keep a rather low profile, contenting himself with checking the Inspector's observations and noting carefully how and what his 'opposite number' chooses to inspect.

In contrast to the tension which can develop with other members of the team, independent Experts rarely quarrel during an Inspection. There is usually mutual respect, even *cameraderie*, and the more likely risk is that the 'home' and 'away' Experts left to their own devices would choose to amble round the plant checking this and that ... and then happily 'decide the case' together over a cup of canteen coffee.

Asking for a re-run

Occasionally a production disaster occurs during a process demonstration; it is then up to those demonstrating to suggest a 're-run'. They may do so, or they may elect to produce 'off-spec' product, which is declared as such. Too frequently they will say nothing and hope that the Inspector has not noticed. If they do not make any statement or take any remedial action, this is tantamount to suggesting that the defective production is 'normal', that is to say 'within the production tolerances usually applied'. This suggests comparison with QC records.

Again, it is not up to the Inspector to start a row by pointing out the obvious defects. But he will be wise to note the operating parameters at the time of the debacle and to request additional line samples at various parts of the production line for subsequent laboratory characterisation.

Product Inspection

Product inspection (and sampling) is nearly always the final stage of a plant inspection. It is accepted practice for the Inspector to take samples of the product at various times during each run. These may be taken to the QC lab for immediate testing in the Inspector's presence or he may be given copies of the routine day/time QC sheets used in the plant covering the days of the demonstration. In any event, it is wise for the Inspector to have a few of these tests duplicated on retained product by an independent laboratory.

In product liability work, the usual 'inspection' stage often corresponds to this last stage of process inspection. The venue is frequently a large warehouse, stacked sky-high with allegedly defective product, which will have to be sampled at random and then tested, as previously described. The main problems are:-

• devising a statistically-valid random sampling procedure of manageable size which is consistent with reasonable access to the material in the warehouse, often stacked on palettes, or in piled containers; and

• agreeing between the Parties a schedule of laboratory testing, the results of which can be taken as indicative of 'fitness for purpose'.

Some years ago the author attended a first inspection in order to assess these problems in respect of a huge quantity of communications cable which, it was alleged, had mysteriously begun to exude large quantities of oil some time after installation.

Further visits and testing proved unnecessary. A cursory examination of the most accessible material at the top of the stacks showed that the majority of the suspect cable did not contain our client's identifying coloured thread and had therefore been supplied by other manufacturers.

A formal request was made to the Plaintiff for our client's products to be presented for examination separately. No attempt was made to carry out such a separation which would have involved a mammoth inspection project in its own right. The case settled shortly afterwards.

Agreement of the facts: the Report on Inspection

The Report will be prepared by those who offered the Inspection and the sent in draft to the Plaintiff's solicitors for approval as an 'agreed report' of the inspection. Besides correcting any errors of 'fact' (readings, etc), this is usually the point at which the Expert can add a short, unemotional account of any obstruction or hindrance he has encountered which was not properly resolved during his visit to the factory. This is unlikely to be accepted by the Opposition as part of an agreed report but it will stand as a minority account ... and be put before the Court in the bundles.

As with the Experimental Reports discussed in later Chapters, there is every reason to agree as much as possible so that the Court perceives an area of common ground between the Experts from which it can proceed to evaluate the reasons for any differences between their opinions.

Litigation experiments are carried out to establish scientific 'facts' (really 'high probabilities': see Chapter 3) which it is hoped can and will be relied upon at Trial. Prior to Trial the results, particularly when demonstrated, can also serve to weaken the resolve of the Opposition who may perceive that its case is built on a less solid technical foundation than had formerly been supposed so encouraging movement towards a settlement. Certain Experiments may also be designed from the outset to quantify damage or loss so that they can also help to establish a financial basis for settlement.

- In Patent litigation, some common reasons for experimentation are to establish infringement (or non-infringement) of a Patent and/or to establish its validity (or invalidity), that is to say whether the teaching of the Patent is correct.

- In Product Liability litigation, the accent is usually on fitness of a product for its purpose or the existence of abusive conditions which might have caused or contributed to premature failure ... and so on.

- Prior to a public enquiry following some large-scale disaster, Experiments are usually carried out to establish the likely cause and perhaps indirectly to point the finger in the direction of those who have behaved negligently.

All these examples have in common the purpose of supporting the opinion of an Expert or other witness by presentation of experimental data which will make refutation of his Evidence more difficult.

Design of Litigation Experiments

Despite the potential risks outlined in Chapter 6, other than by experiment it is often not possible to obtain 'factual' evidence. Although that experimental evidence is rarely if ever 100% cast-iron certain, this should not diminish its value to a Court concerned with the balance of probabilities. Nevertheless it is important that such evidence, while acknowledging a (preferably quantified) penumbra of uncertainty, must never be self-contradictory. The risk of self-contradiction rises rapidly with increase in the number and complexity of the Experiments. One experiment, using the most appropriate method, which shows simply and reproducibly that 'A is twice B' is reasonably 'safe' i.e. defensible. Two Experiments, one of which shows that 'A is twice B' but the other of which shows that 'A is three times B', can be fraught with difficulty. While it is true that both Experiments purport to establish a fundamental truth, that 'A is *larger than* B', the variation of result between methods is an open invitation to the other party to devise and perform Reply Experiments. These may demonstrate other relationships between A and B, allowing the Opposition to impugn both methods of test and to suggest that the many different results are artefacts of the test methods so that no conclusion at all can properly be drawn from any of the results. Moreover the failure of the first party to select the single most appropriate method and then to rely on it, could be seen by the Court as a hedging of bets which so often signals uncertainty or division amongst its Expert advisers.

Danger of the pre-emptive strike

As a matter of tactics, unless there is a history of activity in other jurisdictions or in the Patent Office it is usually better not to design Experiments-in-chief with a view to forestalling criticisms which have not yet been made since this could suggest attacks which might otherwise not occur to the Opponent's Expert advisers. The Opponents will see the case in their own way. This particular way will naturally become clearer when they notify their own Experiments. If such Experiments imply an attack on the validity of one's own experimentation, then the appropriate place to deal with this is more properly in the narrower context of Reply Experiments (discussed in Chapter 9).

There will usually be no shortage of suggestions for more complex experimentation from the client's research department, some of it in part by way of justification of purchase of the latest equipment for the corporate laboratory. Such suggestions should be seriously considered and put into rehearsal at an early stage, not so much for use 'in chief' but rather bearing in mind their potential value in Reply. Unfortunately some research directors try to insist on first developing a 'nuclear warhead' and then proudly delivering their Mark I version in the first wave of attack. Some counsel are too readily seduced by this sure-fire, quick knock-out, total-war approach without facing up to the risks which always attend the demonstration of unfamiliar technology.

A minimalist approach

Unless one 'inherits' client experimentation from another jurisdiction, usually the USA, it is usual to perform only the minimum experimentation-in-chief in the simplest conceivable manner to establish the technical 'facts' without which, in counsel's view, the Action cannot be won. If as often is the case the simple markers so put down 'in chief' are subsequently attacked by a comprehensive barrage of opposing Experiments, these can first be analysed for internal inconsistencies and then further and more comprehensive Experiments-in-reply (or, later on, -in-rebuttal) can be devised to throw doubt on the quality of the opposing 'answer'. These can also, incidentally, reinforce the sterling qualities of the original Experiments-in-chief. Alternatively if there is no experimental defence or counter-attack by the Opponents, or only a weak one, then this may amount to an affirmation of the first party's facts as established in Chief. In using this initially minimalist approach, it is desirable to select Experiments according to the criteria listed below. Because they will be simple to carry out, and so relatively quick and cheap to execute, there is no reason for a client to limit the number of replications prior to drafting of the Notice of Experiments for reasons of time and/or cost. It is important to be completely confident in the opening experimentation; it is a foundation upon which your side may later choose to build.

Design criteria for Experiments-in-chief

Many years experience of the design and performance of litigation experiments has taught that there are a number of criteria which must be considered and satisfied in order to give a high probability of success. These principal criteria are as follows:-

- directly related to the Pleadings (and the Patent-in-suit)

- clear relationship to 'real-life' conditions

- sound theoretical basis of chosen test methods

- relatively simple, fully proven experimental techniques

- high reproducibility of results

158

- easy demonstration to the opposing Experts

- easy and unequivocal explanation to the Court

Importance of flexible design

We have seen (particularly in Chapter 4) that what actually happens in conferences with counsel is usually an iterative process. Successive approximations are made of likely construction(s) by Counsel and of the appropriate and relevant technology by the Expert until, in the run-up to Trial, the various interpretations of 'Claims', 'Examples', and 'Expert Knowledge' are tolerably synchronised. Unfortunately by the time that full synchronisation is achieved the litigation experiments are usually complete and one may then have to live with a series of results which are 'second-best' in the revised context. An experienced Expert Witness can therefore contribute immeasurably to the success of an Action by *anticipating* at the experimental design stage what kinds of experimental data will prove most useful at Trial. By designing into the Experiments a modicum of flexibility, which allows the results to be used in support of the widest possible range of possible legal constructions, best use is made of the client's not inconsiderable investment in this part of the proceedings.

'Purposive' Experiments

Today's Judges are usually more concerned with the industrial *purpose* delineated by a passage in a document (the so-called 'purposive construction' introduced in Chapter 5), particularly the intended teaching of the inventor as understood by an ordinarily skilled reader, than they are in a 'literal construction', the detailed semantics of a passage as drafted in a Patent. This approach of the courts spills over into the design of litigation experiments which should not now require the deployment of high-calibre scientists working at the frontiers of knowledge but should ideally be performable and easily interpreted by the horny-handed 'skilled man' (Chapter 5). It follows that it can be quite pointless to plan and execute elegant theoretical experiments which have little or no bearing on the practical purpose of a patent claim or the actual function of a commercial product. Because the 'elegance' of academic research is greatly prized, many university investigations are carried out on a 'model' basis which is capable of yielding clear-cut results on which it is hoped can be based more general 'laws'. But unfortunately, put crudely, real-life properties of anything are often much more complicated than many university research workers are prepared to admit.

•   Let us say that Professor Bloggs did excellent pioneering work to show that, under certain carefully-controlled laboratory conditions, many aspects of the behaviour of the mineral Bloggsite could be predicted and/or explained by means of the Bloggs equation. His students, and certain external laboratories, took up and extended the original work so that there developed a corpus of knowledge which gave general credence to the correctness and applicability of the Bloggs equation. Faced with litigation on a mineral with similar properties to Bloggsite, the appointed Expert (perhaps the Professor himself) would naturally wish to use the well-established Bloggs equation, together with the experimental techniques which seem to have authenticated it, as a basis for litigation experiments.

So far so good, but it is at this point that some Experts find that they lose sight of the inherent limitations of their available technology. The Equation does not in fact predict *all* the properties of Bloggsite ... in fact there are some unexplained anomalies which, if aired in public, might prove embarassing and even interfere with the Professor's future Fellowship, Nobel, and CBE. Scientists are human. They need future financial support from those who only reward 'success'. Bloggs and his co-authors have naturally written up the positive results and have generously left the field open to the research students who follow them to win their spurs by identifying and investigating the failures. And Bloggs himself may have latterly become too great to countenance any failure[1]. In the event, it transpires that the conditions under which the Equation is applicable cover only a *part* of the service range in which Bloggsite is commercially useful. Certain properties of commercial importance are among the anomalous ones and the real-life service conditions lie at the extreme end (and beyond) those which have been satisfactorily set up in the university laboratory. All the cited academic laboratories have chosen to use a well-characterised, highly purified Bloggsite ... whereas the material in this commercial dispute is rather poorly defined and only 'supposed' to have a similar structure. Moreover as used industrially it contains a modicum of blue asbestos, canine detritus and iron-filings.

---

[1]   Henry C. Beeching (d. 1919) "I am the Master of this College, What I don't know isn't knowledge" The Masque of Balliol

To further complicate matters, the 'Bloggsite look-alike' seems to work equally well in its industrial application when mixed with an equal weight of silver sand, in which form it has been energetically marketed to unsophisticated customers at a slightly lower price as 'Grade II material'. The Opposition's Experiments-in-reply subsequently establish that several other minerals, which (theoretically) would not be expected to obey the Bloggs equation, do a sufficiently good job to be surreptitiously substituted by the manufacturers to even their Grade I customers without detection ... but only of course to help them at times of difficult supply.

To generalise ... it can be dangerous to hang your client's experimental hat on one single too-clearly labelled theoretical peg. This is a point which has to be carefully monitored when accepting advice from even the most distinguished academic Experts.

The value of using standard tests

A cognate argument applies when choosing test methods. They should be impeccable: precise, specific and, if possible, internationally accredited. They should preferably be used routinely and reliably in the relevant industry. Usually it is safe to employ test methods published by the major international and national testing authorities: International Standards Organisation (ISO); British Standards (BS, for the UK); American Society for Testing Materials (ASTM, for the USA); DIN (for Germany); and so on. It is certainly difficult for opponents to criticise the validity of such test methods, though they may be able to say that the particular choice of test is inappropriate in the context of the dispute. When 'industry-wide' *non-standard* tests are employed, their provenance and application needs to be carefully checked and 'evidence of fact' prepared as to their widespread application. The author prefers not to recommend the inclusion of such tests in a Notice-of-Experiments without having first seen the tests performed on a variety of materials by a competent and experienced technician with whom it had been possible to discuss the techniques used.

Experimental Variability: the Importance of Statistics

As explained below, taking one reading, or even a few readings, in an inherently variable system is likely to give you a seriously misleading 'answer'. Since most litigation experiments involve close comparison of a measured value with some specification limit, the adoption of such a Russian Roulette methodology is in general unlikely to assist either the Court or the client. Despite this, it is surprising how often suggestions arise for an Experiment of enormous complexity and cost which will need to be done 'only once' in order to clinch the case; and it is even more remarkable how many Experts are complaisant about this approach. Rather, the Expert's aim should be to combine simplicity (which is normally allied with explicability) with the highest quality. There is no room for second-rate experimentation in litigation. First-rate experiments require strict and demonstrable repeatability. Moreover 'simplicity of experimentation' and 'high reproducibility' of experimental results do not automatically go hand-in-hand. In practice, it is unwise to assume high reproducibility of an intrinsically simple litigation Experiment without establishing this statistically. Even if statistics are hated by judges and counsel alike, as is sometimes rumoured to be the position, they are a fact of life in high-quality experimentation[2].

Assuming that the results of a given test fall on a normal (Gaussian) distribution curve, the spread of results can be characterised by a number called the 'standard deviation' (sigma, σ) such that about 95% of the results would fall within a spread of $\pm 2\sigma$. If the test itself is imprecise, but is the only one available as is the position in much technology and engineering, or if the test result is itself inherently variable, the distribution of results will be *wide* as shown by a high value of the standard deviation. Conversely a low standard deviation, indicating a narrow distribution, is indicative of a well-controlled test applied to a well-defined property. Given the messy industrial subject-matter of most litigation, the distribution is more likely to be wide so that an individual result obtained at random (in, say, the Demonstration) may turn out to be 'very low', 'low', 'high', or 'very high', in comparison with the 'true' value ... normally the arithmetic mean of all results ... which marks the peak of the distribution curve. If one were to make even a simple measurement (say) six times, one would be likely to obtain six somewhat-different results from which it would be a simple matter to calculate:-

- the 'mean' or arithmetic average of the result; and

[2] A really useful statistics primer is: M. J. Moroney Facts from Figures
Penguin Books, second edn 1953

- the distribution of the results, in the form of a 'standard deviation' or 'range' within which any *random* measurement is likely to fall.

This calculation is only easy for a 'normal' distribution; crudely that is to say a distribution in which the chance of overshooting the 'true' measured value is the same as that of undershooting it. Many measuring methods satisfy this criterion but other measurements and properties can lie on a 'skew' distribution such that the consequences or probabilities of under- or over-estimation are not equal. In such cases more complicated mathematical techniques are needed to extract meaningful data from the experimental measurements. Furthermore if one now asks someone else to carry out the six replicate measurements on the same product, it is likely that slightly different results will be obtained from the first set. This is due to 'operator variation' which can easily be allowed for in the statistical treatment of the results. Many tests require a different sample of material or product for each test and these samples, while nominally identical, will often show slight 'sample' differences. The question of 'representative sampling' is therefore of the utmost importance but the details of how this should be carried out in individual experiments are too varied for review here.

An independent Expert should know how to design statistically valid experimentation appropriate to the subject matter and be in a position to advise his client. He should give special attention to this feature of his side's experimentation and insist on adoption of the best practices used in the relevant industry. He should likewise be critical of the work of the Opposition should such criticism be justifiable.

The importance of proper statistical design of litigation experiments and statistical interpretation of the results diminishes as the difference between two critical values increases. Supposing that there is a penumbra of uncertainty about a parameter which the Experts and the literature broadly agree to be about ±10% of its absolute value, then an unequivocal experimental demonstration of (say) a 50% or greater difference between the values is usually decisive. However at a difference of 30% or less, major pre-planning of experimentation begins to become necessary. At a demonstrable difference of 15% or less in this example, the Expert may need to devote exceptional care both to experimental design and interpretation of data.

Proving 'identity' of values

The need for statistics is at its most acute when an Experiment is required (usually by the lawyers) to show that two values of a given parameter are 'the same'. Even when the most stringent precautions are taken in experimental design and implementation together with a very large number of replicate samples it is only possible to establish the likelihood of the two values being identical at some finite level of probability, whether 95%, 99% or 99.9%, which may or may not impress the Court in the context of the decision that has to be reached.

One tries to avoid recommending such design of experimentation if there is any satisfactory alternative. However it is frequently required in evidence to Criminal Courts, particularly as proof of identification (see Chapter 14). For such purpose, which only involves sending the innocent down for twenty years or letting murderers go free, it would perhaps appear that '90 or 95% certainty' may sometimes be good enough. However, where 'losing money' is concerned, 99.9% may on occasion be argued strenuously to be insufficiently close to 100.0% to constitute the necessary proof of equivalence. While there is considerable public discussion and numerous high level committees are debating the 'registration' of forensic scientists and their various laboratories, it is not abundantly clear to the author that the basic difficulty is a lack of relevant 'experience' and of proper 'government regulation'. Instead he wonders could it be a fundamental difference between 'good' science and 'bad' science and their use and abuse in Evidence, as discussed in Chapter 3, here, and elsewhere throughout this book?

Implementation of empirical test procedures

In Patent and related litigation there is usually a basic document (often the Patent-in-suit) which sets out a test or tests which should be used as a yardstick for measuring infringement. Often reference is made to specific national or international standards or, for more novel subject matter, to a paper or papers in some reputable journal. However occasionally an inventor will design his own test procedure and/or criterion and build this into his specification. In nearly every case, some ambiguity can arise as to the precise implementation procedure to be used when testing is carried out.

164

•   In a recent dispute now settled, the Plaintiff's Patent-in-suit specified a crucial colorimetric titration which was " ... derived from that described ..." in a cited reference. Whereas the short description of the titration procedure given in the body of the Patent made no reference to the addition of Oracet Blue (OB) as co-indicator, the citation stated that benefits in determining the end-point accrued from its use. At the Defendant's research labs, after exhaustive tests involving a number of different analysts we convinced ourselves that it was only possible to obtain a sharp endpoint in the presence of OB which we thereupon employed in our Experiments-in-chief. However the Plaintiff took the alternative view that since there was no specific instruction to add OB, and the method was only "derived" from the citation, the co-indicator should be omitted, teaching of the citation notwithstanding. Their Experiments, carried out by an independent laboratory, therefore omitted OB. Either interpretation could have been favoured by the Court. Unfortunately the titrations with and without OB appeared initially to give different endpoints, the 'without' indicating 'infringement' and the 'with' generally indicating 'non-infringment'. In this instance, further work involving other analysts began to indicate that with care and experience substantially the same titration results could be obtained using either method. After a great deal of research tolerable accord was therefore achieved between the Parties.

What the 'skilled man' is taught by the document

It has been emphasised that in attempting to resolve problems such as this concerning the teaching of a technical document, the Court will seek evidence from a man *ordinarily skilled* in the relevant art who is expected to read the instructions set out in the document together with any cited references and then apply his common general knowledge of current procedural practice (as of some relevant date) in interpreting these instructions to make the required measurements. In order to do so, he must not need to add anything whatsoever inventive to his own skill and the documentation he has (readily) available.

•   A celebrated case involving an 'arbitrary yardstick' for determining infringement arose in *General Tire v Firestone*. The parameter in question was called the 'Computed Mooney Viscosity' (CMV) of the very tough high-molecular-weight rubber which was the subject of the invention. Mooney viscosity, obtained by measuring the resistance to shearing of the polymer, was a well-established method of characterising both 'raw' rubbers, and also their compounds with carbon black and sundry additives. But the materials of the invention were so tough and elastic that the rotor of the Mooney instrument slipped against them instead of shearing, this giving a false reading. The Patentee therefore directed compounds to be made containing sufficient oil to soften the rubber to a shearable consistency and provided a mathematical means by which the actual test readings obtained could be extrapolated back to the much higher values which should have been recorded by the raw rubbers in the absence of oil had direct measurements been possible. Hence the CMV was not an experimentally accessible parameter but could be inferred from other measurements. There was legal controversy as to whether such extrapolation was scientifically justified and whether or not the artificial number obtained represented a shear viscosity at all, particularly as the material in question had proved so shear resistant. Nevertheless the Court found that the skilled man was able to perform the required tests as delineated in the Patent and to obtain a number, or 'index', for comparison with the limits set in the Claims. This was enough to satisfy the Claims. Whether or not the Computed Mooney test had any scientific or technological validity did not concern the Court. The questions:-

- Are measurements specified? and

- Can such measurements be made (by the skilled man)?

were both answered in the affirmative by the Experts and the arbitrary 'index' so obtained defined the limits for infringement purposes.

More than a generation has passed and this ruling still generates controversy among lawyers and Expert scientists alike but surely it is completely consistent with the requirements of the Act that the Patentee must define how the invention should be carried out though he does not need to know how it works? Not only this but also if the inventor innocently discloses a seriously misleading, or even wrong, explanation for his inventive step he is certainly not penalised by denial of grant of his Patent; neither can the error be grounds for its Revocation. Any conceptual difficulties arise only at a level *above* that of the hypothetical 'skilled man' who is only required to read the directions and carry out the test using his ordinary knowledge of how such things were done at the relevant date. An independent Expert, often author of several scores of original papers and patents, is really not content with this naive approach. But it is really 'the Act' which he is attacking, not the teaching of any particular Patent.

•   A rather different example of an arbitrary index arose in *Gore v IMPRA* (Phoenix, USA) and a parallel action *Gore v Kimal* in the English High Court. In the Gore Patents cited against IMPRA, one parameter chosen to characterise the inventive step, the easy manufacture of a highly-expanded cellular plastic material, was Matrix Tensile Strength (MTS). Very briefly this was the tensile strength that the porous plastic of the invention 'would have had' *if it had not been porous*. In other words MTS had a clear physical meaning as the specific strength of the material constituting the cell walls of the spongy product. The formula given to calculate MTS involved division of the actual TS by the specific gravity of the porous product. By way of example a TS of 1000 pounds per square inch and an s.g. of 0.2 was characterised by an MTS of 5000 p.s.i. Since very highly expanded, and therefore highly porous, materials were claimed, these were of very low density; as a result high MTS values were calculated of above 100000 p.s.i. as a property of the expanded (i.e. porous) product, an impossibly high value for the 'true' *tensile strength* of an ordinary plastics material.

There are genuine experimental difficulties in measuring specific gravity of an expanded plastic and in estimating the s.g. of the unexpanded material which also figured in the prescribed calculation. There was also considerable doubt as to which of a number of possible standard tests should be used to measure tensile strength, these involving a number of different strain rates which had a marked effect on the results. All this gave rise to a large penumbra of uncertainty concerning the actual *values* of MTS which were obtained in various experiments carried out by the parties. However, the Defendant was in particularly high dudgeon about the use of what seemed to him the 'bogus' parameter, MTS, and its implied relationship to the so-called 'true' tensile strength of the product. He thought that it ought to be mandatory to limit the use of the term 'tensile strength' to apply *to the product* despite the clear teaching of the inventor that the strength was introduced "into the polymer". In the (albeit unpopular) view of the author, who in conference stoutly defended the view of the Opposition against that of his clients, there was no great conceptual problem associated with MTS which was really no more arbitrary that that of the 'denier', a parameter widely used to describe the strength of thread made from bunched (i.e. voided) filament in the textile industry.

167

As an independent Expert, it was Smith's job to persuade solicitors and counsel that their earlier, critical approach needed to be softened which, after some months, with a good grace, they conceded. Had he not succeeded, his acquiescence could have returned to embarrass him during cross-examination.

Difficulties of precise specification

It must be admitted that previous generations of inventors (and their patent agents) were sometimes rather lax in the proper definition of specification tests. This throws a heavy load on to the latter-day Expert to decide what was actually in mind at a particular date. At worst as we have seen, under the old Act a delphic Patent could be bad for ambiguity or insufficiency. However such are the circumstances of the inventive process that there is often little to record of a scientific nature which can assist precise characterisation of the product. The inventor guy just did it, but he didn't know quite how!

• In the aforementioned US case *Gore v IMPRA*, Robert Gore testified in his depositions that the invention was made late one evening after an unrewarding day in the lab stretching samples of PTFE plastic in a more or less controlled manner. Taking the last sample rod from his oven, Gore angrily seized the ends and pulled them rapidly apart to the limit of his outstretched arms. Lo and behold was borne the regular, porous low-density product they had been seeking on which is based the whole of the very successful Goretex breathable plastics industry! But in turning 'rapid stretching of hot plastic' into a patent specification, laboratory and engineering work was carried out which caused more than a slight risk of obfuscating the simple result of that first hand-held test. How fast? How hot? Which materials will work? ... and so on; such questions turned out to have more complicated answers than had originally been supposed.

State of knowledge

Because different Experts often express different views on what they now believe would have been done as at the relevant date, this can often lead to alternative implementation procedures which are sometimes capable of yielding quite different experimental results. Such conflict of Expert opinion is not uncommon and has to be resolved, often with difficulty, by the Court.

Where resolution is difficult, if not impossible, it is understandable that the Experiments of both sides may have to be disregarded, although the Court will still have to find some basis for choice between the testimony of the rival Experts.

Design for easy, effective and reproducible Demonstration

Demonstration of Experiments, whether to the Opposition or to the Court, is yet another matter which is best borne in mind at the design stage. While photography and video records are used extensively for this purpose, it is often important to choose techniques and observations which are inherently 'photogenic' if the subsequent presentation to the Judge by Counsel is to make the required impact. Too often this aspect of experimentation is relegated to an afterthought and many elegant experiments have been seen to fail in their impact for just this reason.

For a satisfactory professional result, all Experiments which are to be demonstrated must be rehearsed, not until they 'may go right' but, rather, until they 'can't go wrong'. Scientists and engineers tend to be optimists and it is sometimes difficult to persuade laboratory management and technicians of the enormous effort which perfection of performance will entail or to convey the disastrous consequences of a failure, particularly during a Demonstration before the Opposition.

When rehearsal is adjudged to be satisfactorily completed and everything is in place, *absolutely nothing must subsequently be changed.* This is the hardest regimen to impose on most laboratories and requires the constant vigilence of the independent Expert to forestall the introduction of eleventh-hour 'improvements' by the too-enthusiastic technicians.

• In a recent Action, as Defendant's our Experiments-in-chief were fully rehearsed in-house in the presence of the author and yielded results consistent with those given in the Notice of Experiments. However we had not bothered to rehearse the relatively trivial though important business of taking samples of intermediate products for each side and for the Court, feeling that this was likely to be uncontentious and could not possibly affect our results. We decided that this could be sorted out with the other side before the Demonstration began.

169

The technicians, some very bright girls, were present at this preliminary discussion and in subsequent talk among themselves they realised that the extra material required by the sampling would limit the amount of material actually available for their test work. Being acute to the need for a trouble-free demonstration, without reference to the litigation team they quite sensibly increased the amount of polymer taken and the aqueous medium in which it was to be dissolved by 50%, from 100 ml to 150 ml of solution. The solubilisation procedure involved fitting standard 200 ml bottles into a tumbling device and leaving the contents to slop about for several hours until visual inspection showed the absence of swollen lumps of undissolved material. The fixtures of the device could only receive 200 ml bottles so that these were still used, though now containing 150 ml instead of the tried and tested 100 ml of solution. Some of the test polymers dissolved satisfactorily but the less soluble materials still remained as lumps after many further hours of mixing. As a result a large part of the programme had to be abandoned and the demonstration reconvened a month or so later at not inconsiderable additional expense. What went wrong? The technicians had not thought that the simple act of increasing the amount of material in the tumbler jars had reduced the ratio of dead space to material from 1:1 to 1:3, so drastically interfering with the efficiency of solubilisation.

Scale of Test

Most litigation experiments involve product and/or process testing. To save cost, the scale of testing obviously needs to be as small as is consistent with 'making the point'.

• If in say a product liability case, the resilience of a dock fender is in question, it would obviously be preferable cost-wise to test a number of tiny laboratory samples cut from real fenders in an impact machine rather than contemplate docking a cross-channel ferry at a number of different speeds in Dover harbour. One advantage of the 'laboratory' over the 'service' test is that at the higher impact speeds there is less chance of 10000 tons of boat cleaving through the quay-side, the warehouses and the customs shed, and coming to rest in Canterbury or Ashford.

However, the possibility of substituting the cheaper tests will depend on the pre-existence of a properly-established and well-authenticated 'correlation' between the laboratory results and service performance. For this reason, and in order to avoid criticism based on lack of relevance, whole-product tests are often preferable to model tests which purport to artificially isolate some relevant property but have not been shown to do so. It is often a strong approach to support a product test with model calculations based on well-established theories which demonstrate that the experimental results are in the same ball park as predicted by the theory.

Process tests, to be carried out on full-scale manufacturing plant, are often proposed by client management without sufficient consideration of the difficulties and disruption and enormous costs which they entail. It is in the author's view rare to see a convincing litigation experiment conducted on full-scale production plant, although it is sometimes necessary to make a witnessed trial batch of some special material during which the plant is allegedly operated 'normally'. Sometimes such an exercise can be combined with a process inspection, as described in Chapter 7.

Perilous demonstration of plant experiments

Difficulties often arise during plant experiments. Anyone who has worked in industry must be aware that 'normal' operation can cover a wide range of actual operating conditions which are often left to the discretion of shift personnel. They are likely to be singularly unimpressed at disturbance, and attempts at definition, of their time-hallowed 'suck it and see' control methods by a 'bunch of lawyers'. They may wonder if it is the prelude to the eventual replacement of all the process technicians by a computer!

When the run is witnessed by the other side's Experts, the latter will eagerly honour their appointment by recording actual values for all the plant parameters which they see under proper control together with comprehensive notes on parameters which they believe should be under control but are not. Subsequent comparison with Discovery data for the plant in question will often establish variations in operation which will be sufficient to throw doubt on the 'normality' of its operation during the Demonstration thus vitiating the whole expensive exercise (see Chapter 7).

Furthermore prior rehearsal of a 'plant experiment' is often virtually impossible, because of non-availability of the plant which is usually fully utilised in commercial production and partly because the works manager already "knows" that what he thinks is wanted "can be done 'on the day'".

He therefore sees no reason to over-exert himself more than once for a remote and special cause. 'Confidence' is a hall-mark of the average plant manager. This likewise limits the scope of the external Expert as a would-be Cassandra since he is not then in a position to brandish shambolic rehearsal data in front of a terrified management and their legal advisers to reinforce the portent of his gloomiest forebodings.

•   In an Action during the 1970s, the Defendant decided to run a full-scale test in its embossed flooring materials plant in Montréal, Canada. During the week of the Demonstration, daytime outdoor temperatures were into three figures (deg F!) and the processing units involved high temperature rollers and gelling ovens which added their not inconsiderable calories to the steamy factory atmosphere. During a brief apology for a rehearsal, any attempt to communicate directly with the plant operatives was forestalled by their refusal to speak in any language other than the broadest French-Canadien. However, no doubt mollified by the anticipation of bonuses, they agreed to carry out some of the litigation trials during the evening when the plant was expected to be be cooler and there would be less disruption of normal production.

Had things gone to plan, our team should have been through and back in the bar of Ruby Foo's 'Executive Hotel & Chinese Restaurant' by about 10 p.m. at latest and, initially, the experimental run looked quite promising. However at about 9.45, the 'line' broke depositing a good few square metres of partly-gelled plastics sheet straight on to the heaters which belched forth a great cloud of vaporised and partially degraded dioctyl phthalate (DOP) plasticiser. Choking and retching, lawyers, managers and experts, for once united in their purpose, rushed out into the open and waited an hour or so in the cool night air (-- it was down to about 93 deg F by then --) for the line to be remade and the start of production of a new batch of flooring compound. At about mid-night the same line failure happened at about the same point in the gelation process but this time the result was more explosively dramatic because the operatives had meanwhile turned up the oven temperature in an attempt to obtain a faster gelation and so a more rapid increase in sheet strength.

Impregnated to the core with health-giving DOP-vapours, we again sought the somewhat cleaner lead-lined environment of the sidewalk of Decatur Boulvd. Returning to the factory at about 1.30 a.m., one was reminded of the London smogs of the 1940s but, just before 3 a.m., success was achieved and the night shift had reeled up the first batch of product. Staggering back to a locked Foo's stinking foully of plasticiser, we demanded bar facilities and some supper which were sternly refused. In retrospect, it is amazing that we were even admitted to our rooms. However they served a good breakfast from 6.30 a.m. which enabled the next part of the Experiment to start again in the factory ... 'on schedule at 0730hrs' ...

Use of pilot plant

If plant data are really necessary, it is often better to persuade the clients to make available, on a dedicated basis, a pilot plant, preferably the same plant that was used to provide the scale-up design figures used in construction of the production plant. Although release of these figures can raise questions of design secrecy it does ensure that comprehensive correlation data are available to satisfy the opponent's Expert. Subject to recognition of the scale of costs incurred in operating even this reduced-scale plant, adequate rehearsal is usually possible and most of the snags can be ironed out before the Experiment is subject to the opponents' scrutiny. Nevertheless all such large-scale experimentation is fraught with difficulty and other avenues should usually be explored fully before embarking upon it.

Long-term and environmental testing

A special type of testing, which is common in product liability actions concerns premature environmental deterioration. Strictly speaking the only appropriate test may well be 'in the field' which can involve exposure of test products matched to control standards in a number of typical sites, perhaps varying in ambient temperature range, hours of sunlight, wind, rain, condensation, industrial fall-out, vibration and so on. However for many high-quality industrial products deterioration can take years, even decades. This suggests the use of 'accelerated ageing tests' such as are commonly employed in a number of industries.

The results of such tests are sometimes found to correlate poorly with those obtained in field testing. Nevertheless, if the results are reproducible they may sometimes be sufficient to transfer a burden of proof to the Opposition who will find it difficult to establish that their inadequacy is such as to vitiate any indication of *relative*, if not absolute, quality.

173

To summarise: in designing and executing litigation experiments:-

- Establish the minimum experimental data needed

- Choose the simplest experiments to obtain those data

- Rehearse until near-perfect reproducibility is established

- Do not alter *any* parameter at the performance, so that the Demonstration is an exact repeat of the Notice.

The practical implementation of Experiments

After the preliminary drafting of a short list of Experiments-in-Chief, the Expert is necessarily involved in the decision as to where they should be carried out. There are usually two alternative possibilities:-

- In-house: usually in the Client's corporate laboratory

- Out-house: in a contract research or university laboratory

The pros and cons of these are as follows:-

Pro in-house:-

- experienced staff and specialised equipment

- generally higher quality laboratory facilities

- cheaper, as conventionally costed

Con in-house:-

- resentment of 'irrelevant' (i.e. legal department) work

- often sloppy lab techniques, giving poor reproducibility

- laboratory often far distant from legal centre

174

- need to call technician witnesses to give evidence

Pro out-house:-

- familiarity with the requirements of litigation experiments

- independent witness available to testify to results

- dedication, associated with presentation of invoices

Con out-house:-

- lack of detailed industry knowledge or special equipment

- more expensive, as conventionally costed

- lack of large-scale (e.g. production plant) facilities

Setting up 'in-house' litigation experiments

It is apparent that many of the 'cons' listed against the in-house corporate laboratory can be ameliorated by the direct involvement of top-level management. In order to achieve this, it is advisable that if possible the Expert attends a short prior discussion with the managing director and the technical or research director, so ensuring top-level commitment with a Board interest in the outcome. Given this initial *imprimatur*, the way can then be smoothed as follows:-

- Experimental protocols are drafted by the independent Expert in collaboration with client's R & D department, with properly worked out time & cost estimates.

- Legal department again reminds the Managing Director (MD) of the importance of the Action, particularly the large difference in estimated costs between winning and losing and the consequent effect on his P & L account.

- MD discusses this with the Technical or Research Director (TD/RD) and any senior plant personnel, and agrees a rough budgetary allocation for expenditure in support of the litigation which thereupon becomes a 'cost centre'.

- Necessary expenditure is sanctioned by the Board, with appropriate safeguards including 'over-run' limits. Board requires on-going progress reports.

- TD/RD discusses with his managers the allocation of the highest-quality dedicated staff, who can both accept the demanding nature of the work and be released from other duties as required during the progress of the litigation. The appointment of staff should be portrayed as an accolade for the chosen few. It should be clearly differentiated from 'side-lining' (to be followed by an ignominious early retirement).

- This litigation cost centre (LCC) team liaises with the external Expert(s) through its manager:-

     -- to organise procurement of any special equipment; and then

     -- to set up progressive 'rehearsals' with statistical evaluation of
        the results.

- The Experiment(s) are formally demonstrated to the home litigation team (including counsel) and senior members of the firm who may carry out (or simulate) aggressive 'observation' by the Opponents and make comments and criticisms aimed at fine tuning of the Demonstration.

- After drafting and serving the Notice, the Experiment(s) are demonstrated to the Opposition by the LCC team in a dedicated laboratory specially cleared for the purpose with enough room for the necessary observation, sampling of materials and so on. There must also be proper provision for recording and agreeing all the data obtained.

This method of working is not cheap but it does get the best results. Also, the skills sharpened up in the rehearsals and demonstration of litigation experiments will usually linger on in the corporate laboratory to upgrade its more routine work. Perhaps the most serious residual 'con' is then the apparent lack of independence of the staff involved in the experimentation, a matter which is unlikely to be of significance in most Court proceedings. Most judges do seem willing to hear evidence from current corporate employees who can speak with particular authority as 'witnesses of fact' and they are content to form their own, usually favourable, opinions of the employees' objectivity and veracity.

Choice of an external laboratory

For commercial reasons, in many instances a corporate decision is made at top level NOT to involve the in-house laboratories in litigation experiments. In this event the choice must be between independent laboratories, such as private research companies and university or polytechnic laboratories.

When placing work in academic laboratories it is often preferable to do so via the university liaison bureau or company which is normally prepared to enter into a formal contract showing that the necessary management is in place to achieve agreed results within the necessary time scales. Litigation is performed against the clock (see Chapter 6) and its inexorable progress to Trial on a cost-effective basis has not always been fully understood or appreciated within university departments. When dealing directly with senior academic staff it is therefore quite important to establish that, subject to appropriate payment of appropriate direct and overhead costs, any such 'litigation' funding is not simply a contribution towards the Department's general research budget 'in the pursuit of knowledge'. Fortunately the steady encroachment of cost-centre management in universities is already making it easier to do business with them.

Using the lab of the independent Expert

Given adequate management and appropriate motivation, there is perhaps not a great deal to choose between academia and the private sector. Sometimes it may be helpful to place experimental work in the Department of your academic Expert. In that case he may be seen to be performing the Experiments himself, adding a somewhat contrived verisimilitude to his evidence. However it should be borne in mind that many of us are some little way from the bench, having been insulated therefrom for several years by serried ranks of technicians and research students. Indeed, if we make a mess of demonstrating an Experiment in front of the whirring video-cameras of the opposition, this *gaffe* may later return to haunt us in the witness box at Trial. Also, the 'hands on' image does not necessarily cut any ice with the Court. The author well remembers Mr Justice Graham saying of him:-

"He's a Professor. He directs the work. He doesn't *do* experiments"

As an alternative, it usually costs much more to have a programme carried out and demonstrated in a research company but the availability of qualified staff with recent industrial experience who will often have a clearer view of what is required of them may well make the extra expenditure worthwhile. Before making a final decision, it is absolutely necessary to review the available knowledge and experience, technical and information facilities, specialised equipment, and track-record in similar work, of a short list of at least three candidate laboratories.

Coordination and control of the Experiments

The novice Expert will meet a range of approaches to the coordination and control of litigation experiments. Formerly much of this work was delegated by the Instructing Solicitor to the independent Expert who was both cheaper per hour and also better qualified to get on with it. More recently, the new technically-qualified IP solicitor is showing a tendency to draw the supervisory work into the partnership usually delegating it to suitable (science) graduate assistants, a method of working used for many years by Patent Agents and a useful training for the firm's future partners. This can work well provided that the assistant is of genuine partnership material and that adequate communication with the independent Expert is maintained at all stages of the work, as is generally the case.

However in product liability and much other commercial work, the 'technological lawyer' is still something of a rarity and delegation of supervision to the Expert is still the best way. The novice Expert needs to know that in these fields it is an unwritten and sometimes unexpressed requirement to summarise the continuing progress of the experimental and other technical work for his instructing solicitor in ordinary language. This is a useful exercise in reducing the technical jargon of the typical laboratory report to facts and concepts relating to the Action. In many such Actions the Expert does more than this, acting as translator between the lawyers and laboratory experimentalists who are finding the 'facts'.

Demonstration of the Experiments-in-chief

The Notice-of-Experiments is usually served by agreement of the Court, which sets a timetable for Demonstration of such of the Experiments as cannot be agreed by the Defendant. In current practice, the Plaintiff must be prepared to repeat *all* of the Experiments. There are several reasons why the Defendant may require this:-

•   Failure to understand from the Notice what the Experiments consisted of, and therefore the full significance of the reported results.

•   Suspicion that the Experiments were not originally performed as defined in the Notice, so that the reported results may be bogus.

•   Doubt that (all of) the values reported in the Notice were actually obtained and/or that the reproducibility of the Experiments was poorer than indicated.

•   Interest in the techniques used, and their execution, with a view to subsequently criticising them in Court.

•   Hope that some lapse may occur during the Demonstration, which will yield radically different data which fails to support the 'facts' asserted in the Notice

•   Opportunity to further instruct Counsel in the technical content of the Case

•   General fishing in the river of a competitor's technology

As procedures stand at present it is almost certain that at least part of the Notice will have to be demonstrated. In fact the author cannot think of any Action in which he has been involved wherein the right to a demonstration was foregone.

Failure to require demonstration of any part will indicate either agreement of the results by the Defendants' Experts or, more likely, advice by their Counsel that the facts thereby established can have no possible bearing on the case.

Demonstration results count more

It seems to be tacitly accepted in legal circles that 'the results which count' are those obtained in a Demonstration in the presence of the other side's Experts. This is probably sound insofar as it reduces the likelihood of cheating but it is less satisfactory in that it limits the available experimental data from which statistically-valid conclusions may be drawn.

•   To quote an example based on a distant past experience, certain tests were carried out by Defendants against my Plaintiff client according to a standard procedure in an open laboratory in the English countryside. For purposes of the Notice of Experiments they had apparently been done at least four times by different operators on a range of samples so that their in-house experts believed that they had a good idea of their statistical reproducibility. Come the morning of the Demonstration by the Opposition there had been heavy overnight rain followed by hot early-morning sun. As a result the humidity in the non-air conditioned lab rose to an exceptional level. The results obtained in the Demonstration were substantially different from those reported in the four preliminary runs, from which their experts concluded that a new and unsuspected fact had suddenly emerged, namely that the test procedure was apparently humidity-dependent. Putting it another way, the Experiment was something of a wash-out.

When such an unexpected result is obtained, a decision has to be reached by those running the Experiments as to whether to abort the Demonstration of the tests at considerable cost to both Parties or whether to continue on a path which may require the Experts to present results to the Court which they believe to be untypical of the product or process, at least as previously tested. When the Experiment involves the trouble and expense of say a special production run on a plant, perhaps even an overseas plant, the difficulty of making such a decision is exacerbated.

The mechanics of the Demonstration

Demonstration of experiments is not of itself an easy matter. Neither in industrial nor in university laboratories are technicians used to performing to timetable before a critical, questioning and, just occasionally, ribald and bad-mannered audience, some of whom may make little effort to conceal their desire for the show to be a fiasco. As a result technical misjudgements can

180

and do occur which would most probably be avoided in a less stressful ambience. Not unreasonably, technicians often expect the 'performance' to be similar in atmosphere to that of the cloistered calm of a practical science or engineering examination with which they are of course familiar from their graduate studies. One novel and unwelcome feature for the operators is usually the close photographic and video observation of what they are doing which, when overly invasive, can sometimes be interpreted as a personal assault. It should be explained to them beforehand that such records may often be required by the observers to prepare meaningful reports. Special rehearsals involving use of such techniques should help to acclimatise them to attack by the intrusive lens and sudden flash. It is a matter for those with experience of Demonstration *mores* (such as the lawyers, patent agents and independent Experts) to prepare the staff for what will actually occur and, on the appointed day, to try to control the event itself so as at least to avoid the atmosphere of a post-prandial livery dinner, not to say a Roman Carnival. A strict 'no booze at lunchtime' rule is desirable to maintain the serious and dedicated conditions of a legal procedure and the two-glass rule set as the limit for any chronic hydroxy addicts[3]. It is most desirable to lay down and agree between the Parties, at the outset of or even before the Demonstration, a code of practice for behaviour in the laboratory including sampling of materials and the witnessing of measurements.

Suggested pre-organisation

When the Expert's advice is asked or he is delegated the organisation of a Demonstration, he will usually choose to proceed as follows:-

•   Prepare in advance data sheets for use by the technicians containing blank spaces for all observations and readings together with details of the calculations, leading to further blanks for the results of calculation.

•   Arrange a pre-experimental briefing session in the laboratory, at which agreement is reached with the Opposition on working practices, safety and procedures/locations for observations and for sampling of materials and products.

---

[3]   "Drink not the third glass .. which thou canst not tame
        When once it is within thee"
        George Herbert (d. 1633) The Temple The Church Porch i

- Ask all the technicians to call out readings as they are taken and then enter them directly on the data sheets in front of the other side's experts who will be provided with photocopies of all the sheets at the conclusion of the tests.
- Require that all questions be addressed to the senior lawyer or patent agent in charge of the experiments who will obtain answers from the technical staff at a suitable break in their schedule.

The Data Sheets need to be prepared in consultation with the technical staff and used at the 'dress rehearsal' of the Experiments so that all the technicians are thoroughly familiar and comfortable with this change of routine. They will learn to write down only the numbers or other observations which are required by the Notice of Experiments and record no other comments or data whatsoever. The correctness of this record is best witnessed by the independent Expert.

At the 'pre-experimental' briefing session, comments and questions on equipment and procedures will be invited from the Opposition. They will also be shown instruction manuals or handbooks for operation of sophisticated equipment and be invited to indicate any pages which they would like photocopied for study by their Experts. It is often convenient to arrange for the technicians to demonstrate the main techniques using 'dummy' materials; such demonstration can then easily be interrupted for explanations to the other side's Experts without prejudicing the actual results which will be obtained in the ensuing Demonstration. This is an important point because many chemical reactions are sensitive to the speed at which operations are performed. Introduction of an enforced dwell period, while the technician waits patiently for lawyers to finish arguing about the admissibility of a particular technical question, can constitute a significant departure from the normal test procedure and so give a different result from that habitually obtained.

- By way of example, in some recent litigation experiments in the USA our technician, an otherwise most competent operator, spent considerable 'extra' time at the Demonstration showing, of his own volition in minute detail to each one of the observers, the spotlessly-cleaned vessels which he had used for quantitative transfer of materials. He was justly proud of the quality of his techniques and determined to rub the noses of the other side's Experts in his personal and corporate excellence. As a result certain crucial dwell times were exceeded. We were lucky to escape with only a distinctive, though not disastrous, change in consistency of our product in comparison with its description in our Notice of Experiments.

The *quid pro quo*, for all the assistance to the other side in the form of prior detailed briefing and pre-documentation, is therefore the rigid enforcement of non-interference with the work of the technicians during the Demonstration proper. Experience shows that, given the extent of prior disclosure and explanation here indicated, Opponents are generally content to observe quietly and without interference.

Handling questions

Under no circumstances should questions be addressed to the technicians and, in case this rule be inadvertently broken, the technicians should be trained not to reply. Of course, the other side's observers must be free to challenge any observation recorded by a technician but this needs to be done without physical obstruction and through the communication channel provided. If no challenge is made, approval of the observation can be assumed. If one or more challenges are made and subsequently found to be ill-founded, the credibility of the other side's Expert(s) will necessarily be seriously impaired.

This regime actually works very well. The author has only occasionally come across technicians who have tried to 'cheat' and this has usually been done in such a clumsy way that they have been found out rather quickly, usually to the genuine embarassment of their own instructing lawyers.

Good and bad rapport

Normally some rapport will quickly develop between the technicians, who are simply 'doing a job', and the other side's observers who are themselves sufficiently expert to appreciate the skills necessary to carry out accurate experimental work under these rather artificial conditions. However, problems do sometimes arise in less well regulated programmes.

•   Smith recalls attending a series of experiments by Opponents in a rather disreputable (US) contract research laboratory some twenty years ago in which conventional rules of fair play were strained, apparently as a matter of routine, presumably in order to give their client the result he was paying for. For instance test runs were aborted without explanation, data and materials being destroyed despite the Expert's requests and protestations. Pre-cooked samples were substituted by sleight of hand for those less-than-perfect examples resulting from the Demonstration procedure. Materials were taken from unlabelled bags which mysteriously contained insufficient excess to provide a sample and so on.

To add to our troubles as observers, our team's conference room was 'bugged', which we discovered by accident after a private conversation between colleagues about a change of flight which plan had mysteriously become known minutes later by our host organisation. Tired of whispering, we had to repair to the local Diner to discuss tactics over a 'submarine' and Diet-Coke.

Faced with such problems, what does an independent Expert actually do? The best our team could manage was to take full notes of each incident and, had cameras been permitted, we would have taken a full visual record. Smith then reported each infringement to his instructing solicitor who protested vehemently on each occasion always to receive the answer that the Expert had been "mistaken". We doubled up on observers, including our patent agents, and confirmed what was happening, still to receive the same bland answer:-

"That was not what you saw, you were all mistaken".

One would like to retail the destruction of the opponent's so-called 'Expert', who was responsible for these 'Experiments', under cross-examination but he was "saved by the bell". Actually during his cross-examination we heard that the case was to be settled world-wide, unhappily against our client, before such retribution could be effected.

Fortunately today's Expert observers are unlikely to be faced with such severe interference in their activities. One reason may be that most Experiments in laboratories are now fully recorded by both sides on video tape which makes it difficult and dangerous to indulge in such flagrant cheating. The only exception to this may be work carried out in a factory, where there is likely to be a general prohibition on photography of any kind. This is discussed in some detail in Chapter 7 under the heading 'Process Inspection' and most of the remarks made there apply equally to the special 'factory experiment'.

Experiments which fail

After taking proper precautions, as herein outlined, litigation Experiments should not 'go wrong' at Demonstrations. But if, despite all precautions, they are seen to have failed, a decision has to be reached quickly, usually on the spot during the attendance of the other side, as to what action can best be taken to recover the position. The reasons for failure of a properly designed and rehearsed experiment are likely to be found under one or more of the following headings:-

- Operator error, including unauthorised 'improvements'

- Materials selection and/ or variation (e.g. impurity levels)

- Equipment adjustment, or defective pre-calibration

- Equipment temporary malfunction, or break-down

- Mis-identification of samples

The first will be usually detected quickly by observers from both sides. The error should be conceded, followed by a repeat. The second is usually, but not invariably, avoided by using unopened manufacturers' containers with the same batch number for rehearsals and for performance. The third is usually a matter of diligence before the event, though sadly an all too common reason for variation. The fourth can often be demonstrated by on-the-spot calibrations, followed by running repairs including the fitting of immediately available spare parts or the substitution of stand-by units, preferably followed by an immediate repeat performance.

Problems of inherent variability

Unfortunately, some kinds of problem have a knock-on, if not a knock-out, effect:-

- In some litigation Experiments carried out by an otherwise competent academic laboratory in the north of England, the Defendants synthesised samples of polyphenylene sulphide and tested their melt viscosities by a standard method. This involved forcing the hot polymer through a tiny orifice under controlled pressure and weighing the amount of material which emerged in a given time, a rather ordinary plastics flow test. In their Demonstration the viscosity of the polymer obtained was much lower than had been expected and the steaming hot yellow liquid squirted through the hole in a trice like an Alsastian in a children's playground before the required standard test pressure could be applied and stabilised. Since the synthesis had required many hours in complex, high pressure equipment, an ill-considered decision was reached not to repeat it and, instead, to construct alternative *ad hoc* low-viscosity testing equipment in order to retest the original samples. However these still gave variable results, involving ultra-short and barely measurable flow times. Had these results been tested in Court, it is more than possible that they would have been found wanting. If so the Experiment as a whole, one of great expense, length and complexity, would almost certainly have been judged unreliable.

The aftermath of failure

If all is still awry after exhausting the possibilities for repetition, it is still open to the Party to deny reliance on the results. It is usual then to offer to repeat the Demonstration on such mutually-convenient later date as may be agreed. This will again add substantially to the costs. Moreover there is nothing to stop your opponents relying on your 'bad' demonstration which they have observed, particularly if they disagree with your diagnosis of a fault in the procedure. For this reason, the decision to abort must be properly considered. It is usually best delayed until after the Demonstration, when a calmer atmosphere will prevail and then conveyed to the other side in the solicitors' inter-party correspondence. The independent Expert can help here by considering the totality of the results and the probable consequences of deciding to 'live with' the less-than-perfect data obtained during the Demonstration.

Effective use of photographs and videos in litigation experiments

There is an increasing tendency to try to visually record every detail of litigation experiments. While as has been said this probably acts as a deterrent to the very few would-be cheats, the many hours of a video record are not easily distilled down for evidential use into a coherent technological elixir. Moreover any use in presentation of the case will usually be subject to criticism by the Opposition. There is often a laudable temptation to 'save costs' by giving the video camera to someone with no special 'producer' or 'camera-man' skills whose main or only qualification is that he or she would have to attend the sessions anyway either as 'gofer/dogsbody' or by way of genuine familiarisation and training. Junior assistant trainee professionals are very adaptable; they have strong arms and backs and endless patience. Nevertheless, like any other professional enterprise, the making of a good technical film does require technical skills which most amateurs do not possess. Besides which, peering through a view-finder for hour after hour is not the best way of familiarising oneself with the Experiment. The videotape, if properly indexed, is therefore best sampled occasionally in order to settle disputes of observation and afterwards quietly buried. If 'presented' as evidence, it will need to be edited, for instance on the basis of 'time lapse', 'split frame' and so on.

Attempts to use an ordinary professional editing house without special technical experience to prepare something less than the monumentally boring for showing to the Court are almost always totally useless. The editors will like-as-not suggest jolly coloured credit titles and soothing background music ... perhaps 'the Pie Jesu' or, thinking of the budget, something 'out of copyright' like the ubiquitous 'Four Seasons' (with 'our Nige' dancing on the platform, and Vivaldi quietly spinning under it). They will press strongly for some human interest ... or the next best thing such as Professor Smith explaining 'science' while stroking his dog ... blending into a distant view of Queen Mary & Westfield College seen through the drizzle and spray of the Mile End Road.

Given good quality material, specialist scientific film companies can of course do a miraculous job but 'at a price' and with lengthy and costly involvement of the Experts who will have to give very clear instructions to the editors as to exactly what they want to show. In so many cases the quality of the crude tape they present for editing will be below that which the editors expect and the end-results will disappoint everyone. Although there are now a number of excellent commercial companies with more general experience in making, editing and captioning highly technical, serious films for presentation to educated lay audiences, unfortunately many of these are often too busy to take on work at short notice.

In contrast, most Experts find the 35 mm camera an invaluable aid to observation and an essential supplement to their contemporaneous notes.

Among colleagues and associates, choice of equipment varies but typical is a reasonably light-weight motor-drive TTL reflex with autofocus (and manual over-ride), motor drive, built-in electronic flash, 28-135 mm motor zoom lens with maximum aperture of about f4 and sundry 'macro' close-up facilities. Such a camera is relatively cheap; it currently costs about £350. As film Kodacolor 400 is generally satisfactory (or 100/200 if colour rendering is particularly important) although the author has been forced to use 1000 - 3000 ASA under special conditions in a telephone exchange where even electronic flash photography was prohibited. The standard 36-frame films have always proved satisfactory, the more so since reloading modern cameras is now achievable in but a few seconds. One soon develops the sense to change film early and waste a few frames rather than try to break the 'changing-time record' during a hot spot in the action. Most of an Expert's camera work has to be done without any special lighting, that is to say using ambient laboratory or factory lighting supplemented, where necessary and permissible, by flash. In fact even a tripod is rarely needed, it being good enough to steady the camera on a rigid shelf or, when hand-held, backed up against a wall. Good processing is obviously important but many 'High Street' developing and enlarging services can be quite adequate without recourse to specialists.

In some cases, agreement is reached between the Parties to swap prints of all photographs taken by their Experts; however this is difficult to police. It is more normal to allow each side to take its own pictures and to use them subsequently as it wishes. Since some at least of the subject matter may be confidential, it is usually prudent to hand over the negatives, together with a set of prints, to instructing solicitors for their retention.

Photography as a part of the Experiment

The foregoing applies to photography in support of general observation. But it is also common to build in photographic, film, or video records into the Experiment itself, usually with a view to obtaining a permanent objective record which can subsequently be presented to the Court as 'unvarnished truth'. In such cases it is more usual to seek professional advice as to how best to record the crucial phenomena, usually of a non-quantitative nature, on which it is proposed to rely. This gives the opportunity to use improved resources, particularly special lighting, and to 'rehearse' the shots or frames so as to maximise visual impact. In a recent Action, Smith advised his client to rely on a Reply Experiment which involved video-microscopy; this is described more fully in Chapter 9 which can serve as an example of how such more professional photography can be deployed.

Effective presentation of Experiments to the Court

However the Experiments have been conducted, there is still always the problem of presenting them to the Court in such a way as to constitute useful evidence. This is made much easier by consideration of presentation techniques and any likely presentation problems at the pre-planning stage. Judges are always mindful of the cost of Court proceedings and they look to the Parties to present their evidence clearly and succinctly in the minimum time that this requires. Just as they insist on hearing only relevant witnesses, they are usually only prepared to tolerate photo presentations which either:-

•   present crucial observations which cannot readily be verbalised; or

•   enhance their understanding of some difficult key issue.

They do not generally take kindly to presentation of lengthy 'documentaries' made by the corporate film-maker to glorify the world of pipes, tanks and the romance of tall chimneys. Neither do they like low contrast, out-of-focus, uncaptioned stills or movies which do not immediately or obviously support the argument which the ardent Expert seems to be trying to attach to them. It follows that, as in editing the total video record, in the search for effective presentation of a clip for the Court there is a narrow passage to navigate between the Scylla of a professional, but often marginally relevant, market-oriented 'glossy' and the Charybdis of a worthy, boring, crudely-edited kind of 'home movie'.

Role of the Expert as 'producer'

Preparation for the Court often reverts to the Solicitors guided by the Experts, with the consultant assistance of Counsel. For this reason, in order to be fully effective it is becoming important for the independent Expert to gain some knowledge and experience in video presentation. This experience can range from leisure study of the excellent examples, such as Sir David

Attenborough and others frequently present on television, particularly parts of 'Life on Earth', to actual attendance at studios or on one of the many courses which are now available. What cannot easily be taught or learned is the whiff of the actor or showman which an Expert may sometimes need in order to bring his technical commentary on a photographic sequence to life. But where this skill is missing and cannot be imparted by those instructing, Counsel will usually be glad to make up for any deficiency of the Expert by repainting his more sober and perhaps even sombre testimony in brighter hues. To the question 'How long?' one must answer 'As short as possible?'. But this should not preclude some repetition of perhaps only slightly different examples which will confirm to the Court the generality and reproducibility of the phenomena being presented. In such cases the first example can be discussed (and captioned) in the necessary detail, the remaining ones being dismissed with a rapid 'more of the same'.

Drafting and agreeing the Report on Experiments

An important function of the Expert is to check the Report which is normally drafted by one of the junior solicitors who will hopefully have been present throughout the tests and have recorded all relevant data during the course of the experimentation.

Since litigation Experiments sometimes take longer to complete than the parties expect, such accurate recording requires constant vigilance over long periods, sometimes from say 8 a.m. (or even earlier) until well after midnight, for six or seven days on end. The load can be lightened by adopting the formal presentation procedures previously advocated but those who have the foresight to do this usually rehearse properly and so seem able to maintain a civilised time-table in their Demonstrations. In this way the problems of failure and consequent 'over-run' are minimised.

The Agreed Report

The object in drafting a Report on any Litigation Experiments is to obtain a factual account, including all relevant data but omitting constructions and opinions which may form the contentious subject-matter of the Action. The reason for such omission is the hope that an agreed Report can be settled between the Parties which the Court can regard as undisputed legal 'fact'.

Despite its manifold advantages, this desirable objective is almost never achieved at the first attempt. This is often because the lawyers find it difficult to resist trying to include the occasional tarantula among the bunches of bananas. An initial compromise is commonly reached, in which a large 'core' section is agreed as common ground but each party inserts snide observations or commentary denied by the Opposition. These minority passages are often interesting and revealing as signposts to future battlegrounds. On the other hand, other reservations can be included simply from ignorance and nit-picking. It is encouraging that so many outstanding points of difference on the Reports are nowadays resolved between Solicitors. This is assisted by good rapport between the professional firms.

It is important for the Expert to advise the Solicitors clearly from a technical viewpoint which language can safely be conceded and what may be a 'key point', even a technical Trojan horse, in the future conduct of the Action. For instance it is truly amazing how the presentation of digital data in analogue form, particularly as various forms of 'smoothed' graph or bar diagram, can act as spearhead of a future argument. It is the Expert's job to advise his team what he believes constitutes 'conventional representation' and where this breaks down into clever special pleading.

The result of whatever measure of agreement can be achieved, called the Agreed Report, is a compromise document which should contain all the 'raw data' (i.e. the actual measurements as made without any mathematical manipulation) and such simple representation of the data as is needed to support the sponsoring Party's contentions in its Notice. To the extent that agreement has *not* been achieved, an Appendix may be included indicating this ... or the Report may be produced in two different fonts or type sizes indicating 'agreed' or 'disagreed'.

Where no measure of agreement between the Parties can be achieved, the Court will be undesirably lumbered with two completely different versions of each Report. Instructing Solicitors in such cases have been known to receive a reprimand from the Court. If the Judge refuses to try to resolve such conflicting evidence[4] at the Trial, all the work will be wasted and each side may wonder how wisely it has spent its clients money.

---

[4] "Who hath believed our report?"
Holy Bible Isiah liii

9   Other Experiments

There are many other circumstances in which Experiments or 'Tests' are used to reinforce opinions in litigation. This Chapter covers those which have one feature in common: all are planned to *answer* some existing argument which has been advanced against one of the Parties and which, being false, merits factual rebuttal. In this respect they differ somewhat from the Experiments-in-chief described in the previous Chapter which usually purport to establish basic 'facts' from which arguments can follow.

In Patents work, Experiments-in-chief may be countered by Experiments-in-reply, occasionally followed in turn by Experiments-in-rebuttal designed to overturn the conclusions of the Reply experiments. In Claims and Liability work, the claim might start with an assertion, for instance that a machine involved in some accident was 'not properly guarded'. A first line of defence might consist of an Expert opinion that the design of the guard did fall within existing safety regulations or best practice for the industry. But this opinion could be strengthened by a practical test in which it was shown that, in normal operation of the machine as guarded, an accident of the kind which had taken place was of negligible probability. The Defendant's experiment could perhaps be developed further to show that unauthorised tampering with the guard mechanism could easily lead to the sort of accident which had actually occurred. This result could then invite a presumption by the Court of 'misadventure'. In which case the Plaintiff might elect to demonstrate by an experiment-in-rebuttal that a *badly maintained* guard could slip in normal use, giving a similar result to that resulting from abuse and so re-establishing the possibility that the employer was to blame.

In a superficially different group are the large-scale simulation experiments which usually follow some major public disaster, whether it be a plane crash, a motor-way pile-up or a structural collapse of a public building. While these may appear to be carried out to 'establish facts', they are almost always performed principally to quell the often irresponsible but sometimes well-founded speculation on safety standards by the media prior to consideration of the disaster by a public enquiry charged both with apportioning blame and making recommendations to prevent a recurrence.

The Expert designer of these experiments is necessarily part scientist and part politician; he is using his technological craft not simply to establish any basic scientific principle but rather simply to counter a point being made against his Employer, whether this employer be a commercial IP litigant, a possibly irresponsible factory manager, a perhaps careless but also unfortunate workman, or a soft-target local authority or government department.

Experiments-in-reply

In reply to what? Strictly according to the regulations for Patent Actions, Experiments-in-reply may only be carried out to challenge and refute the results of Experiments-in-chief already completed by the other side. However in practice they can sometimes also provide an opportunity to usefully extend one's own Evidence after the details of the Opponent's case have become clearer.

A first option is not to do any reply experiments. This carries the implication that Counsel has advised that his client's case is so strong that any and all of the Experiments-in-chief carried out by their Opponents were:-

- completely irrelevant, in the context of the dispute;

- utterly defective, in that all data obtained are unreliable.

If our side is subsequently proved wrong about these sweeping dismissals, the opposing Experiments will stand unchallenged and our lack of response will almost certainly be taken as acquiescence in their results. It is therefore unusual to choose not to reply. Perhaps we may not because our clients have been secretly convinced by the Opponent's Arguments and Experiments that he is 'right after all'. They have thereupon decided not to waste any more money on a feeble and ineffectual Reply when they have by now set their minds on the negotiation of the best possible financial terms for release from the Action. Such 'instructions', which will be given to the Instructing Solicitor, may not always be quick to filter through to the humble Expert.

In nearly every instance, Reply Experiments in patent litigation are selected and designed quite deliberately with the sole object of proving that the apparent Evidence derived from the other side's Experiments-in-chief is, in some important respect, defective. Reply Experiments are intellectual Exocets designed to degrade or destroy a portion of the Opponent's Evidence.

If they succeed in doing this, they will prove useful. If they miss the mark, it should be possible to dispose of them harmlessly, that is to say without detriment to their launcher's case.

In choosing to reply, our side is therefore acknowledging that something seems to have been established by the Opponents in their Experiments-in-chief which is, or could be, potentially damaging to our case. And how we orchestrate our reply will necessarily alert the Court to the significance of the techniques used and data obtained by the Opponents in these earlier experiments. Drawing the Court's special attention to the importance of these Experiments and then mounting an elaborate programme of Reply Experiments which succeeds only at best in inflicting a light flesh wound upon them, will simply risk dignifying the Opponent's experimentation to the level of an oracle[1]. The Expert designer of Reply Experiments must therefore strike at the heart of the opposing Experiments-in-chief by:-

- invalidating the Opposition's techniques; and/or

- obtaining significantly different results which both support his Party's case and also speak against that of his Opponents.

Nothing short of a complete 'knock out' will usually be helpful. The sporting analogy here is probably 'bowls', or perhaps 'petanque', where the last wood/boule sometimes needs to break up the cosy pattern established round the jack as a result of earlier strategic play itself settling in the closest position. At the same time, while satisfying the court rules by being clearly addressed to counter specific points arising in the opponent's prior experimentation, really well-designed reply experiments should ideally gather more and/or 'better' data to contribute to one's own positive case. But the main purpose is to demonstrate that the other fellow's argument is based on some false premise. Of course, had we planned them more perfectly, such data could probably have been gathered in our original Experiments-in-chief but experience teaches that there will always be something missing, particularly if one bats first. This is probably because:-

- our original Experiments were planned on too short a time scale, before the thoughts of the home team of Lawyers/Experts had fully gelled;

---

[1] "For if it be but half denied,
'Tis half as good as justified"
Samuel Butler (d. 1680) Hudibras iii

194

•	it was good policy to do the minimum 'in chief' so as to avoid exposing key areas of sensitivity at too early a stage;

•	as a result of reading Discovery and seeing the Opponents Experiments-in-chief, the contentious technical issues are now fully exposed and better understood.

A somewhat delicate balance has therefore to be struck in designing reply experiments which fall within the rules, that is to say which are not simply a second attempt at Experiments-in-chief. And the same standards of scientific integrity are obviously needed in their design as were used 'in-chief'. When the 'Notice of Experiments-in-reply' is served, the Opponent's solicitors will often trail it in front of the Judge hoping to have any experiments bearing on new arguments (or new experiments having a second bite at old cherries) struck out. However Courts are often quite tolerant of the generally broad scope of such Notices and with good reason: the Court wishes to have available the best experimental facts which the Parties can muster and to this end will generally admit them. They are:-

•	Experiments which purport to demonstrate fundamental defects, whether in the Defendant's Experiments-in-chief or in those of the Plaintiff

•	Experiments which also provide unrefuted (and preferably irrefutable) evidence in support of key arguments.

To be provided with properly resolved experimental evidence is obviously much more useful to the Court than to be told that 'mistakes were made' in the original Experiments but that procedural niceties prevented the modifications which would have corrected these mistakes.

In order to establish the essential characteristic of a 'reply', it is usual to base one's reply experimentation firmly on one or more of the Opponent's *key* Experiments-in-chief:-

•	Let us say that Dr Zeitgeist has made his name and published many learned papers, well-reviewed by his peers and his fellow international conference-goers (and dining companions), on the allocation of a small infra-red peak (at exactly 393.16 cm^{-1}) to the presence of 'rheumatic acid' which is a key compound in the litigation. He has therefore been retained to provide the key evidence for its concentration at a given point in a process;

this he has apparently done competently by properly sampling the Process on a statistical basis and then conducting an impeccable Experiment-in-chief, confidently reporting the concentration to three decimal places. However the Opponent's Expert finds out that the method has not yet been adopted by any national or the International Standards Organisation (ISO). The Expert who, besides being an eminent analytical chemist also happens to be chairman of his college's wine committee, subsequently has no difficulty in conducting a Reply Experiment which shows that the crystalline residue from a mid-range white burgundy (of the year 1986) gives a similar IR peak due in this case to the ubiquitous tartaric acid. The Judge, while perhaps faintly interested in the provenance of the burgundy, necessarily fails to be impressed either by Dr Zeitgeist's identification and estimation of the key infringing ingredient or by his competence as an Expert. He is therefore minded to reject Zeitgeist's evidence for the concentration of rheumatic acid and may begin to wonder whether much of his other evidence, on which his client's case depends, is equally unreliable.

Given the Court's permission, it is then open to Zeitgeist to scrape the residue of his Experiment-in-chief off the floor by conducting Experiments-in-rebuttal. For instance he could perhaps test a wide range of organic acids and find that tartaric is the only one which gives an interfering result. And go on to show that there is no way in which tartaric acid can be generated in the chemistry of the Process, so that the result of his original analysis was valid. But it is often an uphill task to overcome the judicial prejudice against an original over-confident assertion.

As illustrated in the foregoing example, the classical format is to effectively repeat the Opponent's experiment using his own techniques but with some apparently minor variant which yields a quite different result. This leaves the Opponent's Expert fighting defensively on his own ground when he should really be engaged in planning sorties into the camp of his Opponent's major Experiments. It is an old, if risky, military strategy[2]. Experiments-in-reply are undoubtedly opportunistic but they are directed to the good and worthy cause of pointing up flaws in the Opponent's original arguments. The resultant clarification will help the Court decide in favour of the validity of one or the other set of experimental data.

---

[2]   "For 'tis the sport to have the enginer
Hoist with his own petar; and it shall go hard
But I will delve one yard below their mines,
And blow them at the moon."
William Shakespeare (d. 1616)   Hamlet iii

A successful Reply Experiment

•	In a recent High Court Action, the Defendant had opposed Plaintiff's simple demonstration of infringement with an elaborate programme of tests intended to draw conclusions as to both validity and non-infringement by comparison of two contiguous layers in a sheet material, layer 'A' being chemically crosslinked but layer 'B' being uncrosslinked. The Plaintiff's reply experiment was able to demonstrate migration of crosslinking agent from layer 'A' into layer 'B' which had occurred during manufacture and storage of the test materials prior to testing. Layer 'B' was therefore far from being the uncrosslinked 'control' material required by the Defendants in support of their arguments but was in reality a diluted version of 'A' containing a lower, and uneven, distribution of crosslinks through the thickness of the layer. Moreover the chosen technique of video-microscopy used in the Plaintiff's Reply was able to indicate that the extent of crosslinking resulting from the migration was substantial, so that layer 'B' did not have anything like the control composition and reference properties attributed to it by the Defendant.

By knocking out this keystone, a whole arch of the Defendant's experimental evidence was weakened, a classical result of a 'simple' reply experiment with specific and limited objectives. The down-side risk of such a targetted experiment was virtually nil; its essence was concentrated in showing that the Defendant had effectively invalidated his own experiment by using a defective 'control'.

And a less-successful one

•	In a second reply experiment, the Plaintiff offered an additional experiment to resolve a dispute. His Experiments-in-chief had shown a large difference in strength resulting, he asserted, from crosslinking. Defendant's Experiments-in-chief showed a much smaller difference which he maintained was insignificant and could be explained by factors other than crosslinking. In the Plaintiff's Reply experiment, samples were exposed to artificial weathering and showed large improvements in strength retention when crosslinked. At Trial he argued that even if the Defendant was right in asserting that the original strength difference was small, at least this small difference which he claimed to have established on a reliable statistical basis, was indicative of better weathering properties, a principal commercial benefit of the Plaintiff's invention.

This second Reply experiment was a 'compound' reply experiment. It did not of itself indicate that Defendant's prior tests were erroneous or invalid. *Prima facie* it did seem to introduce new material, which was strenuously opposed by the Defendant at preliminary hearings. However the very relevant argument that even a small difference in initial strength could burgeon as a large difference in commercial performance was powerful and was readily accepted by the Court as a proper response to the Experiments-in-chief.

The anticipated result of this Plaintiff's Reply Experiment was intended to neatly side-step a dreary potential conflict of Experts (and their attendant statisticians) each supporting a particular set of strength tests. It appeared to have the added bonus of fixing the Court's eye firmly on the commercial ball of 'enhanced service life' i.e. a better product, rather than small differences between test values which were used as indices of quality. But the actual result of this Experiment, although technically impeccable, was not accepted by the Court because the Opponents, in a Rebuttal Experiment, were cleverly able to show that the crosslinking agent reduced the concentration of hydroxyl groups in the polymer, so diminishing the water absorption of the material, and that this, rather than the increased crosslinking, could have explained the better weathering properties. You cannot, in truth, win them all!

Simulation tests

An important special case involves the simulation, under supposedly controlled and monitored conditions, of some uncontrolled or poorly controlled event which gave rise to the dispute. This is most common when dealing with large-scale disasters such as the collapse of a bridge, an aircraft crash or the burning of a building when there is never any shortage of 'plausible explanations' usually provided by non-technical journalists writing in the Sunday papers. It is convenient to regard forensic evidence gathered from the site of the disaster itself as equivalent to experimentation-in-chief so that the large-scale 'simulation' is by nature of a Reply Experiment which fills in the missing links, explaining why events took place in the way that was actually observed. To be of any value to the Court, such simulations must have high scientific and technological integrity and be carried out by wholly independent laboratories. Very often a number of independent laboratories are instructed by the various parties to a major loss Action, representing respectively the architects, construction companies or manufacturers, the operators or carriers, the principal insurers, the disaster victims and their families and so on.

•   For instance, the rapid destruction by fire of the entertainment complex 'Summerland' in the Isle of Man in 1974 gave rise to considerable duplication of effort including that of the author's then company QMC-IRL.

It was encouraging to those of us who worked in the field of litigation experimentation that all of our various laboratory simulations were planned in a generally similar way and led to virtually identical conclusions as to the source of the fire (arson), the torching of an external hut by some youths, and the mechanism of transfer to the interior of the public building via the heating of the cladding with flash-over occurring in the cavity wall. The cavity was lined with an inflammable board and was not 'fire-stopped', so contributing to the enormously rapid propagation of the conflagration which killed and injured many. So on the basis of rather unanimous technical evidence, the ensuing Public Enquiry had little difficulty in establishing the technical facts and apportioning blame.

Large-scale simulation tests

Occasionally, the scale of the simulation is of the utmost importance in properly representing what occurred.

•   The tragic burning of the Stardust Club, Dublin in the February 1981 was found difficult to simulate until the Fire Research Station carried out a full-scale simulation burn, including a set of furniture and furnishings, which showed that the particular geometry of the hall caused substantial radiation from the ceiling on to polyurethane foam upholstery which degraded adding rapidly to the build-up of fire gases prior to flash-over. So an apparently minor and potentially controllable fire incident suddenly became a holocaust. During the F.R.S. simulation[3] at their full-scale test facility at Cardington, the stage at which the build-up of heat and gases led to flash-over was graphically captured on video with appropriate sound-track. On

---

[3]   P. L. Hinkley, H. L. Malhotra and W. D. Woolley   Report to the Artane Fire Tribunal
UK Dept. of the Environment, Fire Research Station of the Building Research
Establishment: Note N7/82 (March 1982)

each and every occasion when the video used to be shown in public, at the moment when an ignited fire-ball roars out from the test rig in the direction of the camera, chairs have been pushed back and a minor panic has ensued in the audience, to be followed by shame-faced laughter. The real value of these tests though is not simply the provision of a frightening film record to impress the Court or the Enquiry but the carefully placed temperature-measuring devices and gas-analysis sensors which can show which materials are contributing to the disaster at which stage in time of its propagation.

So important are such records that it would be highly desirable to have some information of this nature during the incident itself rather than having to rely on post-hoc analysis of the simulation. To this end, fire-fighters have been equipped with portable gas-sampling apparatus, gas chromatographs or infra-red detectors, in an attempts to gather such 'real time' information which may subsequently assist the Coroner, the C.I.D. and the materials manufacturers. Unfortunately the centre of a major fire is not the most relaxed environment in which to indulge in the impartial and dispassionate collection of scientific data and there has not yet been any wide-spread adoption of this analytical equipment by the fire services.

•   One of the largest-scale simulations in which QMC-IRL was involved was the Ronan Point test. 'Ronan Point' was an appartment block in the East End of London the corner of which collapsed like a pack of cards following a relatively small gas explosion in the kitchen of one flat. After some years it was decided by the authorities to demolish the block but, before this was done, the UK fire authorities and other interested parties were permitted to conduct a test on the quality of sealing between floors under full-scale fire conditions. This fire simulation experiment, which also took place during the 80s, involved starting a large-scale furniture fire in one flat and monitoring the build-up of smoke and toxic gases in flats above, and adjacent to, the fire source. Suffice it to say that the inter-floor sealing was somewhat less efficient than we had been led to believe and both the Fire Research Station and our team suffered a slight loss of equipment. We we were probably lucky not to write off any of our staff as 'consumables'.

Because of the high cost of full-scale simulation experiments, a competent laboratory will usually try to devise reduced-scale tests from which actual performance can be inferred. It is difficult to provide rules by which scale-down can be applied which may vary with different kinds of technology. Almost always significant reductions in scale down to 'model' dimensions will attract criticism of some kind when results are presented in court. A decision often has to be made whether to test (say) a model bridge, at one-twentieth scale, to destruction or whether to spend the available budget in fully instrumenting (e.g. with strain gauges) an actual component of the bridge and showing that stresses could have occurred which were sufficient to cause failure of that component. If one chooses to work with components rather than with a whole structure, one must then be prepared to face arguments based on the suggestion that the component in situ is not subject to the calculated stress distribution or other chosen condition used in the small-scale experimentation.

Rebuttal Experiments

We have seen that rebuttal of arguments based on earlier experimentation is an important objective of Reply Experiments. But it is certainly possible to run formal Experiments-in-rebuttal for the sole purpose of zapping bogus Reply Experiments of the Opposition. In theory at least the Court may give permission for further experiments to rebut those 'in rebuttal' .. "and so *ad infinitum*" .. but as the Trial date approaches time runs out and the Court's patience wears thin. In fact even a first tier of 'rebuttal', with its attendant Notice, Demonstration and Agreed Report, is a relative rarity. Two bites, 'in Chief' and 'in Reply', are usually considered to be enough!

In time past, rather than apply for formal permission for rebuttal experiments with all the time-consuming procedural difficulties this entails, together with risk of refusal of permission by the Court, the Expert Witness was occasionally encouraged by those instructing him to give an impromptu demonstration from the Witness Box. Indeed this still seems to be quite common in US litigation when the Witness will illustrate his answers with Exhibits of all kinds: photographs, videos, samples of materials and so on. The only sensible criterion controlling this would seem to be 'Does it add anything to his answers?'.

• In *Mechanical Services v Avon Rubber Co [1975]* in the English High Court, the author connived with his Counsel, that quintessential English gentleman the late Geoffrey Everington QC, to smuggle into the Witness Box an empty wine bottle, a cork and a 'corking machine' which compresses the cork radially allowing it to enter the neck of the bottle wherein it slowly expands to an interference fit so as to retain the precious fluid. During a rather soporific post-prandial session, while answering questions about the introduction of the rubber strips into an elastomeric bearing using a patented pre-compression technique Smith suddenly waved his bottle and began inserting a cork, the while lecturing on the age-old principle of the corking machine. Anguished cries from opposing Counsel:-

"M'Lud, the Witness is doing experiments in the witness box .. there has been no Notice .. terms of the Order .. matter of following the proper procedures ..."

activated Graham J. who, ignoring the hubbub, appraised the demonstration in a single glance and then addressed the Witness directly:-

"Is that an ord'n'ry claret bottle you have there, Professor?"

In due course the Judgement drew attention to the patented method being nothing more nor less than an obvious application of the age-old principle of the corking machine. But the machine itself became a court exhibit and, for all one knows, remains so, hopefully in constant use, to this day. Whether or not today's judges would be so tolerant is a matter of doubt but one feels that little harm can come of a practical demonstration which may be worth twenty pages of tedious transcript. However there is of course always the difficulty of conveying the bouquet of such a demonstration to the Court of Appeal.

It certainly seems to be permissible for cross-examining counsel to hand up all sorts of bits and pieces to a witness for his observation and instant experimental assessment in the Witness Box.

• One unfortunate Expert, supposedly testifying to the excellence of the PTFE-coated, low-friction screw thread of a patented automatic corkscrew was recently handed such a device in the Box. She was asked to remove the cork of a (full) wine bottle, which task she accomplished with ease. Counsel asked her if she had had any difficulty and, being reassured "no", revealed that the screw of the device he had handed up was *not* in fact plastic coated, being made using the bare metal thread prior to coating.

• The author was more fortunate when testifying in a US court-room on the important difference, in respect of failure strength, between 'adhesive' and 'cohesive' failure of a bonded joint. His cross-examiner suddenly bounded up to the Stand and whipped from behind his back an 'easy open' blister pack, sealed with a soft adhesive closure, which he had apparently purchased from the corner store during the lunch break. This he required the Witness forthwith to rip apart, intending a demonstration of 'adhesive failure' which was at the heart of his case. Smith did as he was asked, taking care to use a high strain rate, and was delighted to note a considerable residue of paper fibre adhering to the torn-off blister. He was thereupon able to explain to the Judge that this was a good illustration of a bond failure which occurred *not* by adhesive failure, as had been suggested to him, but rather by cohesive failure in the weaker substrate ... exactly the way in which the Defendant's product failed, just as he had been explaining in evidence!

In each of these examples, luck, bad or good, played a major part; so that, faced with a snap decision in the Witness Box, one can only reflect[4] :-

"And of all axioms this shall win the prize, ..
'Tis better to be fortunate than wise."

It is not suggested that sleight of hand is a technique to be developed by an Expert Witness called upon to give serious evidence to a Court. Neither is it a matter of 'winning' against the odds. But when faced with trickery, rather than argument, it does no harm to have developed some sense of the street wise for use in one's own self-protection. This theme is developed further in Chapter 11 in the context of unfair cross-examination.

---

[4]   John Webster (d. 1625?) <u>The White Devil iii</u>

10   Expert Reports

In years past presentation of Expert evidence in chief was partly by submission of sworn affidavits but always supplemented by a relatively lengthy 'Examination-in-chief' by his side's counsel. This could last for several days and was of mixed quality in terms of evidence, depending on technical mastery of the subject matter by the interrogator and quick-wittedness in the event of accidents by the Expert.

It also had the disadvantage to the Opposing Counsel that he had no inkling of the detailed technical arguments to be advanced by the opposing Experts he would be cross-examining until they opened their mouths in the Box. This required quick reaction to what was being said *as it was said*, the evaluation of the technology being a job which fell to *his* independent Expert. The Expert's initial comprehension had to be followed by instant translation into ordinary English for the benefit of Counsel who would then immediately conduct the further cross-examination on the basis of this intellectual snapshot. The result was stressful, ultimately rather superficial and often unsatisfactory. Perhaps it derived from the old-fashioned Anglo-Saxon love of justice by ambush ... as exemplified by the Trials of witches ... rather than by the supposedly more logical but possibly equally unfair processes preferred by the courts of many other countries.

To improve the rigour of the system and as part of a general policy to shorten hearings so as to reduce expense to both the Parties, Courts have recently become disposed to receive Evidence-in-chief in the form of unsworn though signed 'Expert Reports' which are popularly supposed to be a substitute for such Examination. They are in practice the Expert analogues of the Witness Statements commonly submitted by Witnesses of Fact. In theory an advantage is now that each side knows in advance from the Reports what technical arguments will be advanced by each Expert, this prior knowledge being used to prepare analysis and counter-argument with a view to sharpening the quality of the subsequent cross-examinations. However vestiges of the old system remain; in particular a sometimes lengthy supplementary Examination-in-chief is still permitted, both on the subject matter of the Report 'by way of amendment and clarification' and also to introduce new material which may have assumed importance after the Report was submitted. If such changes of emphasis are extensive, a quick decision has to be reached as to whether in whole or in part they constitute a substantial recantation so that, at worst, counsel must tear up his cross examination notes based on that Expert's Report and proceed on a hand-to-mouth basis. During such an exercise, the hand will receive numerous hastily scribbled notes from its own Expert which are transformed into instant mouth in the old manner. Counsel seem to enjoy this sort of virtuosity and they, one suspects, are probably reluctant to abandon it. Needless to say Courts do not encourage these long oral examinations ... but in practice they often permit them on the basis that it is the up-to-date, maturely-considered view of the Witness which they are seeking.

The advent of the Report certainly underlines the central role of the Expert by defining the perimeter of the technical battlefield more clearly and in much greater detail than do the Particulars of Objections (Chapter 6). While it is early days yet to form an assessment of the efficacy of the new procedure, one can already see emerging a rather different technical strategy in the conduct of cases. Expert Reports from the Plaintiff and from the Defendant are exchanged concurrently so that there is no temptation or opportunity to tailor views to meet opposing arguments ... but there is opportunity to present supplementary Reports at any time up to and including the period of Trial, subject only to permission from the Court. Rather than being a substitute for Evidence-in-chief, the first and principal Expert Report may therefore be drafted to keep a substantial portion of its powder dry until there has been an opportunity to study the Report from the other side. Such study will hopefully reveal the contentious areas and confirm common ground so that the first Supplementary Expert Report can hit hard at those arguments upon which a decision may turn.

This stage-wise method is not necessarily a bad way of proceeding; on the contrary, such clarification should be of assistance to Counsel and the Court in seeing the wood for the trees. But there is a difficulty of timing under the present system in which, for tactical reasons, the first Reports are often submitted late in the run-up to Trial leaving little or no time to research and present the crucial more-detailed Supplementaries. While the courts naturally want to eliminate more than the necessary minimum of paperwork, the present procedures do seem to be rather less than satisfactory. If such a preliminary battle of technical papers is confirmed as the best way forward, it would be helpful to require the exchange of the first, more general, Expert Reports at a somewhat earlier stage. This should be followed by a second round of Supplementaries, requiring virtually all of the serious technical data and arguments to be included, at least four weeks before the start of Trial. This matter is raised again in the context of pre- and post-Trial briefs.

More seriously, under the present rules there is a temptation for the Expert, often under instruction, not only to omit crucial arguments from the Report but also to deliberately introduce numbers of red herrings into the text so as to waste the Opposition's pre-trial time in preparing detailed rebuttals of arguments which are never going to be seriously pressed. It is suggested that such suggestions, if they are made to the Expert, are really best resisted.

In some Proceedings, the necessary thinning out of the contentious technical issues can be achieved not by exchange of preliminary reports but better by calling an off-the-record meeting of the Experts who will debate the matter. However to be effective this meeting must be followed up by an agreed note stating exactly what common ground has been conceded. As was indicated in earlier chapters, given reasonable behaviour between the parties this form of dispute resolution, which has been tried by the courts from time to time, can be quite effective.

The Expert Report: what it can cover

So far as the author knows, there is no generally-agreed 'table of contents' for the first Expert Report. Neither is it usual for the Court to define what should be included at the Preliminary Hearings. The following topics are usually included in a typical Report:-

- Brief technical subject area: basic principles and 'state of the art'

- Teaching of the Patent-in-suit or other central technical document

- History of the matter, particularly 'the invention', as shown for instance by Discovery documents

- Prior art and other technical publications: relevance and teaching

- The crucial technical questions which appear to have to be decided

- Evidence from Process Inspection, Litigation Experiments, etc

- Reasoned Conclusions

- Appendices giving data, calculations, detailed quotations, etc

These are the bare bones ... but they need flesh on them which will vary considerably from case to case. However the Report should never be too long. The body of the Report should demonstrate that the Expert has properly considered all the relevant information, that any conclusions are properly based on the available documentation and that his personal data-base has been reviewed in the light of his common general knowledge of the field. While personal experience is worth quoting, and often highly prized by the Court, it is often more impressive in a setting of what was known, or generally believed, at the relevant period as shown by relevant documents.

In a first Report, while pointing out contentious matters which are relevant to one's own conclusions, there is usually little point in inveighing against the errors, omissions and general skull-duggery of the other side. If such special pleading is included in a version prepared for the Expert by someone else, which incidentally is a thoroughly bad way of setting about the drafting, the Expert should take the greatest care to edit out the offending passages. These can subsequently be delivered in a much more savage way by Counsel who does not carry on his shoulders the twin responsibilities of 'independence'and 'integrity of evidence'.

The Court will look particularly to the Expert Reports for:-

•   established scientific 'facts' (see Chapter 3); and

•   cogent technical arguments based on these facts.

Inclusion of any other kind of material could therefore detract from its impact.

It goes without saying that the language of the Report should be regular English with proper definition of any necessary technical terms. Any 'sciencese' should be restricted to its Appendices, whence it can be sniffed out and devoured by the Experts on the other side. What is so extraordinary is the scant attention to accuracy which characterises so many of the Expert Reports which are served in support of an Expert's oral evidence. When approving a Report for service on the Opposition, Experts do not seem always to place themselves in the position of the Opponent's legal team receiving the Report and, with undisguised glee, using all means at their disposal to find fault with it. If they thought of this scene in advance, they would surely take much more trouble to prepare documents which were directly relevant to the subject matter of the dispute, were closely argued and properly referenced to the chosen citations and other documentation and which were seen to lead to unequivocal though moderately-expressed conclusions. Attendance to such details of presentation would both enhance the Expert's credibility in the eyes of the Court and assist the lawyers in a proper presentation of their client's case.

One reason for the slip-shod nature of so many Reports may be the tardiness of those instructing in arranging for the necessary meetings at which the quality of drafting is finalised at a sufficiently high standard. Perhaps they believe that a little bumbling is welcome as indicative of the innate honesty, naivity and innocence of their Expert Witnesses ... but should we not at least be guided by the thought[1]:-

"The Moving Finger writes; and, having writ,
Moves on: nor all thy Piety nor Wit
Shall lure it back to cancel half a Line,
Nor all thy Tears wash out a Word of it"

As our friendly Expert confesses in Chapter 11, there were at least two occasions in his career when he would have liked to move his finger back, either to cause or rather to avoid a wash-out and, as a result of these salutary early experiences, his Reports have over the years become relatively blob-free compared with those of some of his opposite numbers.

In a Patent Action, the centre point of the Plaintiff's Report will usually be the establishment of the infringement by the Defendant of the client's valid Patent-in-suit. This often relies on Inspection and Experiments, which require detailed accounts, analysis, and conclusions. But surrounding this will be a more or less detailed discussion of the whole technical case. Outside the Patent field, analysis of the Discovery documents including inter-Party correspondence usually takes precedence.

• For instance in a recent dispute a new technology Prospectus had been issued by Defendant in a successful bid to raise a substantial sum of money from investors. By analysis of the Discovery documents, the Expert for the Plaintiff was able to develop a detailed chronological history of the technical development which he could compare with the wordings of detailed claims made in various public statements designed to elicit funding. This

---

[1]   Omar Khayyám (d. ?) <u>Rubáiyát</u> (transl. E. Fitzgerald first version 1859)

was a major task, involving much detailed analysis and cross-referencing of documents which resulted in a substantial Report of over one hundred pages. However it was designed to enable the Court conveniently to compare the claims of the Prospectus and other offer documents with the actual state of development of the technology, and to draw conclusions as to whether fraud had occurred. Such Expert Reports are often very detailed. They do not make light bed-time reading[2].

Analysis and criticism of the opposing Expert Reports

Despite the often daunting prospect, on receipt of the opposing Reports it is the duty of each Expert to burn some midnight oil in an attempt to grasp in a few days the full impact of the technical case against his client. It is unusual at this stage to be faced with any revelation in principle, since the Particulars of Objection and the Notices of Experiments should have given a good general idea of how the opposition is thinking. However it is quite normal to be faced with detailed argument or explanation of experimentation which causes one to have to acknowledge the correctness of what is being put forward and therefore to rethink certain areas of the case. The usual position which emerges from the review is in the form of a check-list of detailed action points:-

•   to be answered from papers already in the case

•   to be answered using new citations (to be sought)

•   to be answered by new calculations or observations of samples, photographs and so on, resulting from the Experiments.

The check-list is actually an order of preference. Existing documentation will be well known and have to be dealt with anyway. New citations so often serve to answer one point but can often raise several new ones.

The Expert's conclusions must then be discussed with the solicitors, patent agents and counsel. Counsel will also delineate points which, though apparently against our client's case, are in his opinion not relevant to the matters which the Court must decide and so which may be safely left

---

² "The Statements was interesting, but tough"
Mark Twain (S. L. Clemens) (d. 1910) The Adventures of Huckleberry Finn

unanswered. It is important that the Expert also keeps track of these and forms a personal view as to their relevance, for fear of being caught out when left alone under cross-examination by opposing counsel who may take a different view .

Once the citations and analyses have been completed and fully discussed, the Expert should normally prepare a further Note which will indicate the areas of technical 'common ground' between the Parties and delineate the residual differences with explanations of their origin. In particular the Note should make it quite clear as to where the opposing Report is 'right' and where it is 'wrong'.

Best of all for presentation to the Court is to be able to prepare an amalgam of Plaintiff and Defendant Reports showing that by a small change, perhaps of certain assumptions, differences of opinion with one's opposite number can be reconciled to yield a unified technical framework into which all the available data from Experiments, Inspections, Discovery and so on, can be fed. If this cannot be done because the stumbling block preventing such rationalisation is one or more passages in the Opposing Expert's Report, this is the time to consider drafting a Supplementary Report drawing specific attention to his errors.

Supplementary Reports

One possible reason for producing a Supplementary Report is to give the Opposing Expert due warning that he has made errors which he will have time to research and either acknowledge or defend. Another common reason is to take into account the result of a late test or other technical Evidence which was not available when the original Reports were drafted.

Supplementary Reports are usually quite short and do not mince words. They state why your opposing Expert is wrong and, if you know, how his thinking can be put right. They identify new technical facts, draw conclusions and explain why these further improve the already strong technical case presented in one's original Report. They append crucial new citations or data on which the new arguments depend but they do not usually extend the general review which was previously presented as a background to the case.

Reassessment

Once the technical arguments are fully understood, it is vital to discuss the consequences of such rethinking with one's side's Solicitor and then with Counsel. No Expert is omnipotent and so the reassessment of the technical position may even have to include the possible abandonment, or at least substantial modification, of certain 'corner-stone' arguments upon which the Lawyers had proposed to depend heavily. These arguments will be modified or abandoned by Counsel with great reluctance and, if extensive, such changes can occasionally attract a veiled suggestion that a better Expert would have seen the snags earlier on so that he would not have allowed these basic arguments to mature. This may well be a fair criticism which the Expert will have to learn to live with. But the fact of the matter is that he is presently 'the best they have got' so that any such recrimination in the heat of battle is ultimately pointless.

This is a moment when it is essential to reassess the appearance of one's case, warts'n'all, to seek solutions to problems raised by the opposing Report(s) and, if no solutions can be found, to advise that the technical position seems hopeless. This will at least allow the possibility of settlement before Trial, a cheaper and more satisfactory alternative to 'coming a bad second' in the Trial itself. But the foregoing represents a 'worst case' scenario which the author has had the good luck or judgement not yet to experience personally. What a professional Expert must *not* do is continue in acquiescence with previous arguments, believing or even knowing that they will be overthrown in Court but hoping against hope that 'something will turn up' to improve his client's position.

The Reassessment depends intimately on the detailed analysis of the Opponent's position as revealed not only by the Report(s) but also in the light of citations (such as those comprising common general knowledge), the principal Discovery documents, experimental results, inspection data and so on. It is a task which the Expert should perform with diligence. His work will be the basis on which his client's case proceeds to Trial.

A 'primer' for the Court

In a 'difficult' or complex technological case, it is usual to provide an introduction to the technology underlying the industrial art for use by the

Judge. Preparation of this 'primer' is generally the responsibility of the independent Expert and in some instances it can most appropriately form the first section of his Expert Report. However there are good reasons for preparing it as a separate document, not least that it can be readily kept to hand as a *vade mecum*. Perhaps ideally, the contents should include:-

- Expert's c.v. and qualifications

- A short history of the relevant art, particularly its craft origins

- An account in simple terms, using diagrams where appropriate, of the underlying science

- Production developments, including any relevant engineering

- A plain man's guide to the technology of the dispute

- A glossary of the principal terms which will be used by the Experts in their Reports and in subsequent oral evidence

For an English Patent Judge, the level could be approximately that of the first-year undergraduate textbook but for other courts it may be recommended to stick to the sixth-form school level. Probably the latter target is preferable, since a clear and balanced Primer is an essential document when presenting the case to the upper court on Appeal. For a Jury, all the ingenuity of the 'TV presenter' will have to be called into play: polymerising monomers becoming 'little red (or other colour, except white or black) men joining hands'. This is in no wise patronising, but properly reflects the low level of scientific knowledge of the man-in-the-street.

The Primer may often be the Judge's introduction to the technology of the case, a few days before Trial. It should deal with non-contentious matter as a background to the arguments and conclusions expressed in the Experts' Reports. If contention is successfully avoided, the Primers of the Plaintiff and the Defendant may most desirably be combined into one 'agreed' document to be acknowledged as a 'court bible'. However it is sometimes difficult to agree on the content, one or other of the Parties feeling that they may be disadvantaged by the selection for inclusion of even non-contentious subject matter. In this case the Court will be furnished with two primers, one from each of the Parties, a rather confusing position for him. A compromise may be to present a joint document based on what *can* be agreed but also having two Appendices putting forward the dissenting views of the Parties.

Experts should give careful attention to the drafting of their Primer because it is the technical background which the Judge will use in assessing their Evidence. In particular, without going to 'heavenly length' care should be taken in underpinning any difficult or lengthy concatenation arguments by defining in the primer the underlying science of each stage. Opinions differ about the introduction of citations into the Primer. The author is generally in favour of reference to established teaching texts at the appropriate level, provided that these are by accepted authorities and that the cited chapters are well tuned to the subject-matter of the Action. If they are *not*, the Opposition may take delight in pointing out that later on in the Chapter that you have cited, the author appears to be teaching *against* your Evidence; this could leave you fighting an embarassing rear-guard action based on a truthful but halting justification of the omission of this part of the Chapter's teaching[3].

The use of a video-tape or other visual aid can be helpful in assisting the priming task but only if it is 'bang on the point'.

A general view on written Evidence

There seems to be a strong a case for involving Experts more directly in preliminary court procedures and for using more written Expert evidence, followed by interparty discussion, to thin out the technical differences before they ever come before the Judge. Quite often much of the Court's precious time is presently wasted while the parties wrangle over the inadequacy of inspection facilities, the detailed conduct of experiments and so on. This sort of detail could be resolved and the considered views of the Parties included in a memorandum to the Judge rather than wasting hours of court time in procedural bickering. This matter is discussed again in Chapter 12 in the context of Pre-Trial and Post-Trial briefs, used extensively in the USA. Sufficient here to say that one shouldn't have to bother the headmaster every time a boy is found smoking in the toilets.

---

[3] "'I can't explain *myself*, I'm afraid, sir' said Alice, 'because I'm not myself you see'
'I don't see' said the Caterpillar.
Lewis Carroll (d. 1898) <u>Alice in Wonderland</u>

11   At Trial

Novice Experts are sometimes surprised to find that considerable stamina and dedication may be needed to perform well as a witness at Trial. The period of intensive preparation for a major action is unlikely to be of much less than six weeks duration. These weeks may often involve very long days, extending through the evenings, and substantial weekend work. Like an actor after a lengthy series of rehearsals, the Expert may really be 'ready for a rest' at the moment of opening. It is therefore quite important to actually be reasonably rested, if possible even to have taken some holiday, before the preparation stage and to shed superfluous commitments whether social or professional during the run-up to Trial and certainly during the Trial itself. The author finds that there is a lot to be said for dining, not too late, with clients and colleagues but returning to nearby accommodation to read the day's transcript, enjoy a Haydn Quartet, a couple of chapters of Wodehouse or a 'Philip Marlowe' before turning in. 'Nearby', because the irregular hours, early starts and extra fatigue do make it impracticable to work from the country on the basis of daily commuter travel involving the uncertain British public transport system.

Such an ordered existence is not always possible and for the young perhaps less necessary. Sometimes there is work to be done on citations or calculations in the 'war room' (see Chapter 6). Often there is a need to assist Counsel with one's own examination material or with suggested cross-examination questions to be directed at the other side's witnesses. The efficient operation of a litigation team including the independent witnesses is such that every member has to be prepared to do what is needed when it is needed. After working very late, to say after 10 p.m. during a trial, rather than suffer from loss of sleep Smith sometimes misses dinner and contents himself with a late-night sandwich and a beer 'back at base'.

By way of contrast, life in the Witness Box ('on the Witness Stand': US) is relatively calm. The Expert has only one job to do, to give coherent evidence. Also he must keep in mind only the limited range of documents relating to his own evidence. Those with a rather labile and easily erasable memory can usually revise this documentation each evening in an hour or two of concentrated reading: it is often preferable to read in the mornings, before "Court", and go to the theatre in the evenings. While this makes some sort of social life just about possible, a witness under examination is often preoccupied, this making him poor company on an evening out.

At the High Court

In London on 'opening day' the first problem of the novice Expert is often to find his Court ('Court-room': US). Some still come by car ... and are amazed to hear that there is no official provision for parking. Parking bays at Lincoln's Inn Fields are replete by soon after 9 a.m. and neither are there reliable underground car-parks nearby. It is better to use public transport, usually by Underground to the Temple (District and Circle line) or taxi from a main-line station. Most Experts will have little or no difficulty in finding the bulky nineteenth-century Royal Courts of Justice (the 'High Court') building in the Strand which is close to the Church of St Clement Danes but, after struggling through the (token) security check, they may be amazed to find built into its rear and flank elevations a vast complex of newer edifices all interconnected by dingy, dank and occasionally wind-swept corridors peopled by outsize effigies of distinguished past alumni. One needs to allow plenty of time to find one's way about, particularly to wait for the inadequate elevator service to some of the upper reaches. If your Solicitor has supplied you with the name of the Court building and the number of the Court then all is normally quite straight-forward. Otherwise there is a list of the Actions to be heard, the parties, the time and the place, in the fine central hall of the Victorian section so reminiscent of the old St Pancras railway station. Once in the correct Courtroom, at the beginning of the Trial the Experts are temporarily side-lined except in one important respect, that of technical adviser to their Counsel. Indeed for a brief while there is plenty of time for the novice Expert to sit back and enjoy the show.

On this appointed morning, usually soon after 10 a.m. ready for a 10.30 start, the solicitors' assistants and counsels' 'clerks' arrive with complete sets of the pre-arranged 'bundles' all on trolleys and partially protected from the rain on the way from 'chambers'. With luck and foresight their arrangement and pagination has been pre-agreed with the opposing solicitors. Each side usually has a minimum of four full sets of bundles: for the solicitors who occupy the front bench; for the leader (row 2); for junior counsel (row 3); and for patent agents, unemployed Experts and other riff-raff in the back row. These bundles are balanced precariously in rather flimsy wire racks or makeshift cardboard bookcases placed on the too-narrow ledges between the rows. Some law firms employ rotating carousels which cause endless diversion when they fall over, scattering folders and documents in all directions, pursued by any under-employed assistants who happen to be in attendance. A dedicated set of bundles has also to be provided for the Judge, desirably but not alas invariably with the same arrangement and pagination as has been agreed between the combatants. Another similar set is supplied for use by the Witnesses when they are under examination. This stack is therefore erected within reach of the Witness Box.

Old hands among the Experts know that other than 'in the Box' it will often be difficult to see documents as they are referenced in the heat of battle because of the intense competition to have sight of them between the patent agents, the client's representatives, a few score of overseas lawyers sitting in on the case and so on. Provision of an 'extra set' can theoretically ease the problem but the architects of British courts still seem to live in a Pickwickian age before the photocopier had been invented and so document space is at a premium. With the advent of 'improved' modern architecture to replace the 'out-dated' Victoriana, which has so much 'wasted' space', more & more complex Actions now seem to be heard in smaller & smaller courts. Soon we will be trying 'original sin' in a match-box! One does not really know whether to blame today's architects or those ill-informed litigation managers, presumably civil servants, who must have failed to explain the complex functioning of a modern court-room to them. As a result, in contrast to the palatial court-rooms in the USA, there is usually no room to swing a proverbial cat let alone line up eighty or so bulging lever-arch files for quick retrieval and return without causing an avalanche.

As Trial proceeds, the Expert will view with greater equanimity the use of every square inch of floor space to throw discarded or soon-to-be-needed reference books, documents, trolleys and tape. This seems to be regarded as part of the charm of this particular battleground for no one seems seriously interested in improving matters. Maybe the squalor reminds us all of home. The novice Expert with some knowledge of 'means of escape' regulations for public buildings will be particularly intrigued to see the constructions of cardboard libraries built of old archive boxes (... not wine-cases, as was once maliciously suggested ...) which loom and tower in every aisle. It is rumoured that at full moon a grizzled, prematurely aged and disgraced Expert may emerge from these, covered in toner powder and requesting "the price of a cup of tea".

The novice Expert will also soon get used to the endless comings & goings during the Action, like an airport concourse during the rush hour. Here someone with reference book, there a relief shorthand writer, now a messenger from chambers, then a Solicitor's secretary with a just-received fax ... one only needs a milliner, a bird-seller, a hairdresser, a brace of orphans, a couple of pimps, a dog-breeder, a flautist, and an italian tenor to complete the opera[1]. As they enter or leave, each bows respectfully in the direction of the Judge ... who seems to be concentrating too much to notice but is in fact usually well aware of all that is taking place in his Court.

After about twenty minutes in the court-room, the new Expert will become aware of a nagging stiffness in his back caused by the non-ergonomic design of the furniture. At this stage he should not worry unduly about this... he will get used to it as it steadily gets worse during the course of the Trial. In fact it will be at its most intense during periods of duty on the front bench of the older courtrooms where, as we shall see, it is exacerbated by the necessity for frequent 180-degree rotations of the spine. The distress may be ameliorated by introducing a proprietary back support[2] which could be very useful and effective were it not usually 'tried out' by one's silk early in the Trial and subsequently appropriated by him for the duration. Perhaps it is worth taking in a brace of these to allow for inadvertent wastage[3].

Expert's documentation

A canny Expert will collect most of the documentation he is going to need for himself during the preparation phase and keep his personal copies in his 'Charlies', the large personal document cases beloved of the law profession (and, so I understand, of airline pilots dedicated to a heavy weekend away from home). 'Charlies' are named after an old-time Chicago lawyer, Charlie Merriam, who kept them in three sizes: standard. big, and jumbo (which seemed to need two or three men to lift when loaded[4]). Two jumbo Charlies (or, alternatively, large shell-type suitcases with wheels) should see the average Expert through most international trials ... but a monogrammed pair in fine leather is not obligatory. Since the bigger bags are only marginally portable, the Expert will also need a large briefcase or 'standard Charlie' wherein to carry documents from his perch in the war-room to numerous in-trial conferences. These may be held not only in various chambers but also

---

[1]   "Als Morgengabe!" Baron Ochs 'negotiating' his marriage settlement with a Notary in the rather overcrowded anteroom to the Marschallin's bedroom, from Richard Strauss <u>Der Rosenkavalier i</u> (libretto by Hugo von Hofmannsthal)

[2]   A useful product is the "Backfriend" made by MEDesign Ltd.

[3]   ... of the Backfriends, not the silks.

[4]   The bag loaded, not the men.

in cafés, hotels and sundry local pubs round the Strand. Litigation people in the vicinity of the courts are said to be instantly recognizable, because they have one arm 50% longer than the other and are permanently extolling the virtues (or grumbling about the inadequacies) of their osteopaths.

Setting the Stage

Facing the steeply tiered 'Mappin Terraces of Litigation' is the elevated ensemble of the Judiciary. The Judge will sit high above his court, resplendent in his robes and, so it is understood, rather hot wig, beneath the Royal Insignia of Office. He will be the last to enter the courtroom when the pre-session chaos has at last subsided. As the Usher shouts "Court rise!", all will stand and bow. The parallel explored in Chapter 3 is irresistible to anyone familiar with Byzantine art and Orthodox churches. The same respectful, indeed 'courtly', pantomime will take place when the Judge rises[5]:-

"   With grave
Aspect he rose, and in his rising seem'd
A pillar of state: deep on his front engraven
Deliberation sat and public care;
And princely counsel in his face yet shone,
Majestic though in ruin"

On the left of the Judge's seat, as it were 'at the mid-height', is the Witness Box which will remain untenanted during the opening skirmish. In front of the Judge, at a lower level but still rather elevated compared with the mere contestants, are a row of Court officials including the Usher, whose main functions are to try to control our behaviour in the court-room and to provide glasses of tepid water and bibles as needed, and the Registrar (now renamed the 'Associate'), also bewigged and begowned, who has to swear in the witnesses and to identify, label and list any Exhibits which are put to the witnesses. To assuage the novice's curiosity, it appears that wigs are made or horse hair (or cheaper nylon monofilament). They are also worn by counsel, some of whom find it necessary to scratch under them from time to time, a somewhat distressing habit at least for those whose resting place is just behind them. Gowns are of some modest dark material. Some wigs and gowns are worn and venerable, possibly needing cleaning and renovation

---

[5] John Milton (d. 1674) Paradise Lost bk ii

since they have been passed from wearer to wearer for decades. The more historic could probably be rejuvenated by a quick rinse in Betnovate, provided that this treatment would not diminish their value as antiques. Most other countries manage to conduct their trial proceedings without the use of special costumes and there is currently pressure to abandon such regalia in Britain. This trend is being successfully resisted. Like abolishing the monarchy, their loss would be bad for our tourist industry. It would also make the 'robing room' redundant, so eliminating a rich source of anecdote and gossip.

Next to the Officials, or elsewhere perhaps nearer to the witness-box, are the official Shorthand Writers with their singlehanded dictation machines backed up by portable tape recorders. Experts should have considerable respect for the shorthand writers, as does the Court. Within the span of a few days, the same shorthand writer may be recording argument or evidence on the biotechnology of genomes, the results of finite element analysis of a bridge design, flow patterns in the continuous synthesis of poly-4-methyl-pentene-1 or causes of spinneret blocking in a xanthate textile fibre plant. Furthermore many witnesses who will give evidence on any such technical subject under the sun will give it in other than their native tongue or in such regional dialect as we politely describe as a 'charming burr'. It is an old problem[6]. As for syntax, one has only to recall the English description on the box of that Korean doll which shrieks so convincingly when your child[7] tosses it into the air:-

"Cries while you throw up".

While it is true that foreign witnesses are allowed to give evidence in their own tongues through translators, the latter are seldom scientists with a knowledge of the art in dispute so that the result is not always wholly satisfactory[8]. Thus the long-suffering shorthand writer has to record not only the (presumed) clarity and eloquence of counsel but also the mumblings of the incoherent, the foreign, the guilty, the overawed, the bumptious and any jargonmonger who has been chosen to address the Court on his own particular specialisation. Such, from time to time, may include the

---

[6]   "They spell it Vinci and pronounce it Vinchy; foreigners always spell better than they pronounce"
       Mark Twain (S. L. Clemens) (d. 1910)   Innocents Abroad ch 19

[7]   I must not say 'daughter'

[8]   "Egad, I think the interpreter is the hardest to be understood of the two!"
       Richard Brinsley Sheridan (d. 1816)   The Critic i

independent Expert. Although these shorthand writers are professionals who will cope with anything that is sent to try them, it is a matter of courtesy for the Expert to speak slowly and clearly and even to spell, at its first appearance, an unusual term of art or the name of an authority. If one forgets, and they temporarily lose the drift of your evidence, a short meeting with the shorthand writers when leaving the Box will usually achieve the same result. Neither is this *only* a matter of courtesy. In giving evidence, it is one's objective to teach the Judge to see certain technical matters in a particular way which the Expert regards as the 'right' way. While the Judge will have listened carefully to each witness's oral exposition, as the importance of an argument becomes apparent during the case and eventually crystallises into an 'issue', he will wish to refer back to what each Witness said about this issue several days or even weeks earlier.

For this purpose, he will use the 'Transcript' produced by the official Shorthand Writers as a Court record. It is to this crucial document that both leading counsel will refer during their 'closing speeches' which are often protracted arguments with His Lordship. Furthermore if the case goes to Appeal, the Appeal Court, which does not hear any witnesses, must necessarily rely on what was said in the lower court exactly as it is recorded on the Transcript. An Expert who believes that his Evidence is of importance therefore has a clear responsibility to make sure that it is recorded accurately in the Transcript. Being rather fussy about exactly what he is supposed to have said in evidence, in a lengthy trial involving many hours in the Box an experienced Expert usually tries to see a copy of the Transcript as soon as possible on a daily basis and, if necessary, corrects it. Arrangements can usually be made with the Solicitor to have delivery of the day's transcript at a London address by 7 p.m. on the same day so that any corrections can be entered before bedtime or early next morning before the start of Court. Usually the corrections are few and trivial. If so, these are usually passed through the system and agreed by the opposing junior counsel. Sometimes however there is a matter of substance which is best cleared up before the Court in Evidence as described later in this Chapter.

Curtain up

However, now that all the documents are stowed (somewhere), everyone has found a seat depending on rank and position, the Usher bellows "Court rise", we hush and stand, the Judge enters and bows to us .. as we to him. With a modicum of clatter all are again seated except 'Counsel for the Plaintiff' who is to 'open' ...

    ... "May it please your Lordship"

Counsel first explains who he is appearing for. This is not always as easy as it would seem. It has even be known for absent-minded or poorly-instructed barristers to get it wrong. With a mixed bunch of interwoven Plaintiffs and a similar bevy of Defendants, explanation is not always plain sailing. We have already seen (in Chapter 6) that the listed Action 'Snooks and others v Waferthin Tissues (Bodmin) Ltd' may well turn out in practice to be 'I.C.I. v Union Carbide' or 'Boeing v Douglas'. The Judge may intervene at this early stage to ask supplementary questions about the identities or domiciles of the Parties and refer back to Interlocutory or other intermediate Court proceedings involving the same Parties. This pattern of speech by Counsel, interspersed with questioning by the Judge, is of the essence in the Trial process and it is well worth serious study by the Expert from the outset of the Trial. Some Judges intervene more than others and it is counsel's art to satisfy and even encourage the Judge's curiosity about the case which he has to plead without being thrown off his sequence or line of argument. Some judges bark at counsel whereas others speak gently with great courtesy but none flinch from suggesting to counsel that he is wrong if only to see what further argument he can advance in his client's support. This is merely an efficient clarification process familiar to members of university senior common rooms. The underlying thought is usually[9]:-

"Ah! don't say that you agree with me. When people agree with me I always feel that I must be wrong"

This adversarial stance between the Judge and his home Counsel can sometimes dismay novice Experts (and the more so naive clients who fear that it indicates some genuine and deep-seated antagonism between the two which will automatically result in a 'rough ride' and so an unfavourable verdict). The faint-hearted can often be comforted with the thought that judges were once 'silks' and 'juniors' too, that members of the Bar who appear hostile to one another in Court, at least by the standards of ordinary people, are very often the best of friends outside. Indeed the term of address 'my learned friend' is not without real significance in the law business. In truth the honest Expert has nothing to fear. During the interrogation of lay witnesses whom they realise have not (yet) been 'case hardened' by the

---

[9]   Oscar Wilde (d. 1900) <u>The Critic as Artist</u>

system, in most circumstances a good judge will behave rather like Mrs Todgers[10], adopting an altogether softer style. His initial attitude will be to show his belief that the witness has attended to help him reach a fair decision in respect of a complex dispute. It is only if the witness seems to betray this trust that he will be spoken to at all harshly. The Judge wishes to be respected, not to be feared[11]:-

"Judge not the Lord by feeble sense
But trust him for his grace;
Behind a frowning providence
He hides a smiling face"

He is indisputably in charge of *his* Court and he would like to regard the Expert as someone who is there to assist him in reaching a true verdict. When he can help he will therefore always be pleased to relieve any discomfiture of his witness whether an uncomfortable seat, a hearing impediment, a temporary loss of memory, the mislaying of a document and so on and so forth. The Judge will also protect a witness whom he believes to be trying to tell the truth from (rare) unworthy personal attacks or unwarranted denigration of his professional qualifications and experience by (unusual) hectoring counsel. Such attacks are rare in the UK courts, though more of a way-of-life in the US court-rooms.

Opening Speech

Counsel's opening speech requires the most delicate touch. As we have seen, at this point .. the beginning of the trial .. he does not know in sufficient detail what case his adversary, Counsel for the Defendant, will plead or the quality of the evidence he may call. Although by now thoroughly familiar with his own technical case which will have been fully discussed with his Experts, Counsel still needs to keep his argument moderately flexible until he has heard his Learned Friend's case together with all his evidence. Aside from the Reports and anything from people abroad or obtained under the Civil Evidence Act, which the Judge will have read, there may as yet be no evidence on the record except the written statements which have been exchanged. Counsel does not want to present a case of which the cornerstone

[10] "With affection beaming in one eye, and calculation shining out of the other"
   Charles Dickens (d. 1870)   Martin Chuzzlewit ch 8

[11]   William Cowper (d. 1800)   Olney Hymns

might be knocked out, particularly by clever cross-examination of some uncertain witness whom he himself has called. Moreover, besides advising the Judge what to think, Counsel needs to elicit feedback at every moment, on every document, on every argument, as to what the Judge's own view is likely to be. This stance is not so much to please the Judge as to avoid unnecessarily antagonising him. Many counsel therefore like to commence with readings of key documents, for example in a Patent action: the Patent-in-suit, and then indicating gently by reference to 'the Authorities' (records of old cases and judgements) the sort of 'case law' which they will be pleading. This approach undoubtedly works well. It allows the Judge to request instruction on the meaning of key passages in the documents, at the same time showing how he is viewing the case, and to express his preliminary views for instance on the construction of the Claims. As a result, each leader can accurately assess the task ahead of him and instruct his team accordingly. The Expert is well-advised to follow this dialogue carefully and to compare what is said with his own personal views. Unfortunately for counsel, and occasionally for the Parties, in a unilateral but wholly praiseworthy dash for greater cost-effectiveness some judges have recently taken the view that such preliminaries are a waste of the Court's time. They may say at the outset that they have "read all the documents", they are "aware of the Law which should be applied" and so, prematurely, without really being able to investigate the mind of the Judge as to his regard for the key issues, Counsel may be virtually forced to lead his first Witness. Counsel have been known to dig in at this point and *insist* on instructing the judge, whether he likes it or not. But this has the risk of turning the earlier productive intellectual sparring into naked aggression:-

"I don't want to hear any more about this at this stage, Mr B, and please remember it is I who will make the decision" ... "Very well, my Lord, but it may be reconsidered in another place".

The threat in Counsel's riposte is of course reversal of the lower court judgement by the Court of Appeal. Experienced counsel have however become adept at avoiding such confrontation, for instance by dressing up the introduction of their technical interpretation in the clothes of novel 'points of law' thus often interesting the Judge and at the same time subjecting him to the desired teach-in as part & parcel of the legal argument.

• A favourite technique used brilliantly by the late Sir Lionel Heald QC when addressing the Court was to make a simple technical mistake in a key passage from an important document. This was usually seized upon by the Judge who proceeded himself to teach Counsel the correct technology he had gleaned from the 'primer', eliciting on each occasion a grovelling acquiescence. By thus returning frequently to the passage, as his own discovery it assumed greater and greater prominence in the Judge's mind. With today's more sophisticated and technically literate judges and counsel, this sort of ploy is rarer and must require considerably more disguise in its delivery. Neither do our present-day Leaders usually mutter under their breath during their learned friend's 'speech', jangle coins and keys perpetually in their trouser pockets or drop a pile of books on to the floor at the denouement of his argument. To the novice Expert, really familiar only with the technical details of the case and tense with anticipation to 'perform', this legal bumbling and sparring can sometimes seem tedious and even unnecessary. However with experience he will find it a most useful introduction to the workings of the legal process as he hears his Counsel trying to pinpoint exactly those areas where the Judge may become confused about the technology and which will therefore merit the most painstaking and precise explanations by the Experts under examination.

The length of the opening is entirely flexible, depending only on the Judge's patience and Counsel's judgement of the amount of education he feels he can impart to the Court without inducing anger or boredom. Mindful of the risk, in opening Counsel uses his teaching skill, with regard to visible and audible feedback from the Judge, to assess the moment when he is in danger of overstaying his welcome. This may be sooner rather than later for modern judges can be quick to punish verbosity[12]. However, in a Jury trial, much repetition is essential. This educational stage is therefore often protracted and, in the USA, usually 'emotive'. Indeed, in these days of mass entertainment, jury trials can often go in favour of the Attorney who is the best actor, especially if he endears himself to them by frequently making them laugh. There is also considerable reliance on simple diagrams and models, plus costly video animations to make the jurymen feel both at home and properly valued by the sponsoring party ... and possibly to stop their weaker brethren from dozing off[13].

---

[12] "Use not vain repetitions, as the heathen do: for they think that they shall be heard for their much speaking"
Holy Bible: St Matthew vi

[13] "He had bought a large map representing the sea,
Without the least vestige of land;
And the crew were much pleased when they found it to be
A map they could all understand.
Lewis Caroll (d. 1898) The Hunting of the Snark

Evidence

Counsel now needs to support what he has been putting to the Judge by calling Evidence. Without prior warning it will seem Counsel winds up his harangue and begs his Lordship's leave to 'call' his first witness: 'Doctor Strangeways'. In court, the suddenness of transition from Argument to Evidence coupled with the sacrificial rendering of his surname can take the novice Expert's breath away. If he is 'first man in' he needs to recover quickly as he strides towards the Witness Box. On being called, some Experts experience the 'Walter Mitty' syndrome[14]:-

"Then, with that faint, fleeting smile playing about his lips, he faced the firing squad: erect and motionless, proud and disdainful, Walter Mitty, the undefeated, inscrutable to the last"

But the novice Expert is by now likely to be far from motionless and temporarily in a blue funk. Fortunately most counsel appreciate the Witness's problems. His likely need to satisfy a final 'call of nature' before being thrown to the lions can be catered for by providing him with a *sotto voce* countdown during the closing stages of the opening. Other counsel will take opportunities to address soothing indications of anticipated duration directly to the Court. Also some judges will begin trying to insist on a time limit for Counsel's opening speech, often to fit in with the timing of a forthcoming recess, almost from the outset. However careful following by the Witness of the friendly duel between Counsel and Judge during the 'Opening' will usually make these chronological indications superfluous. It will be abundantly clear when the overture is reaching its final cadence and the curtain is about to rise on a brave new world of advanced technology. Most counsel will have given their witnesses a rough indication of the overall timetable and they will commonly plan to introduce their first witness immediately after a recess. Nevertheless, however it has been arranged, there is always that sinking feeling when one hears the stentorian bellow of the Usher summoning one up from the well of the court to a higher profile position in the Witness Box. As in any examination, there is fear of a memory lapse or of some obvious physical infirmity ... even tripping over the steps and sprawling on the way up[15].

---

[14] James Thurber (d. 1961) The Secret Life of Walter Mitty
from 'My World and Welcome to it' Hamish Hamilton 1942

[15] "I'm coming, I'm coming, for my head is bending low,
I hear their gentle voices calling 'Poor Old Joe'"
Stephen C. Foster (d. 1864) Poor Old Joe

<u>Order of Evidence</u>

Where there are several witnesses, both Experts and 'Witnesses of Fact' and their Evidence will be of varying duration and importance, Leading Counsel will give considerable thought to the 'batting order'. The Expert needs to know the rule that Defendant's counsel must put his case to Plaintiff's witnesses in cross-examination before calling his own witnesses and/or addressing the Court. In times past, Defendant's Counsel would not know how many or which witnesses would be called by Plaintiff's Counsel during the Trial and so he was forced to put the greater part of his case to the first Plaintiff's Witness almost regardless of his suitability to answer in terms of qualifications and experience simply because of the risk that the 'first' Witness might also be the 'last'. Today matters are better organised and lists of Witnesses to be called are exchanged between the Solicitors before Trial. In addition as we have seen Witnesses are required to submit their principal Evidence-in-chief in the form of written Reports, the form and content of which was outlined in Chapter 10. This is intended to enable the cross-examination of each Witness to concentrate on the subject matter of his Report plus any further points he has made orally.

It is quite usual to call Experts before the witnesses of fact. A common batting order is: a wide-ranging technologist Expert who will be asked to interpret the major documents, followed by more specialised Experts, often distinguished scientists or engineers, who deal with important detail; then possibly a "horny-handed son of toil"[16], the 'unimaginative skilled man' of Patent Law, who will tell the Judge what was really important to him in (say) a production context. Sometimes a statistician will be called to vouch for the excellence (or otherwise) of any experimentation and in particular the validity of the conclusions drawn therefrom. These are usually followed by witnesses of fact: customers who saw the product or process in use, salesmen who took orders or dealt with complaints ... and so on.

The whole parade can often take several days for each side. Of course the planned sequence may occasionally have to be interrupted to hear 'captains of industry', directors and others, usually witnesses of fact who are enmeshed in a 'tight international travel schedule' and who, more practically, at the end of the day are picking up the tab.

---

[16] Denis Kearney (d. 1907) <u>Speech</u> San Francisco, 1878

The Oath; and the onus of "truth"

On arrival in "the Box", the Witness is required to remain standing and, in answer to the Associate, to state his full name:-

Witness: "Dunlop Wensleydale Bonchester Strangeways"

(Usher hands up a small Bible)

Associate: "Please take the Bible in your right hand and repeat after me:
                  'I swear to tell the truth, the whole truth, and nothing but the truth'"

The Witness then proceeds to swear this Oath. As with the word *obey* in the Church of England wedding service, the former coda '.. *so help me God"* is now conventionally omitted ... whether in recognition of the generally agnostic nature of present society or because of the generally better preparation of witnesses the author knows not. Witnesses of other denominations or without belief are permitted to 'affirm' to similar effect, in which case the formula is:

"I solemnly declare and affirm to tell the truth, etc"

As a scientist, one naturally ponders the meaning of this Oath or Affirmation. Our philosophy would teach us to be wary of this degree of commital. If these words simply mean 'give an honest opinion based on all of the available facts' then no difficulty should arise and we could swear away with abandon. But the implication of omnipotence could seem to be both arrogant and distasteful. Furthermore the negative 'nothing but the truth' seems to preclude the expression of an honest opinion intended to bridge the gap between disconnected islands of so-called 'fact', so denying one of the most valuable contributions of the experienced Expert. As discussed in Chapter 3, scientists and technologists can do no more than draw educated inferences about probabilities from a necessarily incomplete body of legal 'fact'. In reality, this is probably all that the Court really expects of them. If so, one wonders if the actual words of the Oath, together with the hallowed swearing procedure, could benefit from a spring clean?

During the swearing or its agnostic equivalent, the Judge is supposed to stare, hard and long, at the Witness in order to 'assess his demeanour', that is to say 'try to guess whether or not he is likely to give honest testimony', while presumably choking back any prejudice against his colour, appearance or accent which may be welling up before the poor creature has uttered a word about the matter in hand. So however frightened you may be in entering the Box, as a witness try to look and sound like someone from whom you yourself would gladly buy a second-hand affidavit. Perhaps it will help to remember the teaching[17]:-

"A merry heart maketh a cheerful countenance"

The Judge will then say in a matter-of-fact but kindly voice:-

"Please sit down (Doctor)".

As a practical matter it is worth adjusting the height of the chair provided .. either now at risk of slight delay or preferably in the recess prior to being called[18]. At five-foot-two, there is nothing worse than following a seven-footer in the Box, to be left dangling from the high stool for the next two hours without any chance of relief from the pins & needles which will invade your lower limbs. Moreover, you should also be concerned to protect the authorities from a slight but significant liability risk[19].

Examination-in-chief

Your own Counsel, either the leader or his junior, as will have been arranged in advance, will now rise to examine 'his' Expert. He will ask (usually!) prearranged questions and you will address your answers to the Judge, referring to him if you need to in the same way as does Counsel as 'M'Lud' or 'His Lordship'. As we have seen, the equivalent in the US Courts and our PCC is 'Your Honour'. It is normal to address Counsel by name ('Mr Brook'). They are senior professionals and should equally deserve the Expert's respect. (And we understand that any Witness is also at liberty to address Counsel as 'Sir', and that there is no prohibition which prevents touching of the forelock.)

---

[17] Holy Bible Proverbs xv

[18] "One never more can go to court,
Because his legs have grown too short;
The other cannot sing a song
Because his legs have grown too long"
Edward Lear (d. 1888) Nonsense Songs: 'The Daddy Long-Legs and the Fly'

[19] "He fell off the seat backward by the side of the gate, and his neck brake"
Holy Bible I Samuel iv

This oral examination is a vestige of the old 'Examination-in-chief' at which the Witness spoke the whole of his evidence on to the transcript in response to the appropriate prompts from his Counsel. Now most of this evidence is provided in the Expert's Report together with any Supplementary Reports which he has prepared, for instance in response to written evidence from the other side. The Report (and any Supplementaries) are formally put to the Witness and confirmed as true under oath. From this point on they are Evidence in the Action and, having been referred to in open court, they are free of confidentiality restrictions, unless Counsel has reserved confidence in, for example, a particular table of commercially-sensitive data. In theory then the new oral examination-in-chief is now of very short duration and largely confined to clearing up typing errors and of course any mistakes of fact in the written submissions which will have been read by the Court. It is also an opportunity to comment on the Report of the Opponent's Expert if this has not already been submitted in writing. Nevertheless in practice the occasion may often also be used for a presentation of new material which has been recognised as important rather late in the preparation period. Judges can become restive if the examination is prolonged but they usually seem reluctant to truncate the presentation of Evidence which may be important in assisting them to reach the right decision. Another use of the 'oral' is to present Exhibits which have not fitted into earlier formats and ask the Expert to authenticate them by way of commentary. For instance in a recent case the author started his evidence by adding a spoken commentary to a videotape of some microscopic demonstrations of a material undergoing dissolution and swelling. Other Witnesses were asked to comment on the adhesion of plastic materials to different films which they had seen tested and which had also been recorded on video for the Court. Others again were asked to identify photographs, samples and so on.

It is an ideal, seldom realised by independent Experts, to give short and specific answers to the questions asked by Counsel whether in examination-in-chief or in cross-examination. There is certainly no call to lard your answers with technical minutiae which have not been requested[20]. If he wants more detail, Counsel will not hesitate to ask for it. Likewise if an Expert wanders off the point he may well be asked, with the utmost civility (at least the first time it happens), whether he would be so kind as to answer the question. Persistent rambling will attract more severe admonitions, first

---

[20] "Merely corroborative detail, intended to give artistic verisimilitude to an otherwise bald and unconvincing narrative" Sir William S. Gilbert (d. 1911) The Mikado

from Counsel and even, in cases of verbal dysentery, from the Judge.

In preparation the Expert will often have been told that he can take his own notes and even marked documents (such as the Patent-in-suit) into the Box with him. But do not count on it! In practice opposing Counsel nearly always seem to object to the use of such private notes by the Witness or, at the very least, to huff and to puff, wanting umpteen copies for perusal and use in subsequent cross-examination. On the whole, unless an Expert's work involves complex mathematical or other such material, it is a better to plan do without notes and learn to refer only to the (unmarked) documents officially provided 'for the use of witnesses'. As to the Witness's general demeanour ... like the architecture of the older English court buildings this should best follow the hallowed tradition of the Victorian public (i.e. private) school or (upper class) nursery[21].

At this point the Expert may face the first requirement to actually deploy the library of Court documents provided adjacent to the Witness Box. At the outset these are in a carousel or on shelving arranged in numbered Bundle order so that selection is not difficult. However as the Trial winds on its way, new bundles and, much worse, loose documents, are 'put in' which sometimes find their way into Bundles ... and sometimes do not.

After each witness has left the Box, the Court Usher is supposed to rearrange all the documents in order but in practice one may inherit a desk-top piled high with discarded paper, the bundles out of order and so on. There is no need to panic. The Judge is quite resigned to this situation and will never hold his manic fumbling with the papers against the Expert. Rather than add to the confusion by activating the Usher, he will often vacate his perch to assist in retrieving a missing volume from the dreary pile of waste.

In all this examination-in-chief is unlikely to occupy more than twenty minutes to perhaps an hour, after which Counsel will usually speak a conventional trigger phrase such as:-

" ... and now I expect my (learned) Friend would like to ask you some questions".

---

[21] "A child should always say what's true
And speak when he is spoken to,
And behave mannerly at table:
At least as far as he is able"
Robert Louis Stevenson (d. 1894)   A Child's Garden of Verses: 'Whole duty of Children'

Cross-examination

Counsel for the other side will instantaneously (if not quite noiselessly) rise with the invariant call-sign:-

"May it please, your Lordship ..."

In a trice, your cross-examination has already begun. It is important for the novice Expert to remember at this point that he is not engaged in some form of medieval tournament in which the objective is to unhorse the knight charging towards him. In other words there is nothing to be gained by taking an instantly aggressive or defensive stance and much to be lost by way of personal credibility. The man facing you is another professional, similar for all practical purposes to your own side's Counsel who, for the present, is doing the same sort of job as you are, that is to say trying to help resolve the complexities, the ambiguities and contradictions which originally caused this case to come before the Court. Counsel will address the Expert politely, though some do so with no special deference[22] ... particularly, one expects, the authors of Expert Witness books ... and the tempo of question and answer is leisurely, as is necessary for the benefit of the shorthand writers. Even under cross-examination, it is rare to hear any bullying of technical witnesses and such, if it commences, will soon be controlled by the Judge. Modern counsel rely on authoritative persuasion to try to obtain the answers they need. The relevant game in this respect is not so much chess but more commonly that of 'Angling', our English river fishing[23]. As we shall see, US court practice is altogether more earthy in respect of handling Expert Witnesses. This makes it much easier, and more of a pleasure, for a Witness to disagree vehemently with his cross-examiner. As a friendly Attorney in Arizona put it to the author:-

"A century ago we'd have shot it out in the dust in front of the courthouse"

The adversarial system requires Counsel to put the best case he can for his clients. This may include suggesting from time to time that the Witness is mistaken in his facts or the conclusions he is drawing from the facts. He

---

[22] "I regard you with indifference closely bordering on aversion"
Robert Louis Stevenson (d. 1894) New Arabian Nights: The Rajah's Diamond

[23] "Thus use your frog ... Put your hook, I mean the arming wire, through his mouth, and out at his gills; and then with a fine needle and silk sew the upper part of his leg, with only one stitch, to the arming-wire of your hook; or tie the frog's leg, above the upper joint, to the armed-wire; and, in so doing, use him as though you loved him"
Izaak Walton (d. 1683) Compleat Angler ch 8

will go on to propose alternative conclusions and invite the Expert, through his questions, to support these or, at the very least, to admit that there is some possibility of the alternative interpretation. In this way he hopes to distinguish fact and informed opinion from hazy conjecture and surmise. At the same time he prepares the way for putting alternative thoughts about the case into the Judge's mind which will wean him away from the suggestions put by your own Counsel in opening. Although the avowed objective of Opponent's Counsel is the same as yours, to instruct the Judge in technical aspects of the case, it is your job to reinforce what you believe to be true and to clearly reject any inappropriate or misleading alternative proposals he may make during his cross-examination. As Witness one must answer all counsel's questions truthfully with a 'Yes' or a 'No' if this is possible and appropriate[24] or with an explanatory sentence or request for clarification if this is needed. But there is no need to be burdened by this rule to the detriment of a proper explanation.

Although it will not necessarily help the Judge, it is not a disgrace to say that you 'don't know' the answer to counsel's question, if this is the truth. However if you think it could be helpful it is nearly always permissible to add a speculative answer, on some assumed basis or data, *provided that it is made clear that this is how you are answering.* Such speculation must be both relevant and plausible and it should be directed to assisting the Judge to better understand the uncharted nature of the territory into which the Question is leading. Nevertheless artistic license[25] should be restrained and presentation of 'pet theories' may not advance either your own or your client's credibility. It is of course open to the cross-examiner to then probe the new basis of your speculation and to try to suggest that this position is not tenable. But the onus is then likely to be on him to postulate an alternative basis which you may duly have to consider ... and then accept or reject.

A few of the more traditional cross-examiners cannot resist the hallowed form of question:-

"Please answer 'Yes' or 'No': "... Have you stopped beating your mistress yet?"

---

[24] "Let your communication be, Yea, Yea; Nay, Nay"
Holy Bible St Matthew v

[25] "So geographers, in Afric-maps,
With savage-pictures fill their gaps;
And o'er unhabitable downs
Place elephants for want of towns"
Jonathan Swift (d. 1745) On Poetry

When faced with such an 'attack', and the word is used advisedly in respect of this type of question, it is particularly important not to be carried away in an excess of zeal to please His Lordship by giving some monosyllabic answer. Your 'yes' or 'no' will later appear on the Transcript and probably cause endless confusion. It is preferable to reply good-naturedly:-

"Please can we take that in stages, Mr B?"

... and you may be surprised and delighted to hear the Judge, who is well up to all these ploys, echo your answer with:-

"Where exactly are you leading, Mr B?"

... or some such mild reprimand, both to Counsel for playing the wild card and to the Witness for cross-examining him on it. Provided that this does not develop into a stalling tactic, there is never any reason not to ask for clarification, since[26]:-

"It is better to ask some of the questions than to know all the answers"

Occasionally, perhaps through tiredness, you will misunderstand a perfectly phrased direct question with no advocate's hassle implied. Again there is no disgrace in saying so and you will usually be tolerated by the Judge who wants to hear your considered answer to a question you *have* understood properly rather than be led by you into a thicket of non-comprehension. The *considered* answer is perhaps the key to high quality evidence and the Expert should obviously not allow the generally slowish tempo of Question and Answer to accelerate to the point where he has not thought out the implications of what has been asked and of the reply he intends to give. A golden rule is: 'Never allow yourself to be stampeded', and always remember the old North American adage[27]:-

"Do not put mouth in gear before brain is engaged".

So if you do not understand you must say so and, unless you are deliberately avoiding an answer, the Judge will support you. Counsel will then rephrase his question, often simplifying it by presenting it in a series of interlinked sub-questions.

---

[26]   James Thurber (d. 1961) <u>The Scotty Who Knew Too Much</u> Hamish Hamilton

[27]   Anon. Well-known saying in the engineering industry

If you *are* suspected of deliberately stalling, Counsel may have the question read back by the shorthand writer rather than putting it again himself. But some counsel can and do resort to this bludgeon rather prematurely, often as an assault tactic on a determined and intractable witness, so do not immediately blame yourself for stupidity, or lack of attention, if it happens. It may merely indicate Counsel's personal frustration at not having achieved the hoped for 'break-through'. Counsel will never forget, and neither must the Witness, that the object, the only object of this exercise is to help the Judge understand a technical point about the case. As we have seen, this purpose is not served either by garbled multifaceted questions nor by lengthy, rambling theoretical answers. Be as succinct as you can; in court, no Expert ever gets Brownie points on the deferential basis[28]:-

"Of science and logic he chatters.
As fine and as fast as he can;
Though I am no judge of such matters.
I'm sure he's a talented man"

Both debaters, Counsel and the Witness, should try to simplify the dialogue without loss of rigour. If this is impossible, as Witness it is possible to add a caveat briefly explaining the simplification used and that the true situation is indeed far more complicated for certain designated reasons. This invites further questioning, either from Counsel or from the Judge if either feels that any point turns on such greater detail.

Watching the Judge

Some instructing solicitors suggest to the witness that he watches the Judge, as does learned Counsel, both to assist His Lordship's note-taking and to see see how the answer is being received. The author is not at all sure that this is either practicable or desirable. Besides sapping intellectual concentration on one's own clarity of expression, it can turn the Expert into a kind of actor which can easily diminish his credibility. One is not being required to give an answer which simply pleases the Judge, one is trying to give a rational and helpful explanation of a complex process. It is only rarely, for instance in answer to a blanket question such as:-

"Tell his Lordship what you actually saw during the factory inspection"

---

[28]   Winthrop Mackworth Praed (d. 1839)   The Talented Man

that 'watching the Judge' will be helpful. During an Expert's answer to such a question, the Judge may well be making long-hand notes of this 'evidence of fact' and it will be reasonable to proceed at a steady pace which will allow the Judge to do so, enunciating clearly and deliberately any technical terms which have to be used to give a proper answer. In other circumstances, it seems more natural and normal to direct one's answer to the questioner in a slow conversational tempo. Judges certainly do not seem to be incommoded by this. In answer to any such general question, a quick decision has to be made by the Expert as to how to compress three or four days, or even weeks, of detailed observation into a few sentences. In your efforts to do so, your cross-examiner may hope that you will reveal in your selection your own thoughts on the strengths and weaknesses of such observations which will help him to probe the weaknesses, in detail by means of supplementary questions. One should try to start by giving the missing framework, in this example the purpose of the inspection and what one was looking at, what areas of production were covered and so on, often with reference to the process inspection. If the Judge still seems interested in this, and Counsel has not intervened ... usually because he is not really interested in the answer but needs a break to refresh himself from his notes prior to a change of topic or to take further instruction 'on the hoof', the Expert may then continue into the further detail of observations and conclusions, trying to restrict himself to 'highlights' which are likely to be most relevant to contentious matters which the Court will have to decide. At any point, the Judge may himself intervene, taking the opportunity of continuing the examination to obtain answers to questions which arose in his mind when reading the various inspection reports and so on. When he has had enough detail, he will politely terminate the Witness's answer ... for instance by addressing Counsel:-

"Which specific part of the Inspection did you wish the Professor to comment on, Mr B?"

Normal service is then resumed.

Mistakes by the Witness

Occasionally, the Expert is caught off guard.

• A short section of the author's Expert Report in a recent Action cited a technical paper which on close examination dealt with a similar but sensibly different material from that which Smith had actually presumed. This was not readily apparent from the abstract but became clearer in the full text of the paper which was somewhat delphic and which, late in the run-up to Trial, the Expert had not fully absorbed. Put clearly, after the necessary build-up, came the cross-examination question direct:-

"This citation does not support your argument, does it?"

This Expert was here faced with a choice, a long and uphill, true but tenuous, technical justification of how the evidence from one class of material could be used to draw conclusions about another ... or an honest admission that he had made a mistake in his preparation. In the event Smith agreed with his inquisitor, admitting that inclusion of this particular citation was an oversight. The Witness's ready agreement seemed unexpected by Counsel and, as a result, to throw him. In the event the Court heard no more about this small, though regrettably careless, point which did not figure in the Judgement because it was so far from the kernel of the case. In general if an Expert has made a simple error it is almost always better for him to admit it quickly rather than let it assume disproportionate importance in the Evidence and even undermine his credibility as a witness in respect of other matters wherein he, in truth, is more firmly based. A golden rule is[29]:-

"Agree with thine adversary quickly, whiles thou art in the way with him"

Another problem which can arise is the inapposite analogy:-

• In dealing with the state of 'common general knowledge' ('cgk'), the author as Expert had made the point that even quite closely related industrial applications of certain types of material each had their own traditional technological jargon and that there was little communication at the grass-roots level of the skilled man which would allow knowledge in the one field to diffuse to the other. The Judge showed interest in this. Smith illustrated this idea by drawing an analogy of the high valleys of the Pyrenees mountains on the border of France and Spain where villages separated by only a few miles as the crow flies, but on different sides of the chain, had different local cultures and languages. His opposing Expert questioned the analogy suggesting (incorrectly) that the 'cgk' situation was more like that in Switzerland, with many tunnels under the mountains

---
[29] Holy Bible St Matthew v

giving good communication between the valleys. But the truth of the matter is that, despite these advantages, four languages are still spoken in Switzerland and, by and large, there is still little or no intermingling of peasant cultures between the Cantons.

Letting the guard drop

•   In an Action during the 80s, a distinguished scientist (and very experienced Expert Witness) Professor Proudfoot was giving evidence intended to establish the obviousness of the invention-in-suit. Without making any actual 'mistakes', he then fell victim to skilled but fair cross-examination which first played upon his vanity as a fastidious and painstaking research chemist. The Professor had admitted that some 'routine laboratory experimentation' would be necessary to end up with the specific chemicals which the Plaintiff had shown would work and that there were also a number of reaction variables: times, temperatures, pressures, concentrations and so on which could also affect the industrial synthesis in determining practical success or failure. Counsel then appeared to leave consideration of the Patent-in-suit in order to concentrate on the Witness's general approach to the methodology of his experimental work and his wide personal experience in planning and directing research investigations. To all these questions, he received academic 'straight bat' replies indicating a good knowledge of the statistical design of crucial experiments and the necessity of varying conditions over as wide a range as possible, particularly the importance of not drawing sweeping conclusions from too narrow a spectrum of results.

Slowly Counsel began to feed into some hypothetical polymer synthesis a list of variables, the same list as had been agreed to influence the patented reaction ... to which Proudfoot correctly replied that, for each experimental variable one might need to investigate by experiment five or six different values. As the tally increased, the 'front row' totted up the total number of variables multiplied by the total number of values multiplied by the total number of materials which amounted to such a grand total of experiments as represented a research program of many man-years. Counsel quoted this figure and then asked the Witness if he still thought that the invention was obvious ... Needless to add that Counsel's approach had in mind particular case law: *American Cyanamid v Ethicon* and that a finding of 'non-obviousness' based on this authority duly appeared in the Judgement.

What to do if you forget

All novice Experts are overly concerned about the potential consequences of a memory lapse. They should be reassured that:-

* a serious lapse hardly ever happens; and

* a minor lapse can often be dealt with in re-examination.

But if you do mislay some detail[30]:-

"Better by far you should forget and smile
Than that you should remember and be sad"

There is a suggestion of slickness, of a 'lesson learnt', when the Witness answers every time along lines such as:-

"My opinion is 'A B C' .. and this is supported by the paper of Joshua Hickhinbotham, J B Smugley Jnr, X Q Katskradel, and Z Z Z Funk Annalen der Fisch und Meistersingernwändeln Putschchemie (1897), 403 (xvi), 1235-1247"

To forget some of the details is not only more true to life but also kinder on the shorthand writers. It is enough to say, when pressed about the basis for the opinion, that you recall an early paper which covers the subject-matter. An experienced Expert may even suggest, in so many words, that this paper may be located by his side's instructing Solicitor, so directly inviting the paper to be put to him later in 're-examination'.

On the other hand, mistakes which arise as a result of a skilled cross-examination which throws doubt on your Expert understanding of the basis of a process can be a quite different matter[31]:-

"The Centipede was happy quite,
Until the Toad in fun
Said 'Pray which leg goes after which'
And worked her mind to such a pitch,
She lay distracted in the ditch
Considering how to run"

---

[30] Christina Georgina Rossetti (d. 1894) Remember

[31] Attributed to Mrs Edward Craster (d. 1874)

Fun or not, the Toads you will meet in court can ask damaging questions and the Expert cannot permit himself the luxury of such a 'distraction' when giving evidence under cross-examination without falling into the ditch. You are there to give your explanation ... and it is needed *now*. When you enter the Witness Box, you must know what you believe about the technical points in the case and be able to put over your views clearly. This being so, without offering any offence to cross-examining Counsel, his instructing Solicitor or his Expert advisers, if you are prepared take heart that[32]:-

"One man that has a mind and knows it can always beat ten men that havnt and dont"

Mistakes by Counsel

Mistakes in cross-examination are not necessarily made by the Witness. Due to poor instruction or a failure to understand the precise technical issue, Counsel may get his question wrong and this can be quite disconcerting to the Expert. Normally a little polite and good-natured dialogue between Counsel and Expert enables Counsel to canter round the course again and take the jump more cleanly. However if he doggedly persists with his original construction, matters can become embarassing or, worse, hilarious.

•   Some years ago, an Expert was being examined about a chemical reaction which exhibited both 'retardation', a reduction in the rate of reaction, and 'inhibition', the existence of an induction or delay period before the reaction commenced. In questioning him on a 'rate of reaction vs time' plot in a cited document, Counsel, normally clear and incisive, got these the wrong way round stating that 'inhibition' involved a 'change of slope'. Witness replied by simply stating that *retardation* was shown by a change of slope, whereas *inhibition* was shown by an *intercept* where the reaction curve crossed the base line. Meanwhile, a flurry of notes and drawings was passing from the opposition's Experts via juniors, solicitors, patent agents and any other able-bodied messengers, all of which seemed to quite overwhelm the inquisitor. After whispered consultation, Counsel apologised to the Witness and to the Court most charmingly, saying that he had "got it all wrong" and that he would take further instruction and return to the subject next morning. The session continued in the best of humour until the Court rose. But, at 10.30 next morning, Counsel got it wrong

---

[32]   George Bernard Shaw (d. 1950) <u>The Apple Cart</u> i

again. This revealed to a now somewhat sombre Court that the concept of an intercept in this particular context might be beyond his grasp. This time, in order to clear up the matter on the Transcript, the Witness, left temporarily as an unguided missile, felt that he had to seize the initiative and explain the graphs in the cited chapter in some detail: what they taught and how they supported the interpretation he had been proposing. Everyone in the courtroom felt acute embarrassment when Counsel apologised yet again to the Witness for the confusion he had caused. Moreover it was at this point in the cross-examination that the Expert, so he has said, felt unusual emotional strain and for some minutes was conscious that his concentration, with a whole day of further examination stretching before him, was less than it should have been. Recovery after such an incident, as after any minor fall, is obviously important and it is not amiss for the novice Expert to try out some cross-examination practice with a friendly Junior well before his first appearance in the Box.

The perilous Re-examination

After the cross-examination is completed, cross-examining counsel will usually sign off with a formal:-

"No further questions, M'Lud".

The Witness is now available for Re-examination by his own counsel. This can be accident prone. The psychology of re-examination is of course particularly difficult for the inexperienced Expert Witness. He has relaxed after being let off the hook by his cross-examiner. He is tired and, since he was banned from feeding at the same lawyer's trough as his team during the period of 'purdah', probably also hungry, thirsty and dangerously hyped[33]. The novice Expert really wants his torture to end here & now and he may feel that there is no problem in saying anything which comes into his head in response to that friendly face with whom he has worked closely during preparation. As when during a military interrogation the soft man follows the hard man as interrogator, any witness should be aware that this could be his most dangerous moment.

---

[33] "Alas! in truth the man but changed his mind,
      Perhaps was sick, in love, or had not dined"
      Alexander Pope (d. 1744)   Moral Essays Epistle i

Re-examination is really intended as an opportunity for his counsel to clarify, dare one suggest 'to reverse', less than satisfactory answers that have found their way on to the Transcript. A short re-examination may prompt a witness to deal with a point which has 'gone wrong'. However, it runs the greater risk of reinforcing, and so drawing special attention to, the significance of his earlier answer[34]. A long re-examination, a rarity, is almost always an attempt to patch up a lost cause.

•   In *General Tire v Firestone*, Charles Taylor, Firestone's chief chemist, was re-examined on the obviousness of the Patent. As mentioned in Chapter 4, this patented invention was (put simply) 'to include large volumes of cheap oil with the rubber to form viable tyre treads of commercial quality'. Under cross-examination, Taylor was obviously deemed by his camp to have proved somewhat less than adequately vehement in presenting the addition of such quantities oil to rubber compounds as a 'well-known and ancient art', as had been confidently expected of him. As the author recalls it the re-examination question was put by Firestone's Counsel, perhaps rather too directly, rather like this:-

"What was your reaction when you heard that large volumes of processing oil could be mixed into these tyre compounds without deterioration of properties?"

After a longish pause came the Witness's fatal answer:-

"I was amazed"

This was followed by sounds of intaken breath, intermingled with an occasional stifled snigger from GT's side. Sir Lionel Heald QC, leading for General Tire, later addressed the Court at length on the question of 'obviousness' returning frequently to the evidence of the skilled man:-

... "You will remember him, my Lord, that nice Mr Taylor, *the one who was amazed*"

For most Expert Witnesses, there is nothing they enjoy more in a trial than to hearing their Counsel say:-

"I have no questions, M'Lud ... May the witness be released?"

---

[34]   "As a dog returneth to his vomit, so a fool returneth to his folly"
Holy Bible   Proverbs xxvi

Helping with cross-examination of the other side's Witnesses

The reader unfamiliar with Court practice may think that giving evidence was what the Expert was hired for. Now that his "die is cast", he can be pensioned off if not put out to graze. In fact, the really hard work of the Expert at Trial has only just begun. The real test of mental agility is assisting Counsel with his cross-examination of the other side's Experts. And of course if the Expert is acting for the Defendants, he will have to undergo this baptism of fire *before* taking his own turn in the Witness Box.

As described at the beginning of this Chapter, the Expert when not actually 'in play' resides in the back row awaiting his moment of action rather (geometrically, at least) like a rook behind a line of pawns. If this is too crowded, he can sit in the seats provided for a credulous but not usually numerous public which has the advantage that he can better appreciate the antics of Opposing Counsel. For the purpose of assisting his own side's Counsel, he is promoted to the front row with the solicitors, facing the court officials, right under the Judge's nose and directly in line-of-sight with the Witness under examination, not infrequently a friend or associate. This has the advantage of providing him with ready access to the best kept set of documents and he is provided with sharpened pencils and coloured pads from which in favourable circumstances the leaves can be torn almost noiselessly. The purpose of this hitec equipment will rapidly become apparent. More important, it puts him in close contact with the instructing Solicitor who knows better than anyone else the location and significance of every reference and document in the case.

In other words, the Expert, having given his 'aria' from the Box now has to pull his weight as a key member of the ensemble. The musical analogy is particularly apposite because the art of 'cross-examining counsel' is not dissimilar from that of the orchestral conductor who has to unfold the structure of the music while both listening to the playing and simultaneously smoothing out any accidents or infelicities which need correction.

Like the conductor, throughout his examination of the Witness Counsel has to think in three time frames:-

- the future i.e. where he is going in his questioning;

- the present i.e. the answers which are now being fed back to him by the Witness; and

- the past i.e. the consequences of any mistakes or admissions made by the Witness ... insofar as they influence the case as a whole. This on-the-hoof analysis of the 'past' must then be fed back as quickly as possible into a re-synthesis of the 'future'.

In order to carry out this mental exercise, Counsel must:-

- understand the technical answers which are being given;

- ascertain whether they are correct and complete; and

- combine them with other evidence in the case, or with new documentation, in order to rejig his amended examination so as to extract the specific admission which is his goal.

The home Expert is convened to assist him in doing all this and, to be completely effective, he must think with his Counsel and if possible anticipate his needs. The Expert can carry out this task in either of two ways which can be described in conventional management jargon as 'reactive' and 'proactive'. That is to say he can wait until requested to give an opinion on some specific question or he can follow the detailed cut-and thrust of the action, anticipating Counsel's needs, preparing and hopefully volunteering the necessary information at exactly the time that Counsel is expected to need it. This latter 'proactive' approach is of course the more difficult, particularly in the matter of accurate timing. But if carried out well it can make an immeasurable contribution to success; if badly it can prove irksome to counsel and reduce his performance.

Reactive support of counsel

To understand even this easier 'reactive' approach, the reader has need to know that examining Counsel does not content himself in public discourse with his temporary prisoner, the Witness, and with the Judge. At the *sotto voce* level, Counsel is also in frequent communication with his instructing Solicitor in front of him and, less frequently, with his Junior behind him who has a special responsibility for control and management of references in the Transcript. This responsibility becomes more and more arduous as the Trial progresses and the Evidence accumulates.

- The late Professor Hermann Mark of Brooklyn Polytechnic Institute was a frequent Expert Witness in court and he told the author that in his latter years he favoured the reactive approach, after first learning to snatch sleep behind a pile of law books. However he appeared mostly in US litigation, which can indeed be protracted, and in the more comfortable ambience of US courtrooms.

Counsel has an enviable ability to talk, to write and to listen to the answer to his last question concurrently and, in deploying this brilliant gift, he will tacitly expect the members of his team to be able to do likewise. It can frequently happen that, while currently dealing with a topic in dialogue with the Witness, Counsel may pose a question to his Expert and it is the duty of the Expert to instantly scribble (legibly) an immediately-understandable opinion-in-reply. This 'note' (conveniently on a 'Post-it' adhesive sheet) is passed, usually via the Solicitor, to within Counsel's field of vision. Such effort may bear fruit, and be incorporated in Counsel's next series of questions, or it may be wasted. Often, the Expert's note is sometimes best accompanied by a sheet torn (yes .. torn!) from one of the citations, with a passage highlighted, as an invitation to put this to the Witness. With a lively and well-informed (or self-opinionated) Witness, such notes, marked citations, and questions can be flying to and fro at a rate of knots and, at each new statement from the Witness, the topics can change with bewildering frequency.

Counsel will not use every note that the Expert supplies on such a reactive basis. Perhaps he has obtained from the Witness meanwhile a sufficient answer for his purpose and thinks it too dangerous to press the topic further; perhaps the technical position is not as clear as he had believed and his earlier question had implied; perhaps he doubts, or fails to understand, the opinion his Expert has expressed and so needs further background in order to sustain a line of questioning based upon it; and so on. However, if the point is an important one, he may well ask the Witness to 'describe his wife, children and pets to His Lordship' (or some faintly more relevant topic), and, while not actually listening to the answer, engage in a whispered though highly concentrated evaluation of the technical state-of-play directly with the Expert sitting before him. This is physically easier for Counsel than for the Expert who has to twist through the aforementioned 180 degrees in order to whisper back, really requiring (as we have already learned) the services of a resident osteopath. To add spice to the occasion, neither knows how long this local dialogue (on usually a contentious and technically complex point involving data and drawings) can continue without premature interruption. At any second, the Witness or, more seriously, the Judge, can lose interest in the material of the 'entracte' and ask for the opera to continue. In the absence of Counsel's guiding baton, a garrulous Expert Witness in the Box may well become engaged in an alternative dialogue with the Judge who, recalling the excitement of his own years as a leader, sees the opportunity of improving upon the quality of upstart counsel's lack-lustre examination. Or left to his own devices an experienced Witness may use the opportunity to clarify and improve upon some of his earlier answers wherein he felt he had not done himself justice, so contradicting a number of usefully injudicious admissions he may have made earlier.

To avoid such problems, any matter which is critical but complicated will usually be 'referred', that is to say Counsel will pass on to other less contentious points with a view to seeking time for a proper dialogue with his Expert adviser during a recess before returning to the point, better briefed, later in his cross-examination. But this strategy of *reculer pour mieux sauter* may be less than ideal from Counsel's viewpoint because a Witness who was non-plussed by, and so poorly resistant to, the original line of approach is quite likely by then to have had time to think further about the matter, refer to additional citations or otherwise prepare himself to deal with a second wave of such questioning. That he is able to do so will obviously improve the quality of the Evidence he is able to give to the Court but may fatally prejudice the 'success' of the cross-examination.

Proactive support of counsel

Many experienced Experts try to anticipate what may be needed in support of their counsel's cross-examination, equipping themselves in advance with the necessary citations and concentrating on key matters culled from the Report or agreed with Counsel in advance of Trial to be essential to his case. Preparation for this has to take place early in the preparation cycle (Chapter 6). Whereas the preparatory briefings with Counsel are, in his view, mostly opportunities for him to see what his Expert may be able to say in terms of Evidence, they are also from the Expert's point of view tacit opportunities to see what his Counsel actually understands about the technical content of the Case. Mentally, the Expert will define the different areas of technology where Counsel's understanding seems to be strong, adequate or weak. If the Expert is sufficiently self-knowing he will already have carried out a similar analysis of his own abilities .. or had it firmly done for him by those instructing .. without benefit of the psychiatrist's *chaise longue*. Any 'weak' areas of Counsel's understanding which are germane to the Case should be bolstered during preparation by detailed analysis of the opposing Expert's Report and by provision of digests, notes, reviews, diagrams and so on which may or may not be read and/or serve their purpose. Despite such diligent preparation, these weak areas may well still be danger points where the cross-examination of the Opponent's Witness could fail.

Prior to the cross-examination of his opposite number, the Expert should try to work closely with his own Counsel and Solicitor so that the Expert is throughly familiar with the ground plan of the cross-examination, both its detailed objectives in terms of key admissions and the nature and quality of technical information which Counsel can muster in support of each of his attacks. At the examination itself, there will be lengthy periods wherein even the proactive Expert will have rather little to do. These will include much factually descriptive Evidence (except in the rare instances where the Witness suddenly exhibits unjustified 'creativity') and those many areas where Counsel already has a strong understanding and is well armed with material. A closer watch on events may be necessary during examination of the 'adequate' areas but usually only if the Witness senses that he may be able to escape from Counsel's interrogation by retreat into the arcane depths of his subject. And in Counsel's 'weak' areas his Expert needs to maintain a 'red alert', listening to and weighing every word spoken, following every document cited word by word, and preparing notes and diagrams in readiness for a call from Counsel ... which in fact may never come. If the summons does come this pre-cooked material can be served as an immediate response to Counsel's hunger for information while others of the team, usually solicitors and junior counsel, hunt for further references or make additional diagrams.

With some counsel, but only those he knows well enough not to be able to offend, the proactive Expert can scribble note after note during such stormy periods of the examination knowing that they will 'catch the eye' even if their content may not prove of any immediate utility. Certain counsel arrange these notes in patterns or fold them into their own notebooks to accord with their 'future plan'. Others glance at them and immediately scrumple them into a ball. Others still leave them in a pristine pile as if 'returned unread'. But the exact meaning of this 'body language' is something which must needs be worked out between Counsel and Expert. There should of course be a balance. Some counsel would naturally find it irritating to see repeatedly noted references to some key citation, such as "Remember 'Hassocks & Grones'!", under their nose when they fondly believe that they have been most skilfully stalking round the boundary of this much-discussed and equivocal publication with the Witness for the past ten minutes. It is probably a bit like your nervous English passenger screaming "Remember *priorité à droite* !" in every French village. So a hyperactive, even if well-informed, proactive Expert will not necessarily be regarded by his every Counsel as unalloyed good news.

Helping Junior Counsel

One particular aspect of proactive Expert activity *is* universally appreciated. This is an analysis of technical answers from the previous day by the opponent's witness who is still under cross-examination. The results of such overnight analysis are most usefully introduced into the system via Junior Counsel who will already be fully familiar with what has been said and have his copy of the Transcript ready marked up for his leader. It is quite common for technical examinations, particularly of minor witnesses, to be carried out by technically qualified Juniors. This is a good shopwindow for their advocacy. They prepare thoroughly and in the author's experience seldom fail to make a good job of it. But there is one small problem.

Most Juniors rehearse their cross-examination with their own Expert but still need his help and advice if the Witness introduces new or unexpected technology into his answer. Consequently there is the same need for rapport between the Expert and the Junior as there would normally be between the Expert and his Silk. However the Junior occupies and carries out his cross-examination from the third row, separated from the front bench by his leader and an impenetrable barricade of bundles. It is usually beneath the Leader to act as postman. He will ignore the accumulating notes because he is already preparing himself for examination of another Witness or writing preliminary notes for his Speech. In his increasingly desperate attempts to find a perch the supporting Expert can site himself in the back row, overpopulated and bereft as it is of working copies of the documents and without the important liaison with the solicitors to which attention was drawn earlier ... but this is not usually a satisfactory solution, particularly since Junior Counsel has to turn his back on both his Witness and the Judge in order to converse. This is a problem the author has never solved; neither one suspects has any satisfactory solution been found by solicitors and counsel. The only short-term strategem for the keen Expert is to crouch expectantly on his haunches at the end of Row 3 like a badly-behaved family Labrador during the cheese course of a domestic dinner-party, providing further and better grist to the mill of his physiotherapist.

Evidence 'in camera'

Trials are normally open to the public; but occasionally Trials or some portion of them are held 'in camera', that is to say without communication of the proceedings to the public. Procedurally, this is a perfect curse. It also adds to the cost and duration of the Trial. Not only are a number of one's useful assistants often barred from the Court but separate Transcripts of Evidence are required, for the secret bits on the one hand and for those portions in the public domain on the other. In asking questions, giving evidence and so on, one has to be perpetually aware of whether the 'ban' is 'on' or 'off', even when referencing between previous Answers. Judge's are now taking a quite robust view with client's representatives to the effect that old 'commercially-sensitive' information is stale news. They will assert that such documentation is probably already common knowledge throughout the industry and will be unlikely to qualify for special treatment in camera. This has provided a most welcome simplification of Trial procedure.

Video-evidence

In an interesting new development, in order to avoid unnecessary expense, Expert testimony was given via a video link from Japan. The results to date are regarded as only partially successful, problems arising in the presentation of documents to the Witness and in the necessity to repair to smaller premises wired for the relay which can exclude members of the litigation teams and limit public access[35].

---

[35] The author is grateful to Edward Nodder for this information and interim assessment.

12   After The Trial: Judgement; Appeal; Damages Enquiry

The Judgement is the decision of the Court as to whose case has succeeded and whose failed. It also may incorporate or add on an Order as to damages and costs. Though in a short and simple case it can be given *ex tempore* a Judgement is usually 'reserved' ... that is to say the Judge takes away his or her personal notes made during the Trial, the transcripts of evidence and speeches, the documents which have been cited, together with any key exhibits and then prepares a considered review document stating the grounds leading to the decision. The Judgement is traditionally read by its author initially in open court, a somewhat forbidding experience for the representatives of the Parties roughly half of whom present are going to lose their shirts[1]:-

"So having ended, silence long ensewed,
Ne Nature to or fro spake for a space,
But with firm eyes affixt, the ground still viewed.
Meane while, all creatures, looking in her face,
Expecting th' end of this so doubtfull case,
Did hand in long suspence what would ensew,
To whether side should fall the soveraigne place:
At length, she looking up with chearefull view,
The silence brake, and gave her doome in speeches few."

The Judgement is later revised in detail, such as by editing of the Transcript, and handed to the representatives of the Parties prior to publication. If our side has won, a champagne lunch for the team may be in order. But if our side has lost, the event usually turns into a wake terminated by an emollient conference with Leading Counsel who advises on grounds for a possible appeal.

A good Judgement defines the issues between the parties and states the statutory Law which applies, supported by case law usually in the form of quotations from relevant earlier judgements, particularly appeal judgements. Having thus set down the criteria which will be employed to reach a decision, the Judge then examines the *documents*, stating what the key passages mean, the *evidence* that has been given, weighing its quality and relevance, and the *arguments* put forward by Counsel in support of their respective cases. Both the reasoning and wording of the Judgement are of

---

[1]   Edmund Spenser (d. 1599) <u>The Faerie Queen Nature's Reply to Mutability</u>

crucial importance since they are likely to be examined in minute detail at a subsequent hearing before the Court of Appeal. Usually it is clarity itself, but occasionally it may be in part delphic, as if[2]:-

"The quarrel is a very pretty quarrel as it stands; we should only spoil it by trying to explain it"

This, of course, is where the thrust of any Appeal is likely to be concentrated.

How Judges review Expert Evidence

We noted in Chapter 11 that Judges are normally exceptionally courteous and helpful to Expert Witnesses in person. They understand the artificiality of the Trial situation and the unfamiliarity of the surroundings in which an architect, scientist or engineer finds himself. The majority are readily prepared to make due allowance for any hesitancy or lack of composure. Experts are there to help them. Until it becomes clear beyond all shadow of doubt that the man 'in the box' is being deliberately unhelpful, he will be given the benefit of the doubt. However, as we have also seen, it is the purpose of an Expert's appearance at a Trial to impart information. It will often be mentioned approvingly by the Court if this is done succinctly, for instance by directly addressing the questions posed by counsel with clarity and consistently with documentation in the case. Likewise, if this has not been done well, the Trial Judge may draw attention to the fact in the Judgement, particularly if the Witness's answering has bordered on the evasive. The Judge will usually make clear whose evidence he has relied on and the basis for that reliance. Experts are sometimes slow to appreciate that it is not so much their own personal view about the technology which is really being sought but rather a consensus view of 'people like them' in the appropriate industry as at the relevant date. Of course under examination one must say what one really believes but gratuitous presentation of a personal theory of say 'heat transfer' as 'digging among the atoms by little green insects from Saturn' may do little for an Expert's credibility in his field. In fact such an approach may reasonably result in the rest of his evidence being devalued or set aside. This will be as clearly set out in the Judgement as it would in a good critic's review of an opening night.

---

[2]   Richard Brinsley Sheridan (d. 1816) The Rivals iv

Judges naturally prefer the evidence of the opposing Experts to be reconcilable in the form of an overall plan or theory which they can use as common background information to the technology in dispute. Sometimes this can be achieved and, if so, usually results in a satisfactory outcome. If Expert Evidence cannot be so reconciled, Judges will often draw attention to this and speculate that one or the other of the technologists concerned seems to hold personal views not in accord with those of his peers.

While in scientific circles such minority views may occasionally be illuminating, in court it is more likely that they will be regarded as quirky, and it is in such cases that the less orthodox evidence may be devalued or even set aside. It is therefore important that those hiring Experts (see Chapter 3) should be aware of whether or not their man is 'mainstream' or a unique, and probably vocal, dissenter. The pioneer researcher, known world-wide for his fearless expansion of the boundaries of his subject, may be justifiably famous and rightly regarded by his peers as a cult figure. Such is the way that science develops by argument and by often acrimonious debate that his polarised intellectual contributions may have forced a less trendy establishment to assemble the counterarguments of orthodoxy in a much more succinct and credible form. This progress by debate may be vital for the growth of scientific knowledge but it is likely to be of no help at all to a Court until the outcome of such debate has been resolved and generally accepted.

The Court is seeking scientific explanations based on established consensus and belief such as would be selected by the author of a reputable teaching manual which he intended as a firm intellectual basis for first-year undergraduates embarking on a career in the field.

Conflicts of Evidence

Not infrequently there are head-on conflicts of technical evidence. As previously mentioned, these are less likely to be about the facts of a given situation or the data obtained in characterising it (... although this does sometimes happen) than about the interpretation of the data. In such situations the Court is again forced to express a preference for testimony of one witness or group of witnesses over another and to give reasons for this preference. Alternatively, the Judge may discard the views of both Plaintiff and Defendant on this point.

•   For instance in a recent Judgement Aldous J. rejected the evidence of a rather too-dogmatic Expert witness who refused to make any allowance for valid counter-arguments which should prudently have caused him to at least modify his views:-

"Dr White in his evidence-in-chief said that Professor Black's view of how polymerization could occur would not happen because of steric hindrance. He also said that if the PEGDA did polymerize it would separate into a separate phase and would not form an inter-penetrating network.

In cross-examination .. he accepted that the mechanism of polymerization suggested by Professor Black was plausible but maintained that steric hindrance would prevent it. He also maintained his view that if the PEGDA polymerized it would separate out. He said that polymers basically did not mix because the entropy of mixing was too low. He was not aware of the solubility parameters of the materials which were similar, nor did he observe the experiment to see whether phase separation occurred. His opinion that phase separation would occur was based upon his view that, in general, polymers did not mix. I did not find Dr White's evidence, that the ingredients .. could not cure, persuasive. If the mechanism was plausible, then I can see no reason why inter-penetrating networks should not be established. The fact that polymers in general do not mix appears to me to be irrelevant. Here there are materials with similar solubility parameters which are mixed, and I can see no reason why separation should take place during polymerization.

Further I had the impression during Dr White's cross-examination that he realised that his opinions might need qualification, but even so was not prepared to accept that fact..."

This extract (in which fictitious names have obviously been substituted) illustrates the detailed level at which the modern English patent judge will seek to resolve such conflict of Expert evidence. The Trial Judge had clearly expected Dr White to go beyond his repeated generalizations about the difficulty of mixing of polymers and to deal specifically in his cross-examination evidence with the special case of joint polymerization of mutually-soluble monomers to form intermingled polymers of similar solubility parameter, a principal thermodynamic criterion of compatibility.

Rarely, and usually in some desperation, Counsel will have attempted to discredit an Expert by suggesting that he is untruthful. Unless this is demonstrably the position, as shown by major inconsistencies in testimony clearly recorded on the Transcript, this is a risky line of attack which is unlikely to gain the sympathy of most English judges.

- To quote from a judgement dealing with such a case, in which the character of the (corporate) inventor was under direct attack:-

"Counsel for the Defendants submitted that Dr Inhouse was an unsatisfactory witness and that I should not place reliance on his testimony. He submitted that Dr Inhouse had exaggerated the attempts to solve the problem, had misrepresented his involvement .. and also that when being asked about the notebook .. sought to rely upon a matter which he must have known was false ... Dr Inhouse appeared to me to be a truthful witness. I do not believe that his evidence, when read as a whole, shows inconsistencies or exaggeration. In any case I have not found it necessary to rely on those parts of his evidence that were criticised."

It is probably a mistake of tactics for Counsel to bring the Judge into an unnecessary moral confrontation with the Witness. A judge endeavours to carry out his task of balance and assessment on a higher plane than that of the human farmyard which generates his business. Most judges wish to take the detached view[3]:-

"Thus I live in a world rather as a spectator of mankind than as one of the species"

Nevertheless, there have been cases of the court-room discreditation of Experts. These have usually occurred not simply as a result of some crude prompting of toiling counsel but rather through conclusions drawn personally by the Judge in listening to the Evidence and surveying the witness's demeanour under cross-examination. In contrast to the scene here on or beyond the fringe of Europe, in the court-rooms of the USA attempted discreditation seems often to be a first rather than a last resort.

- The author remembers an expedition during the early 80s to the land that is almost-free both to give evidence himself and to hear the cross-examination of his opposite number, an elderly scientist with distinguished credentials and impeccable experience in ivy-league universities and several of the greatest and best chemical corporations. Smith's friendly Attorney waded into his bellicose cross-examination from the opening bell, charging up to his elderly victim on the Stand and waving a Transcript of his earlier

---

[3]   Joseph Addison (d. 1719)   The Spectator No. 1

253

Evidence in his face:-

"You're not much good at this, are you, Doctor?" he ranted "That's what you said to me during your Deposition, wasn't it .. that you were 'not much good at it?'" "Not much good at anything, is that it?" " Is that why you are here giving evidence .. still knowing nothing about it .. ?"

and so on in like vein for the obligatory eight-minute softening up period. Then, rather as an anti-climax, the technical questions began. The Judge showed no special reaction to this immoderate preliminary onslaught and made no mention of it it in his otherwise voluminous Judgement. In other words one has to presume that this sort of behaviour is "par for the course" in US trial procedure.

Appeal

We have indicated that a significant proportion of judgements of the lower Court are appealed. This may take place in the hope of reversing the decision but is just as likely to be for tactical reasons, for instance delay or the need to keep the question of validity open during proceedings elsewhere under corresponding patents. Having won at first instance, and now in the possession of a closely reasoned lower-court Judgement which confirms everything they have privately believed about the excellence of their case for so many years, with regard to the loser's Appeal successful litigants tend to take the simple-minded view[4]:-

"What Judgement shall I dread, doing no wrong?"

But dread they should learn to ... 'right' or 'wrong'. It is perhaps human nature that the losing parties in the lower court will put much more time and effort into preparation of their Appeals than will the smug and self-satisfied 'winners'. This becomes obvious in connection with the further employment of their Experts, who are too-seldom consulted again by their clients or their solicitors after an original win in the lower Court until too late they are told of a fiasco on Appeal. Then the Experts can only muse[5]:-

"But what is past my help, is past my care"

---

[4] William Shakespeare (d. 1616) The Merchant of Venice i

[5] Francis Beaumont (d. 1616) & John Fletcher (d. 1625) The Double Marriage

On the contrary the Experts on the losing side, or occasionally a new team designed to patch up a sinking ship, will have assured themselves of consultancy involvement for the duration. Chastened counsel will now have time and budget to consider their Experts' every revelation, will work up the technology as never before and, come the opening of the Appeal, will continue to refer to the Expert for explanations in dealing with any technical questions raised by the Appeal Judges during the Hearing. The result is likely to be the brilliant representation of a technical case which had perhaps been barely sketched to the lower court Judge.

Contrast this with an erstwhile victor's reiteration of old and tired 'winning arguments' from his lower court triumph, put inappropriately in attempted rebuttal of novel technical approaches which are being canvassed by the now well-schooled 'vanquished' party who have cunningly cloaked them in some of the existing Evidence culled selectively from the Transcript. Finding himself in this situation, Counsel's heart may be in the right place but he can be easily overwhelmed by a flood of new technology for which his work with his Experts prior to the Trial perhaps a year or more before will not have prepared him. Despite a brave face, secretly and inwardly he may well be wishing[6]:-

"Where my heart lies, let my brain lie also"

This expensive and wholly unsatisfactory disadvantage of English IP litigation which seems to be a major cause of reversals seems to be overcome in the USA by the requirement for written summaries of the litigants technical cases in the form of Pre-Trial and Post-Trial Briefs. These avoid to a large extent the element of 'technical ambush' which we have cherished for so long on this side of the Atlantic. They should certainly be tried out in UK litigation.

Pre-trial and Post-trial briefs in US litigation

They are succinct summaries (often only forty or fifty pages in length) of a case, at the stage the technology finds itself as revealed by the Evidence. They are prepared by both the Parties in a dispute so as to show clearly both the common ground and the extent of the remaining differences between them. Being the essence of the legal arguments, their preparation involves

---

[6]   Robert Browning (d. 1889)   One Word More xiv

enormous care and effort on the part of the drafting Attorney who takes every opportunity to consult with his Experts in representing the technical arguments simply and rigorously but, above all, clearly. As a result of reading the 'brief' prepared by the other side, each Party's Expert can then prepare a proper technical agenda of matters which require under-pinning by facts, citations, further consultation with specialists, and so on. In the process of preparation, new and better methods of presentation of the technology to the Court will spring to mind. However above all these periodic summaries mark the development in importance, often the rise and fall of the Court's interest, in the specific technical issues of the case.

Post-trial Appeal briefs will expose exactly where the litigants agree with the lower court's decision and where, and on what specific issues, they believe that the Court was right and where mistaken. This encourages even the 'winner' to make proper technical preparation for an Appeal. In fact in the author's experience the winner normally takes just as much trouble with his preparation for an Appeal as does the loser.

•   A very typical 'winner's' Appeal brief concerns *3M v Johnson & Johnson Orthopaedics* Appeal from the US District Court for the District of Minnesota dated 27 November 1991. Although JJO were the losers in the District Court, the winners did not 'rest on their laurels' and the care in preparation of the 3M brief was such as to re-identify and re-present virtually every one of the many issues, comment on every significant finding of the Court, and recrystallise the case showing clearly why the original decision was correct and should be upheld. Quoted here only by way of example to show the punchy style but without any commital to the rights and wrongs of the argument, the 3M brief deals here with a relatively minor technical point, firmly and fully, as follows:-

"JJO points to certain chemicals used in the 'tacky' prior art for some non-lubricating function such as anti-foaming, and argues that because each of these chemicals, when used in a different form or a much larger amount, is a lubricant of *Scholz*, the prior art is *ipso facto* lubricated. But the district court found that these chemicals, either because in the wrong form or in too small an amount, *did not function as lubricants*. JJO complains that the district court improperly 'disqualified' these so-called prior art 'lubricants'. But plainly, once 'lubrication' is properly understood as not a mere label but meaning something of real substance and function in the context of the invention, the 'disqualification' is compelled."

This passage is extracted from forty-seven pages of detailed argument put forward by a Party which has already had an 'easy' win in the lower court.

Damages Enquiry

Whereas the Trial Judge may make an Order dealing with costs and damages as an addendum to the Trial itself, following a very large and complex case possibly involving a diversity of products a Trial may be followed by a separate Damages Enquiry. Generally the Parties will have agreed to take the assessment of damages or an account of profits as a separate procedure after the Court's finding on validity and infringement.

Much of the Evidence put before the Court at such an enquiry will be of a commercial nature: sales volumes, territories, price codes, discount structures and so on ... together with the dates during which infringement of a valid patent has taken place. Similar information may be presented to the Court in the form of an Account of Profits. It may also happen that composite products are involved, making use of the patent in only a part of their structures; or there may exist non-infringing or marginally-infringing materials alongside a hard-core of clearly infringing lines. In order to assemble an equitably-based catalogue of wrongs which merit financial redress, Experts are often involved. In the biggest and most complex cases the Enquiry may become a 'mini-Trial' involving the presentation of experimental data on the various products which differ from the 'typical product' purchased for the main Trial and used by the Plaintiffs in determining their Proof of Infringement.

The inexperienced Expert, or those instructing him, may be beguiled by an easy win in the lower court into skimping the preparation for the Damages Enquiry. This can have serious consequences.

- Very many years ago in the *General Tire Damages Enquiry*, the author had been giving evidence extending over some weeks for the same client in the Stockholm court and had therefore left a trusted assistant to carry out some crucial litigation experiments for a forthcoming Damages Enquiry requiring the dispersion of carbon black in a mixture of oil and polybutadiene, according to a specific mixing recipe cited in the patent-in-suit. All had apparently gone well with the work and on his return to the UK, two days before the Enquiry opened, he received together with a mountain of other papers a copy of the Assistant's report on the work which gave exactly the test results expected, showing that polybutadiene should be included within the list of infringing materials on which damages should be paid by the Defendants. All seemed in order, the Report was served with the Expert's full approval and he was ready to give evidence on it. In cross-examination, Counsel suggested that an Appendix to this report contained the mixing schedule which had been used. Smith agreed. Counsel asked if it conformed to that in the Patent. Believing it to be so, Smith said "yes". He asked the Expert to take a copy of the Patent and read the details of the test therein specified ... (and his subsequent cross-examination earned Counsel the soubriquet 'MFH' ... but it was really more like gassing a badger!).

As it turned out, the specified ninety-second dispersion period had been extended by the Assistant (without any instruction) to two minutes, and so reported ... a normal sort of adjustment for a skilled technician to make: "just to make sure the carbon black was all properly dispersed", as he confessed rather unhelpfully after the event. But the legal consequence was that the Expert Witness had to admit that the test which had been carried out was *not* identical to the Test specified in the Patent. Though he genuinely believed that this minor alteration would have no effect on the results, he had not actually tried it and so could not be certain of this.

The Court correctly concluded that there was uncertainty over the test result so that oil-extended polybutadiene could not be included amongst the infringing products. As a result of his failure to read every word and check every figure in his assistant's Report including the test procedure stated to be taken from the Patent, the Expert Witness lost for his client a proportion of the back damages to which he was entitled.

As an independent Expert, the author soon found it best not to cultivate a habit of making expensive mistakes like this one. One must quickly learn to give oneself time to read documents properly and always to employ high-grade assistants, familiar with the requirements of litigation work, whom one can trust.

The Damages Enquiry is not a marginally irrelevant 'add-on'. It requires the Expert's full concentration ... and his very best work.

13   Making the Expert cost-effective

Litigation is inevitably expensive and should obviously not be contemplated other than in the context of a realistic budget. Penny-pinching preparation can lead to a lost case. This budget will equate the best possible estimates of the direct costs of winning and of losing an Action against the 'masked' costs of passivity in terms of lost markets and/or low-price competition. A smallish High Court Action in the UK, expected to be heard within a span of (say) five or six days, might involve a minimum direct cost of say £0.5M, to which must be added any damages and/or costs of losing plus the considerable disruption costs of the work of senior members of the organisation. Larger actions, world-wide, could easily budget total costs of £2-3M per annum for three to five years. It is therefore of the utmost importance that a litigation exercise should be budgeted as accurately as possible to give 'value for money'. This includes that part of the budget which provides for Expert's fees and expenses.

It might be thought that the Defendant upon whom the Writ is served will have no choice in whether or not to litigate but, as the earlier chapters 1-4 indicated, there are several courses open to exploration before actually proceeding to Trial. For instance a settlement may be contemplated and discussed between the parties at virtually any time, its likelihood usually depending on the maintenance of courteous, low-key negotiations based on realistic sums in compensation for any possible damage caused.

It is extremely unusual for a writ to appear 'out of the blue'. Most manufacturers, users or importers are fully aware of the nature, strength and ownership of the principal IP in their field of activity and, in consequence, they will be quite well aware when they or their competitors are 'sailing close to the wind'. Bearing in mind that simple notification of a valid patent does not constitute a 'threat', it is quite usual for Directors to have a friendly (or mildly aggressive) telephone confrontation which is the 'shot across their bows'. In the absence of any reaction to this, the aggrieved firm's patent agent will often be instructed to send a formal letter detailing the particular rights which appear to be infringed by a specific product or process. At this stage, if not before, the defending Directors will consult with their own advisers in order to assess the strength of their position relative to that of their adversary. Continuing infringement after this point is therefore a signal that the infringer regards the rights of the infringed as valueless, a view which has probably already been expressed by him in opposition proceedings intended to revoke the grant of the infringed's patents.

Litigation therefore breaks from a slowly gathering storm, giving the adversaries ample time to seek shelter. It should be a consciously chosen course-of-action which must be managed in the same way as any other corporate activity. This includes accurate budgetting in advance of the commencement of formal action. In fact as mentioned elsewhere in this book, many corporations in the USA treat their 'litigation budget' as an ordinary management 'cost centre' and expect it to make its annual target contribution to profitability. Provided that such profit includes saving of the aforementioned masked costs (loss of markets, etc), it is claimed that 'litigation management units' can readily produce a 15 - 20% per annum return on capital. Their existence and activities also contribute to the defence of their company by concentrating the minds of would-be infringers who will know that it is corporate policy to pursue any suspected pirates competently and without hesitation. Such units behave very professionally in maintaining running budget estimates of the cost of litigating versus the cost of settling, so that they are always in a position to choose what appears at the time to be the most cost-effective path.

How Expert Witnesses can be cost-effective

Like any other corporate consultant, the independent Expert should only be retained if he is cost-effective. Cost-effectiveness is measurable in the usual way on the basis of progress towards objectives on a time and expenditure basis. This requires the definition of clear *litigation objectives* which need to be agreed between the Expert and those instructing him and updated from time to time as preparation proceeds, particularly when circumstances may change.

Occasionally, the Expert is asked to estimate in advance his personal time and cost to achieve these agreed objectives but, since litigation is team work and progress also depends on the speed of response from the other side, it is not always easy to be precise about this. The best way is to respond to a draft scenario created by the instructing solicitor indicating the various steps wherein he thinks that Expert help will be required and, if possible, the amount of time involvement which both would or should regard as reasonable for each stage. Using this as a discussion document, it is usually possible to hammer out a costed schedule which will be sufficient for client's internal budgetting purposes.

Typical fee structures

The most usual method of charging by most independent Experts is on a per diem rate plus agreed expenditure on travel, subsistence and approved sub-contract work at cost. Occasionally a 'fee cap' is also agreed, a total which must not be exceeded without obtaining Client (or Solicitor) approval. However others, including the author, do not use the 'per diem' method, preferring a 'per hour' charge rate. This avoids any problem of apportioning time between say two client meetings in London on the same day. In such event each client can be charged directly for the hours engaged and any common travelling time may then be divided between them. Many London solicitors and patent agents also use this system.

The Expert's actual basic rate per hour for preparation, report writing, attendance at experiments and so on, is quite often the same as that which is he charges as a senior industrial consultant to non-litigation clients. However it is normally uplifted by say 50% for overseas work and for attendance in Court. This increase is not so much to reflect the arduous nature of such duties but rather to compensate for the difficulties which result from being incommunicado to other clients for long periods which often requires making costly special arrangements to cover his regular work during these periods and may, at worst, result in permanent loss of business. Subject to the availability of the Expert, on such a plan the client can command more of his time as the case develops, so accelerating the preparation phase. Then if the Expert has no more to contribute, his involvement can be curtailed with consequent saving of fees.

An acceptable basic rate per hour varies according to the qualifications, seniority and particularly litigation experience of the Expert. An experienced Expert learns a new case more quickly, so saving the excessive time otherwise spent in instruction by other expensive professionals (lawyers and patent agents). The experienced Expert commands a higher rate, not so much as is sometimes thought because of his ability to 'think on his feet' or 'perform well under fire' but because he can quickly advise his clients, during careful preparation, of most of the technical arguments which can be put against their case and so can prepare throughly and in advance not only

261

himself but also the rest of his team for the Trial to come. A typical Expert fee range in high-class corporate IP work in the Patent Courts is now from £80 - 230 per hour but in simple cases at more local level rates can be as low as £50 - 75 per hour. These are comparable with the rates charged by UK Patent Agents. These Expert rates include the Expert's own overhead costs and they are reviewed from time to time, often at the end of each calendar year. Rechargeable expenses will comprise first-class train travel, business class air travel, taxis, own car mileage ... plus meals, hotels and any sub-contract work at cost.

It is usual to bill clients quarterly through the instructing solicitors, most of whom settle these accounts within twenty-eight days. If not, they will usually pay on a Statement issued at the end of the month following invoicing. UK value-added tax is added by registered Experts, being shown separately, unless the client satisfies the special Customs & Excise regulations for 'zero rating'. Invoices, when submitted for settlement, should be supplemented by a sheet showing date/ time spent/ work done/ expenses/ fees in abbreviated form. This will help a winning Party recover his costs from the loser. In order to keep fees down to the minimum, prompt payment is assumed. Some solicitors will pay only on receipt of funds from their client but, if this is acceptable to the Expert, he would be advised to confirm that a commercial policy of monthly billing followed by issue of statements is the minimum they employ to achieve settlement of debts. Since it is not appropriate for the Expert to act as banker to his corporate clients and budgetting to do so would unfairly penalise the prompt payers, delayed payments properly accrue interest charges at an appropriate rate such as that fixed in accordance with the provisions of the Judgements Act. To avoid arguments in the future, this provision should best be included in the initial 'letter of agreement'. Moreover in aggravated cases of deliberately delayed payment without proper explanation, it seems not unreasonable to apply the higher rates used by credit card companies and banks when dealing with unauthorised overdrafts. This is a matter which deserves the sympathy of the regulatory bodies and of the courts.

Occasionally, other methods of charging may be preferred by client or may be agreed as suitable for a particular type of project. The most common alternative method is the 'retainer', a negotiated lump sum payable quarterly plus a reduced hourly rate. Rarely, an overall lump sum is negotiated (i.e. a 'fixed price contract'), often with a proportion paid in advance. These methods both have the disadvantage, to client and Expert alike, that it is very difficult to estimate the time likely to be involved, which will determine a 'fair price' for the work actually involved. Moreover settlement of the Action can occur early or late in the preparation for Trial, or not at all ... so that any estimate based on predicated duration or volume of work is necessarily fraught with uncertainty. These disadvantages can be overcome to some extent by negotiating a fixed sum plus contingency fees but only in cases where the 'contingencies' can be adequately foreseen and agreed at the start of preparation.

Costing for the Trial

Since it is usually regarded as essential for the independent Expert to be present in court throughout the Trial, the period involved has to be blocked out of his diary well in advance so that these dates cannot be offered to any other clients. By doing this, the Expert is dedicating himself to the Trial client and in the event of settlement prior to Trial (or its deferment) he will be 'out of work' for this period. An exception to 'time-based' rates is therefore to negotiate a *retention fee* ('retainer') for the period of a Trial. In this event, the starting date is known in advance according to the Court's availability, and counsel can estimate the duration of the Trial quite accurately, often to within a day or two.

This 'retainer' is often handled in the form of a 'packaged tour' contract. About three months in advance of Trial, the Expert is retained for a fixed fee based on the expected hours involved for the period of the Trial. Cancellation of this contract less than two months before the scheduled start of the Trial incurs half fee; and less than one month before Trial, full fee. It is thereby possible to make a reasonably accurate estimate of the cost of Trial which will be of value to the Client when considering the option of settlement of the Action 'at the door of the Court'.

'Value-based' arrangements

Some clients, particularly those with experience of US management habits, may suggest use of 'value billing' in which payments are made to their legal advisers on a scale determined not merely by time but also by the *importance* of the work to the client and the high quality staff, often with unique experience, who must needs be deployed on it. This affects the

Expert Witness too. It is no longer appropriate for the Expert to spend a number of days in the Patent Office library 'mugging up' the detailed subject matter or searching for a few references wherewith to illustrate the common general knowledge in a particular subject area at a particular date. He has had to learn to subcontract this work to competent specialists who charge fees at lower rates.

Likewise it is seldom cost-effective to instruct an Expert simply to go away and 'do experiments'. Rather, the Expert should devise or design the Experiments and then if necessary arrange to sub-contract their rehearsal and performance to others who can perform them most cheaply. Then he will only need to visit the laboratory at crucial points when further guidance or interpretation of results is required and for the necessary rehearsal and demonstration runs which he will be required to conduct or witness. When designing a substantial litigation experiment program, it is useful for the Expert to prepare what is in effect a commercial 'tender document' which can be used by the client or his solicitor to seek quotations for carrying out the experimental work from competing university and private-sector laboratories. Many clients are in favour of this approach since it enables quotations for the work to be compared properly on a like technical basis.

Methods not in use

So far as the author is aware, no Expert in the UK has yet been hired on a 'contingency fees' or other results-related basis. 'No win, no fee' may seem attractive to certain US law firms but it could be highly damaging to the independence of Experts whose objectivity would risk being undermined through the linings of their pockets. The same objections can be made to 'discount billing' in exchange for a fixed or minimum volume of work for the client or 'premium billing' in which a higher fee rate is applied in the event of 'success'.

Such methods may well be ephemera born of recession in which managers are forced to earn their spurs by driving a hard bargain. In truth the most cost-effective method is to hire a good and experienced Expert who needs little or no supervision but delivers exactly what is needed at the right time and in the right place. The exact method by which you pay him is of secondary concern.

Quality of work

It goes without saying that the quality of work required of an Expert Witness is that of the highest grade of international consultant. Not only should the advice be good, following diligent preparation, it should also be 'seen to be good'. That is to say letters and reports should be well laid out and accurately reproduced preferably using a modern laser printer.

The speed of response is also vital and the Expert should remain accessible to those instructing him at all reasonable times. This means having available not only telephone lines but also fax, even electronic mail and other forms of communication which those instructing may prefer to use.

• The author recalls one interesting and relaxed academic lecture tour of South Africa when he kept in close contact with in-house counsel of his US client by fax and phone throughout a crucial fortnight when a much delayed final version of the client's Notice of Experiments was about to be served after several detailed amendments. Corrected drafts came and went with startling regularity, one appearing on a Saturday morning on the creaking office fax of an Ostrich Farm, raising clouds of red desert dust, just before a most spectacular ostrich race.

There is really no difficulty in keeping in touch ... and today this applies to almost anywhere in the world.

Use of assistants

If one or more Assistants are employed by the Expert, this can contribute to his cost-effectiveness. However, it is important that:-

• the standards of the Assistants are not in any way inferior to those of the Expert (see Chapter 12); and

• the sub-contracting of work in this way is pre-agreed with the instructing solicitors or attorneys, who may occasionally wish to seek approval from the client.

Keeping the litigation team informed

The most effective way of saving client's money during the preparation of a case is by establishing prompt and thorough two-way communication, particularly of documentation. Some of those instructing are better at organising this than are others. If the Expert receives documents tardily and piece-meal, he can spend more of his time forming half-opinions which have to be revised with each new information input than if he can receive a complete package prior to starting his work.

Likewise staged progress meetings are extremely beneficial but only when thoughtfully scheduled at points where preparation has actually reached a suitable stage for exchange of views. For instance there is little point in holding a meeting to discuss Opponent's Discovery until the Expert has had opportunity to review all of the Discovery documents and reach interim conclusions. If the meeting is to involve counsel, it is important that the Expert should receive a copy of 'Instructions to Counsel' together with any attachments which will be discussed so that he can follow references to these. Obvious ... but it is surprising how many secretaries and paralegals fail to realise this when sending out the papers.

The Expert in his turn must keep his instructing solicitor fully informed on his own work progress and, if a date has been agreed to discuss one of his technical notes, he must see that the draft of it is circulated a few days before the meeting ... without fail.

•　These may seem to be elementary management points but it is in these areas that the author has found in the past that client's time and money have been wasted.

Working overseas

There are various reasons which may make it necessary for an Expert to travel overseas for his client. These include:-

•　to obtain information about a product or process which is likely to be, or which already has been, the subject of litigation in the foreign country;

- to meet foreign Experts, or potential witnesses of fact, who may be appropriate to call as witnesses in a UK Trial;

- to see experiments or tests being run in overseas laboratories;

- to give evidence in a foreign court.

Again, for the same reasons discussed in connection with 'commitment to client for the period of the Trial', because it is necessary to block out several days in one's diary it is usual to charge an uplifted rate for overseas work. Because of this higher charge rate it is even more important to ensure that the Expert is fully instructed with all necessary technical documentation, to which he has made the necessary responses, prior to the overseas visit.

Given this quality of instruction, experience shows that a coordination meeting held over a weekend in, for instance the USA, can be extremely cost-effective not only in information exchange but also in the forging of direct personal links between scientists or engineers which will be used time and time again (via phone or fax) during subsequent preparation. Such team building activities are crucial in preparation for a successful Trial.

14   The future of the Expert Witness

In this book the idea is advanced that the resolution of disputes through use of Expert opinion is firmly rooted in our western culture. While resolution procedures might be improved, for instance by the substitution of considerably more 'written' in place of 'oral' affirmation, as advocated in earlier Chapters, there seems no need for any modernistic trend to replace present mechanisms, merely a need for steady evolution. Settlement of disputes by the methods here outlined therefore seems to be a 'growth area' for the foreseeable future, whether this be by litigation in the courts or through less formal, ADR processes.

Some current areas of activity: computer software; pollution; biotechnology; new materials

There are certain technical areas wherein there is presently a flurry of activity and considerable litigation involving the use of Expert Witnesses. A number of these are in the areas which are loosely designated 'emerging technologies' in which the technical and/or legal principles are still fluid, the application of the statutes often far from clear and there is a dearth of established case law.

•   Computer Software

The principle IP technique for the protection of proprietary software is the law of copyright. Despite the strenuous efforts of the software houses ... those six-page 'agreements not to copy' (which do any of us read?) that accompany even a $50 notepad package ... the law has proved extremely difficult to interpret and enforce. Instead of relying simply on legal protection, manufacturers have shown some ingenuity in building deterrents to copying into their products which easily defeat the casual would-be infringer if not the professional thief.

•   The defeat of Apple in its suit against Microsoft ('Windows') and Hewlett-Packard ('New Wave') programs came as a bit of a surprise. Many had regarded the Macintosh screen display as one of the unique selling features of their system. The San Francisco Judge found that such basic elements as on-screen 'icons' and overlapping 'windows' were either not covered by copyright or already included in a 1985 licensing agreement between Apple and Microsoft. Apple's defeat opened the way for a user-friendly IBM-compatible operating system which is likely to become ubiquitous. According to one report[1], independent Experts for Apple had assessed potential damages at \$5.5 bn. But an appeal may be pending.

The balance has been redressed to some extent by a recent ruling in the English High Court that copyright may be infringed without necessarily duplicating the actual program source codes. It is sufficient for the Plaintiff to establish that the 'look and feel' of the new program depends on that of the old. Such non-literal infringement of copyright is novel and must rely to a large extent on Expert evidence as to the similar structure and organisation of the two programs.

In Europe, there has been a substantial effort to harmonise divergent laws on the protection of data-bases resulting in a draft European Community (EC) Directive on Database Copyright. The requirements proposed are much less stringent than those presently enforced under UK (and Irish) law and, in consequence, the Directive is unattractive to many of our own data-base suppliers who comply. The draft Directive would provide for:-

       i: 10-year protection against illicit extraction of data from a protected data-base; and

       ii: extension of regular copyright (such as applies already to anthologies of printed material) to a collection of data selected in such an original way as to represent an 'intellectual creation' of its author.

Provision ii obviously provides considerable scope for Expert testimony which will extend from consideration of the originality of the data selection *per se* to its novel arrangement, tabulation, indexing, abstracting and so on which gives the data-base value-added so justifying its selling price. However it is generally in accord with the provisions of the corresponding US copyright law. Harmonisation may not be easy because English law vests the copyright in the text itself, which may be just a collection of words, and does so for no less than 50 years, whereas the laws of other European countries vest rights in the authorship. A view has been expressed that 'intellectual creativity' is not the right criterion but that protection should also be awarded for diligence of a routine nature in making the

---

[1]   Louise Kehoe   "Apple suit dismissed in surprise ruling"   Financial Times 16 April 1992

selection[2]. Again the distinction between 'creativity' and mere hard slog will no doubt, in individual cases, require the evidence of Experts. The whole matter is bedevilled by concepts of 'public interest', not locking away information of value to the public, and 'restraint of trade', the stifling of free competition by award of a monopoly, as exemplified by the *Magill* case which has been appealed to the European Court of Justice. Even more contentious are the proposals regarding compulsory licensing of material not available elsewhere which, if implemented by the Commission, would certainly generate a plethora of disputes.

- ## Pollution and Environmental Protection

Environmental Law is one of the great growth industries in a time of recession and we have recently seen the establishment of the first Chair in this subject at Imperial College[3]. Several firms of solicitors have set up specialist groups and there is now at least one UK journal devoted to legal developments[4].

- The position seems not unlike that depicted, albeit on a smaller scale, in 'Clochemerle'. After a couple of centuries of reprehensible disposal of all our industrial waste at random in seas, in rivers, into the air, and soaked 'away' into the ground, the world's conscience suddenly demands an instant cleansing of both new and old process industries. Vote-hungry politicians rush through the necessary, usually ill-drafted legislation. Faced with election pressures, these try to apply it retrospectively while industry does the best it can to keep in business through an amalgam of overt compliance and covert infringement, the meanwhile competing with less constrained producers who, for various reasons, often geographical, are able to operate more economically outside the regulations. In these circumstances one can foresee litigation, mostly funded by the insurers, which stretches to at least the middle of the next century.

Legal control of the environment is not in itself new, as evidenced for instance by an early case involving the contamination of a well by raw

---

[2] Hamish Sandison, of Linklaters & Paines, quoted by
Celia Hampton in Financial Times 28 May 1992

[3] The incumbent is Prof Richard Macrory, sponsored by solicitors
Denton Hall Burgin & Warren

[4] "Environmental Law Monthly" published by Monitor Press

sewage[5]. But over the past few years there has been an enormous widening of the products, processes and situations which are subject to statutory controls. Except in the very largest industrial companies, the impact of these laws is only just beginning to be felt. Many are worried about the potential cost of all this. Despite its simplicity and perceived 'fairness', it is easier to agree with the principle[6] that 'the polluter pays' if you are unwise enough to believe that it is someone else's money that he is going to pay with. Important sub-divisions of environmental law include:-

- Water purity

- Contaminated land

- Waste disposal

- Environmental nuisances: smoke, smell and noise

These are all in the province of the chemist Expert. By way of example:-

- In even a small (and apparently local) pollution incident, the sums of money involved may be large. For instance, in *Cambridge Water Company v Eastern Counties Leather et al (1991)* mentioned earlier, mixed chlorinated solvents ("perchlorethene", PCE) were spilled and inadvertently allowed to contaminate an aquifer. The aquifer was subsequently tapped by the water company. After testing to new, more stringent EC limits for chlorine contamination, the levels in the water were later found to be too high. So persistent was the contamination that, despite attempts to clean up, the water company was eventually forced to abandon this source and draw from another point on the water table, requiring the construction of a new pumping station. The costs of all this amounted to about £1m which the water company was trying to recover. But the Action failed in the High Court, partly because the Court accepted the argument that frequent experience of small spillages of the noxious solvents, which did not cause such water contamination, could not have alerted the Supervisors to the potential consequences of a larger spill.

This may have been a bad point. To a technologist, it seems rather like saying that the terrorist who detonates a ton of explosive in a town centre

---

[5]   *Ballard v Tomlinson*   (1885)

[6]   *Environmental Protection Act*   (1990)

'could not have foreseen' the devastation it would cause from his limited previous experience with 2 pounders in litter bins. But, in accord with common sense, the Trial Judge Kennedy J. also found that an act which was legal at the time it was committed could not become illegal as the result of subsequent legislation:-

"That there should be an award of damages in respect of the 1991 impact of actions that were not actionable when they were committed fifteen years before is, to my mind, not a proposition the common law would entertain".

Nevertheless, the Appeal Court has recently overturned this judgement on the grounds that the prior pollution was actionable and that liability was strict. From this, it followed that negligence did not have to be proved. As Alan Fisher[7] writes:-

The (appeal) judgement has opened the door to retroactive pollution liability which even the most radical EC commissioner would fight shy of. Furthermore, it has done so without having to answer to any electorate for the economic damage such a ruling might inflict".

This sort of case may provide work for lawyers and Experts for decades to come. While old cases are being re-opened, and the Experts are asked to indicate the probability of historic contamination leading to present loss, green-field sites will be desecrated with new industrial building. Already one can see the price of the former industrial land, which we should prefer to see as the site of future industry, falling in the absence of bidders. True green-field sites, with zero risk of accrued environmental liabilities for industrial use, will be at a premium and there will be further encroachment on the rapidly dwindling countryside.

Meanwhile, contaminated or supposedly contaminated wasteland will remain as the veritable 'blots on the landscape'. The whole problem of clean-up costs and compensation has been described as[8]:-

" .. a nettle that has to be grasped"

---

[7] A Fisher "Guilty before the law .. but quite legal at the time" The Times 8 December 1992

[8] R Burnett-Hall "Land blighted by its registration" The Times 7 April 1993

272

- <u>Biotechnology</u>

One of the major industries of the future, biotechnology already qualifies as one of the most active in seeking patent protection for its products and processes. The costs of this protection may typically lie in the range 5-10% of research expenditure. Global expenditure on biotech patents has been estimated to exceed $100m per annum[9] against a commercial background in which some $1bn of new money was raised in public offerings by US biotech companies during the year 1991 alone. The milestone US patent (to Stanford U. & U.Cal.), for the recombinant DNA processes on which genetic engineering is based, casts a shadow over all more limited successor patents, covering specific processes and/or products in that country. Of course, as mentioned earlier, prior publication in the American style can invalidate foreign filings.

<u>Patents for living creatures</u>

Historically, patents have not been awarded for living creatures, but the impact of genetic engineering, an undeniably inventive interference with 'God's will', has caused some hurried rethinking in the patent offices. For instance, the European Patent Office (EPO) recently granted a patent on the 'oncomouse', a transgenic animal engineered by Harvard University for use in cancer research. This was at least partly because of the importance of such research. This first patent was recently followed by grant of others but there are oppositions in the pipe-line. Such granting of monopolies is being vigorously opposed by lobby groups, so that the future of these cases is by no means clear. The industry is pressing for clear directives, which it hopes will enable it to protect a wide range of engineered animals and plants.

<u>Patenting 'Man'</u>

In the USA, with government approval, the National Health Institute (NHI) recently filed nearly 3000 applications for human gene fragments. These they had identified without in most cases knowing their *in vivo* function. This has upset many biologists and is sparking off IP wars between traditionally collaborative scientific organisations; for instance the UK Medical Research Council (MRC) is said to be planning to patent about

[9] C Cookson & J Clayton   "Of mice, men and money"   <u>Financial Times</u> 3 June 1992

2000 of its own gene fragments. However, subject to expert evidence not yet adduced, it is quite possible that both the NHI and MRC applications may be rejected. Not that any decisions are likely to be reached quickly, in view of the huge backlog of biotech applications awaiting examination which may take up to five years to emerge from the system.

Casualties have already occurred in scientific circles, as witness the resignation in April 1992 of Dr James Watson who was in charge of the US-dominated Human Genome Project. Watson was not alone in taking the view that knowledge of the detailed sequence of human genes was the cornerstone of biotechnology during the next century, including the seeding of a revolution in healthcare products, and that research leading to this knowledge was going to be seriously impeded by indiscriminate claiming of bits and pieces of IP at an early stage of the mapping process.

It is generally acknowledged that, by restricting product and market development, this whole patenting circus is doing untold damage to an important emerging industry and could in the future result in the commercial failure of many innovative companies. But there is as yet no sign of the broad cross-licensing deals which have successfully resolved parallel problems in the electronics business. Since the bio-industries have, as yet, few cash-cow products, and very many ideas which may never make money at all, this obsession with 'rights' and their protection may simply be a symptom of biotechnology's immaturity compared with that of more-established industries. If the industry wishes to approach its projected $50bn turnover by next century, it has not got long to set its house in order. This may be more quickly and easily achieved by ADR and arbitration than by use of legal systems currently lacking a proper basis of case law which can properly guide the decisions of the Courts.

Patents for Agrochemicals

One exception, wherein money is already being made, is the supply of genetically-improved seeds. Typically this has sparked off political rows such as the divisions which have occurred between Members of the European Parliament (MEPs) and the EC. The MEPs want their constituent farmers to be able to re-use such seeds after the harvest without payment of further royalties, whereas the Commission has supported the bioagricultural industry who assert that this will reduce their returns so cutting investment in an important part of the European economy. One looks forward to Expert testimony that a particular crop has been grown from strains of a particular age, with or without the benefit of the necessary 'rendition to Caesar'[10]. However so fast is the current development and emergence of new and better strains of seed that, for the moment at least, most farmers would have little incentive to 're-use', better yields being obtainable by use of the updated products. In other words, it is presently more cost-effective to pay for the newest technology.

In December 1992, the EPO finally confirmed patents granted for herbicide-resistant plants to Plant Genetic Systems and Biogen. These are genetically engineered to resist a specific broad-spectrum weed-killer which would be co-marketed as part of a 'farming package'. At the hearing, Greenpeace submitted that the invention was immoral, and so not patentable, on the basis that it facilitated greater use of herbicides which would cause greater harm to the environment. Whatever the rights and wrongs of this particular submission, the way now seems to be open to cite independent Expert evidence on *the morality of any industrial process* which, if accepted by the Court, could even lead to revocation of granted patents. Ministers of religion: pastors, vicars, rabbis, ayatollahs, ... the Witness Box is yours!

- Pharmaceuticals

Pharmaceuticals constitute a special case in patent law. Because of the the exceptionally long gestation period from filing applications to emergence of a fully approved and certified product, which is commonly ten to fifteen and may be as long as twenty years, the normal twenty-year life of a Patent is not long enough to give the manufacturers adequate protection. In Europe, a short development period of five years or under which is typical of products as a whole will not qualify for an extended patent, but a period of more than ten years will qualify for a Supplementary Protection Certificate (SPC) giving five years of further protection. Development periods of between five and ten years will qualify for a lesser supplement. While the date of application is unequivocal, difficulties may well arise in determining exactly when a particular drug was first authorised for use in the EC. For instance, one can now envisage the need for independent Expert opinion which will distinguish between large-scale testing, test marketing and full-scale sales.

---

[10]   Holy Bible <u>St. Matthew xxii</u>

Claims against the drug companies

The drug companies, themselves extremely active in litigation, and not least in the Patent field, are sitting targets for attacks by a gold-digging public. Since the perfectly genuine and pathetic "Thalidomide" case against Distillers, the Courts have been flooded with frivolous cases which have now reached epidemic proportions. This is the province of the medical Experts and one can only quote from a recent article by Doctor Theodore Dalrymple[11] which portrays the scene, in his usual vein, as a 'black comedy'. He writes:-

"There is a great deal of money to be made from misery, and even more from vague dissatisfaction. First we doctors prescribe tranquillisers; the patients become addicted to them and sue the drug companies; then the lawyers for the patients and the drug companies hire us to testify that the tranquillisers did, or did not, ruin the plaintiff's lives ... We charge £500 a case ... One of my colleagues has seen 170 cases and will pay off his mortgage with the proceeds ..."

The commercial impact of patent litigation between the leading corporations in this industry is serious. To keep in the race, drug companies have to invest heavily in market development before they have establised their proprietary rights in the Courts. One such case is the success, in the US Court of Appeal, of Amgen over Genetics Institute in respect of the anemia-treating drug 'erythropoietin'.

As in the related field of 'biotechnology', there is dispute over the rights which might accrue from the exploitation of natural materials, barks, flowers, and so on, as drug bases. While it may be ovious that to use the natural product as a drug *simpliciter* to treat known conditions cannot easily qualify for patent protection, what about its application to the treatment of new illnesses, or its use as a basis for chemical transformations into new and efficacious products?

This spills over from the commercial into the world of international politics in which developing countries submit to Earth Summits lengthy diatribes about the rape by the developed countries of the Third World's only indigenous assets.

---

[11]   T Dalrymple "If symptoms persist ..."   The Spectator 5 December 1992

- ### New Materials

In contrast with the internecine struggles of the bioscientists, the Materials field seems a haven of well-regulated calm in which the ample guidance of the Statutes is well-supported by a substantial body of authoritative case-law. However this is not to deny that new materials, particularly 'composites', have introduced needs for novel expertise, so that the net for suitable Experts has to be cast ever wider. Perhaps recent advances in super-conductors, novel composites and so on will disturb the equilibrium but, by and large, at present, it is still possible to obtain reliable legal forecasts of the outcome of litigation in a way which has not yet been established in the new areas. Overall, despite the manifold difficulties of the emerging industries, IP law has generally worked quite well in offering a level of protection to innovators commensurate with their expenditure. In this area, it would seem that no one should be looking for fundamental changes, merely for the fine tuning necessary to meet new challenges.

Some other areas where Experts are needed

- ### Products and Structures: fitness for purpose

Every now and then a bridge falls down, an aircraft crashes, or a baby chokes on a plastic toy. Each such tragedy can give rise to an Enquiry at which Expert Evidence is adduced.

- The 'Summerland' enquiry involved an amusement complex on the Isle of Man which was set alight as the secondary result of minor arson in a plastics storage hut adjacent to the main shell of the building. Many died, mostly from inhalation of smoke and toxic (or heated) gases. The Enquiry found numerous departures from recommended practice including the wrong use of materials (fibre-board liners in place of plaster board), lack of fire stopping in the wall cavities, locked emergency exits, and failure of the fire brigade to respond to early calls. Demonstration Experiments connected with this enquiry are described briefly in Chapter 9.

In addition to such large and well-researched incidents, there are myriads of smaller disputes, often involving Trading Standards officers, which are decided at local level and which involve expert evidence of a fairly primitive kind. Such evidence is often little more than informed opinion, unsupported by citations or, in some instances, even test results.

- ### Planning Enquiries

While most of this book has been addressed to resolution of disputes involving technological (scientific and/or engineering) evidence, there are a number of areas in which non-scientists are called as Experts. In particular, architects and town planners regularly give evidence to Planning Enquiries, including Expert opinion on the aesthetic impact of proposed developments. This is again a current growth area as the UK leads Europe out of a serious economic recession[12].

- ### Professional negligence: Malpractice

Malpractice suits have been a feature of the US scene for many years and are beginning to feature also in Europe. Independent Experts are usually practising doctors, particularly specialists in the various fields. There has been a traditional reluctance for the 'healing' dogs to eat one another in this supremely courteous profession and it can be difficult for an aggrieved victim to find a suitable witness to act. Nevertheless, in an industry where cover-ups were formerly not unknown, it must be a healthy trend that more and more doctors are now prepared to be objective about the inadequacies or misdemeanours of their colleagues. Such evidence as they do give is often still overly based on 'professional opinion' and insufficiently reliant on laboratory and field testing. For instance it would be an advance were it to be made mandatory to record all major operations on videotape and all drug prescriptions on a central hospital or surgery computer. Many responsible medical practitioners do this voluntarily and have built in a system of checks on procedures which they operate with colleagues. But it is not these well-regulated individuals that the author has in mind when making his criticisms.

This is a delicate area. There is a real need to protect patients from malpractice while also protecting responsible doctors from the vexatious litigation often started by members of the public supported by an over-

---

[12]   "The Continent will not suffer England to be the workshop of the world"
        Benjamin Disraeli (d. 1881) Speech, House of Commons 15 March 1838

generous legal aid package. Otherwise doctors will change their methods simply to play safe. A present example of this is the very large increase in medical recommendations to pregnant women to have their children by caesarian section simply to avoid any risk to the doctor of being sued as a result of unexpected complications occurring during natural birth. What seems to be needed is a 'health care code' developed with the help of Experts which defines levels of inconvenience, discomfort, natural risk and excessive risk in relation to medical treatment of various common conditions.

- Insurance and claims

Involvement of independent Experts is on the increase as fraudulent claiming by the insured on companies seeking exclusion of liability through their small print has now risen to epidemic proportions. Personal experience as an Expert in this area suggests that one has to be tough to survive.

- In one case, when acting for a major UK insurance company, the forensic laboratory had taken endless pains by reputable techniques to establish a high probability that a valuable listed house had been burned down as the result of arson. Moreover, the torching had been perpetrated with great forethought and efficiency by someone who clearly knew the house and its internal geography very well indeed. On the night of the fire, the Claimant had arranged for a celebratory dinner party in an hotel at which his family and friends were present and at which all the family were ostentatiously introduced to the Head Waiter during pre-drinks. Unfortunately it appeared that, soon after this unusual introduction, his son had chosen to retire to his room in the hotel "to rest for a couple of hours" without drawing attention to this for fear of "spoiling the fun" of the guests. On rejoining the party, revived by his rest, he was again formally presented to the hotel staff, who were later to be called as alibi. The son was a competitive driver whose sports car had been parked close to the hotel; it would have taken about an hour to drive to the house, and another hour back to the hotel ... To everyone's surprise, at the door of the Court, the Plaintiff agreed a settlement involving a large payment to the Claimant and the case was withdrawn. Apparently on this quality of circumstantial evidence, the Police would not assist them. It was not worth the risk to their reputation to proceed with a civil case based on a charge which "might not stick".

Whereas much of this book has been concerned with the resolution of corporate disputes, Expert Witnesses are often called to assist in personal cases which can impose substantial emotional stress:-

• The author recalls acting for an Appellant to the Criminal Injuries Compensation Board to whom the award of £25000 was the difference between subsistence for her family and virtual destitution. The lady's husband, a farmer, had died in his bed from asphyxiation and smoke inhalation. The fire had been started during the night *either* by an electrical fault in the manifestly decrepit wiring *or* by a soldier who, locked out of barracks, had broken into an adjacent barn during the night, slept there and supposedly thrown a lighted match or cigarette-end into bales of straw. If the latter, the widow would receive compensation of £25k; if the former ... bad luck, they weren't insured! On the basis of the Expert evidence, fortunately for her, she won.

• <u>Crime and criminal trials</u>

There has been considerable public disquiet at the nature of "expert" evidence presented by the Director of Public Prosecutions (DPP) at major criminal trials. In fact, many believe that the government forensic laboratories have not been doing the best possible job. The limitations of the in-house (usually 'government') experts who have misled our Courts as to the significance of test results have been fully discussed in detailed publications. As a result it is obviously important to introduce more independent Expert evidence into the Criminal Court procedures and to rely less on those in government service whose advancement could possibly be prejudiced if the Prosecution fails to secure a conviction. Just as the boards of corporations need the leavening presence of independent non-executive directors, it seems reasonable that there should be a panel of independent Experts to be called upon by the DPP before each and every major trial, to assess and vouch for the quality of the technical evidence to be put before the Courts. Most of the Police are honest, and many are trying to do a good job under difficult and often dangerous circumstances with little political support but, in order to restore public confidence, it is important that the Prosecution should also be seen to be 'doing the right things in the right way'. Much 'new science' has recently been imported into the criminological scene, the majority being unquestioned by the Courts as to its provenance, probably because of the 'Minturn' effect[13]. In view of the public disquiet with the conclusions of

---
[13]   see footnote 11 to Chapter 1

many criminal trials, this position will surely have to change. The form that such change could take might be the mandatory employment of *independent* Experts to challenge the evidence of police and government forensic laboratories. Not only could this improve the quality of justice, it would also help to raise the standards in these laboratories and the calibre of their chosen witnesses who can be expected to give reliable evidence leading to conviction. An example is the use of the so-called 'DNA test' as near-ubiquitous evidence of identity. Graham Cooke[14] has pointed out that the overall reliability of such DNA conclusions will depend on:-

• the scientific process of extracting the DNA from the samples, some of which, particularly those from the scene of the crime, might be degraded or difficult to work with;

• the quality of the alleged match of "crime" DNA measurements with "suspect" DNA measurements, and what criteria are used to decide whether there is a match;

• the correctness of the mathematical formulae which may be applied to the usual case wherein more than one DNA result has been found to "match";

• the use of correct and sufficient sample data from which the frequencies of particular DNA measurements in the relevant statistical populations can be properly estimated.

Scientists themselves are now uneasy about the use which is being made of their work. Bown, writing in the New Scientist[15], gives details of the Hammond trial which led to the case against him being dismissed on the grounds that the DNA fingerprinting techniques used to identify the suspect were unreliable. It is not comforting to reflect on the 'tied' nature of the principal forensic laboratories, whatever their competence.

These requirements are not unique to DNA evidence. In fact, some such proofs of reliability are required in all experiments for litigation purposes (see, for instance, Chapter 8). How can this sort of science lottery be controlled to give a better quality 'justice'? Perhaps most effectively by insistence of the Courts on proper statistical evidence for the significance of

---

[14]   G. Cooke   "The length of genetic string we cannot yet measure" The Times 19 May 1992

[15]   W. Bown "DNA fingerprinting back in the dock"   New Scientist 6 March 1993

cited experimental data. One feels that the Criminal Courts have something to learn from the Civil Courts, particularly the Patent Courts, in the proper weighing and acceptance of test results, particularly those adduced using novel and often barely proven technology. There is one acknowledged problem, that technical matters have to be kept simple for presentation to a Jury, but this is a challenge to which independent Experts should and could respond. Following repeated miscarriages of justice in the UK Criminal Courts, 'too difficult' seems no longer an adequate reason for delaying reform. In a recent science editorial, our UK doyen 'Nature' discusses[16] the similar perplexity in which the US Courts now find themselves as a result of legislation introduced in 1975 to admit as evidence almost any opinion from an 'expert witness' who is qualified "by knowledge, skill, experience, training or education" in the subject matter of the Action. In the absence of criteria by which the Court can judge the *level* of these qualities, such a standard is plainly deficient. In an age where the peer review system has often proved fallible, can publication in accredited scientific journals simply be used in deciding the admissibility of published scientific evidence? The Nature recommendation is to adopt, at least *pro tem*, a recommendation of the Carnegie Commission on Science, Technology and Government:-

"The Commission urges the justices to adopt a new standard for evidence that would require judges not to resolve scientific controversy but only to ask three pertinent questions in weighing admissibility of evidence: Is the claim testable? Has it been tested? And is the methodology sound? Courts should not exclude evidence just because it is not accepted wisdom; nor should they allow Defendants to be held liable on the basis of mere hypothesis or speculation. While it is true that speculation is an essential part of science, and true that new ideas may have a hard time gaining acceptance, it does not follow that untested science belongs in court. That would be bad public policy".

In endorsing this approach, one might only add that the Commission still leaves open the question of how a non-technical judge, instructing a lay jury, can evaluate the specific quality of the answers he obtains to his three 'admissibility' questions. The use of Expert Witnesses, as in the English Patent Courts, is fully compatible with these requirements of the Commission and it does provide a very satisfactory model for other courts to follow. Responsible Experts can advise the Court in these scientific and technological matters and, if necessary, carry out witnessed experiments in support of the opinions they express. They should be used more.

---

[16] Editorial Nature 8 April 1993

Appendix A   A disastrous cross-examination

In the imaginary case *"Old Chequers Cooperative v Metallic Chessboards"*, *Moscow (1812)*, Professor Babbling[1] has been called, somewhat ill-advisedly, as a novice Yogi to give Expert evidence concerning the dastardly infringement of the proprietary 'black & white colouring' of his established client's checkered pattern by that upstart firm 'Metallic Chessboards':-

Q: Will you please take the 'Old Chequers' wooden chessboard. Do you have that?

A: Er, yes .. this one isn't it? I can't quite ..

Q: I think it is, Professor. (more gently) In fact, I believe it is the only board in this court made of wood. (laughter) Would you tell his Lordship what you observe about the colours of the contiguous squares?

A: Oh, yes ... I suppose .. Yes! .. they are *black* .. and *white*.

Q: Would you indicate to his Lordship which squares you call "black" and which "white"?

A: Obviously (pointing at two squares) *this* one ... and *this*.

Q: Would you regard these properties of "blackness" and "whiteness", these different colours, as fundamental to the design of the chessboard.

A: Well, yes, they're all like that, these chessboards, aren't they?

Q: Would you look again at the square you described as "white"? Why do you call it "white"?

A: Well, er, well .. for one thing it's lighter than the black square, it reflects more light ...

Q: So by "white", you mean "more reflective than the black"?

---

[1]   Sebastian Brant: "A fool will bare his mind with speed
       (d. 1521)   A wise man bides his time indeed.
                           Far better to be sage and quiet
                           Than let a babbling tongue run riot."
   from   Das Narrenschiff (1494) ch19,   translated by William Gillis as The Ship of Fools
   for the Folio Society, London 1971

A: Er, oh .. yes .. wait a minute .. no ... I mean not necessarily just reflectance .. the paint .. it has a white .. a pale coloured pigment in it .. yes, it's because of the paint .. it looks different to the eye.

Q: I am passing up to you, Professor, a set of colour-matching samples of standard painted surfaces covering a series of colours described as whites, creams and greys. Have you these?

A: Yes, but ... I wonder ...

Q: Would you tell his Lordship which of these colour standards best matches the square you have called "white", that is to say which standard looks 'similar to the eye'?

A: Hm .. yes .. well .. none of them really .. you see they are all on glazed paper so that the patterns have a different texture from painted wood.

Q: So that in making your colour comparison, you would want to take into account not only the colour but also the texture of the surface?

A: Definitely .. well, not always, I suppose .. you could subtract the texture effect .. it depends on whether you are just interested in a different texture ... I mean for contrast reasons ..

Q: Exactly, Professor. Please could you now subtract the textural effect and make the comparison I asked you to make two questions ago?

A: What comparison? .. I'm sorry .. oh, the patterns .. yes .. I suppose No 29 and No 34 are nearest in actual colour ...

Q: Both described as "light grey" in the Notes on the following page, aren't they Professor?

A: Where.. er, yes .. are they? .. so they are .. well, it isn't really a pure white .. yes, I'd settle for "light grey".

Q: Now will you make the same comparison for the square you called "black"?

A: That's more difficult .. er.. perhaps No 87 or 93 ..

284

Q: Both described in the Notes as "deep charcoal grey", aren't they?

A: Yes, that's what it says in the Notes .. but as I said the texture on the board is quite different ..

Q: So that even having two shades of grey, you are telling his Lordship that it would still be possible to contrast the squares by means of different textures?

A: Well .. yes .. if you wanted to .. you could .. er ..

Q: You have told his Lordship, have you not, that the squares on the wooden board are *not* in fact 'black' and 'white' but that they are both 'grey'?

A: No .. I didn't mean to say that .. I said that they *were* black and white .. er, hm .. probably when the board was new the white squares were whiter .. I .. er .. well .. they may well darken in use, just as the dark ones can get lighter .. you see both of these squares have the same texture, painted wood, so the only reason you see a difference between them is because of a difference in the reflectivity due to the different colours .. and I would like to add .. (even more rapidly) .. there is a difference .. in the paint .. in the colour of the paint .. in the reflectance of the paint within the range of wavelengths of visible light .. it is due to the ratio of titanium dioxide to lithopone used in the initial dispersion carried out on a three-roll mill in 3:1::toluene:white spirit .. and there are other additives that are put in to ...

Q: Different shades of grey, but both *grey*, didn't you say, Professor?

A: Well .. I suppose .. er ... ... Yes.

Q: Thank you, Professor. Will you please take the metal chessboard? Does this illustrate the point you were making about texture so that the grey squares are well-contrasted?

A: Yes, yes .. you see they are quite different materials .. different metals .. which reflect the light in a different way .. quite different textures .. yes, I .. it is a question of the angles of the grain boundaries ..

Q: Are the squares not painted on?

A: Oh, no .. they are plated .. what you see is the crystalline structure of the metal which is quite different for the two materials .. that's the contrasting texture .. using small-angle reflectance electron diffraction ...

Q: Are the metal squares black and white, Professor, or would you describe them as different shades of grey?

A: Oh, *grey*, definitely .. *not* black or white.

Q: Thank you, Professor. I have no further questions.

On this Evidence, from the other side's Expert, Counsel for "Metallic Chessboards" successfully pleaded that:-

•   MC's design principle was that of 'textural contrast' not 'difference of colour'.

•   That MC's squares were not 'black and white'.

•   That the successful prior art product was not characterised by squares which were 'black and white' as claimed in their Patent.

•   From this, he went on to develop an argument to attack the validity of the OCC Patent.

Counsel for 'Old Chequers', while manfully suppressing the temptation to re-examine, had to be content to fight a losing 'purposive construction' battle based on the somewhat conflicting evidence of "looks different to the eye". In the circumstances, his clients were, rather unreasonably, dissatisfied with his performance in 'coming in second'.

Professor Babbling felt aggrieved that he had been side-tracked by Counsel's sudden introduction of the colour card and, as a result of his confusion, had forgotten to give his evidence about the difference in *colour* of the metals, which he really thought was what contributed to the definition of the squares. He also felt 'tricked' into his (relatively unimportant) admission that both 'white' and 'black' were 'shades of grey', and thought that as a result he had done rather badly and lost face. (This impression was amply confirmed by his failure ever to be hired again).

In short[2] :-

"He remembered too late on his thorny green bed
Much that well may be thought, cannot wisely be said"

But he probably then lost interest and did not read the Judgement. If so, he
would never have realised the most serious flaw[3] in his Evidence. This was
that he himself had introduced gratuitously the potentially fatal 'new
principle', that of textural contrast, and had then himself been persuaded to
use it to distinguish, unequivocally, the alleged infringing product from the
homotextural product made by his client. He would also have remained
unaware that having first rejected the use of the colour-comparison chart
provided for him, he very soon found himself drawing conclusions from it.
In the well-worn epigram [4]:-

"When they have you by the 'ears', the hearts and minds will follow"

If you want to survive as an Expert Witness it is best to avoid ever letting
them get that first hold.

---

[2] Thomas Love Peacock (d. 1866)   Crotchet Castle: 'The Priest and the Mulberry Tree'

[3] Robert Burns: "O wad some Pow'r the giftie gie us
     (d. 1796)   To see oursels as others see us!
                            It wad frae mony a blunder free us,
                            And foolish notion.
                                     .... 'To a Louse'

[4] Source unknown ...but an oft-quoted management principle

Appendix B   Short glossary of English terms used in technological litigation

Academic   A member of staff of a university, college or other higher education centre, who is experienced in writing, lecturing and research. In this book, usually a professional scientist, technologist or engineer.

Act   Legislation enacted by Parliament for implementation by the Courts.

Action   A dispute formally set down for hearing by the Court using the processes of litigation.

Affidavit   Written opinion/report, sworn under oath. May constitute the technical evidence of an Expert at an intermediate court hearing.

Appeal   Attempt to reverse an unfavourable judgement given by a court of first instance.   In England, usually heard by two or three judges on the basis of transcripts of the evidence given in the lower court.

Art   1: Technological and industrial knowledge based on experience and practice which may not always have yet been underpinned with conventional scientific theory.
    2: All that is published (the 'state-of-the-art') about a particular industrial product or process. See also 'prior art'.

Attorney   US lawyer who 'doubles' the roles of preparation of a case and pleading it to the Court.

Authority   Usually: the written text of a judgement given, or upheld, on Appeal.

Barrister   Lawyer who has trained and is qualified in the art of pleading a case before the Court.   He/she is authorised to give an 'opinion' on the likely legality of a client's position and the anticipated outcome of contemplated litigation. Usually termed 'counsel'.

Bundle   File or group of files containing all the relevant papers pertaining to a particular subject featuring in the Trial. Normally assembled by the instructing solicitors.

Case 1: A dispute between parties which is being, or is to be, settled by legal procedures. When 'set down', the case becomes an Action.
2: A file title used by patent agents and others in the application for a legal monopoly on behalf of a client.

Chambers Building, or part of a building: offices where lawyers prepare their work ('Law Offices': US). A term used by barristers, a number of whom inhabit one set of chambers under the wing of a titular 'head'. However, UK solicitors work in 'offices', administered by a 'managing partner' who sorts out internal squabbles among the inmates.

Claim(s) That part of a Patent which sets out the limits of the monopoly granted to the applicant by the government in exchange for the necessary disclosure of details usually given in the 'body' of the patent.

Clerk The business manager and general administrator of a barrister's 'chambers'. He will arrange the barrister's appointments (with a solicitor or patent agent) and negotiate his fees & expenses. He will also arrange for the barrister's personal 'bundles', together with volumes of statutes and cases, to be available at meetings and in court.

Common general knowledge (cgk) Term used in the patent courts to describe prior art information which is generally well-known by the skilled man in the art at the priority date of the Patent. But in practice can often extend towards all that is published and available (world-wide) about a given industrial art at this date (i.e. the 'state-of-the-art') unless it be in an obscure foreign language without an available translation.

Conference Upmarket term for a discussion meeting at which opinions are sought by those instructing. Formerly referred to meetings with Junior Counsel. A meeting with Leading Counsel, together with his Junior, was known as a "consultation".

Copyright See 'intellectual property'.

Costs Fees required to meet the expense of bringing an Action. If they cannot be agreed, these costs are 'taxed' by the court and only a proportion of the total cost of the litigation is recoverable by the winner from the loser.

Counsel   A barrister ('Trial Lawyer': US) who pleads a case for his client in court.   In order of increasing seniority, counsel may be pupil barristers, juniors or leaders (who have 'taken silk'). 'Silks' are those who have been appointed Queen's Counsel, and are identified by the letters 'QC' after their surnames.

Court   1: A building designated for the hearing of Trials) ('Courthouse': US) (e.g. 'The High Court').

                2: A particular room in such a designated building ('Courtroom': US) (e.g. 'Court No. 27').

                3: The Judge, or panel of Judges, who hear the case and reach a decision and deliver Judgement.

Damages   Compensation for loss suffered by one Party as a result of the actions of the other.

Decision   Verdict of the Court following Trial. The main conclusion of the Judgement.

Defendant   Party accused of an illegal act or of causing damage ... who usually denies it.

Deposition   Preliminary oral evidence gathering, used in US procedures but not in Europe, at which a Witness is examined in the presence of his own Attorney but not of the Court.   The transcript of the Deposition forms part of the Evidence before the Court.

Discovery   1: A novel phenomenon or principle discovered by an inventor, research worker or investigative team.

                2: A legal procedure which requires the disclosure of both Parties in a dispute, each one to the other, of all relevant documentation they have, or ever have had, concerning the subject-matter of the dispute and issues in the Action.

Evidence   Oral or written material offered by a witness under oath in order to assist a just decision of the Court.

Examination   Dialogue between counsel and a witness during a Trial. As explained in Chapter 11, this may take the form of Examination-in-chief (X) by his own side's Counsel, Cross-examination (XX) by opposing

Counsel, or Re-examination (XXX). In the USA and, very occasionally, in the UK, even Re-cross-examination (XXXX) may occur.

Experiment Technical program advised to the other side in advance by a properly served 'Notice of Experiments' which has been admitted by the Court. Usually followed by a Demonstration of the Experiments (see Chapters 8/9) to the other side. In patent litigation, such experiments may often be carried out to prove either 'infringement' or 'invalidity'.

Expert Witness See 'witness of opinion'.

Fact An observation which is so well authenticated, usually by witnesses, as to persuade the Court that it is 'true'.

File wrapper The prosecution history of a (usually) US Patent through the Patent Office, showing objections made by the Patent Examiner and the amendments agreed by the applicant's Patent Agents or Attornies.

House of Lords UK supreme court, which rules only on matters of law referred from the Court of Appeal.

Infringement 1: General term for unauthorised invasion of the property rights of another party.
2: Specific term for unauthorised invasion of the monopoly claimed by the registered proprietor of a valid & subsisting patent

Injunction Order of a Court (usually) prohibiting the doing of some act, such as stopping the sale of a product or the use of a process which has been found to infringe a valid patent. Breach of an injunction can lead to proceedings for contempt of Court, punishable by imprisonment or a heavy fine.

Inspection A formal examination of the other side's equipment, materials, or documentation, which is carried out according to a specified procedure authorised by the Court.

Instruction Appointment (e.g. of an Expert) ... assuming an undertaking by the appointing authority (solicitor, patent agent) to settle the fee-notes or invoices of the appointee.

Intellectual Property (IP)   Legal subject matter concerned with patents, copyright, trademarks, industrial design and confidential information

Interlocutory   A stage in the proceedings which takes place ahead of the Trial e.g. application for an interlocutory injunction to restrict the damage done by a Defendant to a Plaintiff's business pending Trial.

Inventor   The person who first discovers, or puts into practice, a novel process, material or device for which a Patent is, or may be, granted.

Judgement   Initially oral, then written, findings of the Court which details the arguments of the judiciary in deciding each of the salient points.

Jurisdiction   Geographical area subject to rulings from a particular court e.g. the High Court, sitting in London, has jurisdiction for England and Wales but not for Scotland or Northern Ireland.

Lawyer   Someone who has qualified in the Common Professional Examination (CPE), and is using this qualification to practise in accordance with the rules of the legal profession.   Most solicitors and barristers also have degrees in Law. Increasingly, in technical actions, lawyers also possess basic degrees in Science or in Engineering.

Opinion   Any report, for instance by a barrister or by an Expert, which sets out a properly researched and argued point-of-view on the state of knowlege, usually of a topic important to the progress of the litigation.

Paralegal   Person without formal legal qualifications ... but often experienced and so able to take responsibility for many of the routine aspects of preparation for litigation and for Trial. New and useful entrants to the English law scene.

Patent   Monopoly granted by a government in exchange for disclosure of details of manufacture and/or operation of a material or device to a supposedly grateful 'public'. This can, in general, involve a ban on making, using, marketing and importing. Ownership of a Patent does not confer automatic right of use, which may require a licence from the holder of a 'dominant patent' in the field.

Patent Agent   Graduate scientist or engineer who has further qualified as a chartered patent agent (CPA) and/or European Patent Agent (EPA) but usually not as a lawyer. They work with 'inventors' in drafting patents and then 'prosecute' them through Patent Offices. After grant, they may be involved in defence of these Patents against infringers. ('Patent Attorney': US *is* normally a lawyer).

Patent-in-suit   Patent which is the subject of the current litigation.

Plaintiff   The aggrieved party, who seeks legal redress

Plead   To address the Court, using arguments and citing evidence, asking for a favourable verdict or decision for one's client in a dispute. Only barristers can presently plead in the English High Court. Elsewhere, solicitors may plead and, in the Patent Offices and in the Patents County Court (PCC), so can patent agents.

Pleadings   Formal legal document, usually drafted by junior counsel and 'served' by a solicitor, which sets out in outline a party's case which, it is intended, will be presented to the Court during the forthcoming Trial.

Prior Art   Technical-legal term used in patent jurisprudence to designate all that has been published about an industrial technology as at some specific date, often the priority date for application for a patent-in-suit.

Priority date   The officially recognised date of application for a new patent as endorsed by a national or supra-national patent office. As a result of a Patent Convention, this date is usually accepted virtually world-wide.

Professional   Someone qualified by a degree, or equivalent diploma, supported by several years of practical experience in the practice of his discipline and usually subject to rules in exchange for protection of his/her professional title.

Recess   A short break in the Trial proceedings.

Serve   To formally deliver a document (or equivalent material) to the opposing party in a dispute according to the prescribed legal procedure for such service.

Solicitor   Lawyer who prepares a case for his client and 'instructs' barristers and experts who are required in bringing the Action to Trial. In Intellectual Property Actions, many solicitors may also have science or engineering degrees. An increasing number are also qualified patent agents.

Statistics   The mathematical study and calculation of probabilities. Used in the design and interpretation of experimental data.

Testimony   US term for 'evidence'. Since the impact of television, a word used increasingly in the UK.

Trial   The formal hearing of arguments and evidence by a Court, being the 'lower court' or 'court of first instance'. Following Trial, the Court reaches a 'decision' in favour of the case of one or other of the parties. It backs this up with a judgement setting out detailed reasons for its findings.

Witness Box   The enclosure from which a witness gives his evidence in the English Court ('Witness Stand': US).

Witness of Fact   A witness who has made observations of phenomena relevant to the subject matter of the Trial which one or other of the Parties feel will assist its case. The witness of fact is not required to state his opinion of the technical correctness of the background to his observations but may have to relate them to his 'common general knowledge' as a skilled observer (e.g. 'On 10th May I mixed A with B and measured the viscosity increase using the method of B.S. 999 ...').

Witness of Opinion   An Expert Witness who is asked to help the Court reach a decision on technical matters which are in dispute between the Parties. He may do so both by citing his own observations and/or by offering his educated & experienced opinions on the meaning of documents and other material relevant to the Action (e.g. 'In the light of my knowledge and experience of viscosity changes during chemical reactions, the reasons for the increase in viscosity when A is mixed with B are ...').

General Index

295